The GOOD EARTH

A Guide to the Vegetables, Fruits, Grains, Nuts, Spices, and Culinary Herbs of Our Planet

Jon Gregerson

Whitecap Books

Vancouver/Toronto

Edited by Linda Ostrowalker
Cover design and illustration by Warren Clark
Interior design by Carolyn Deby

Typeset by Vancouver Desktop Publishing Centre Ltd.

Printed and bound in Canada by D.W. Friesen and Sons Ltd., Altona,
Manitoba

Canadian Cataloguing in Publication Data

Gregerson, Jon.
  The good earth

  Includes bibliographical references and
  index.
  ISBN 1-55110-032-0

  1. Plants, Edible. 2. Vegetarianism.
  I. Title.
QK98.5.A1G74 1992   581.6'32   C92-091528-0

The Good Earth

C O N T E N T S

I N T R O D U C T I O N

This book is the result of my own quest for information concerning the multitude of food plants that I commonly and uncommonly eat. Here you will find entries for the whole spectrum of marvelously diverse Old and New World vegetables, fruits, grains, nuts, spices, and culinary herbs of our planet combined in a single whole and arranged alphabetically to form a reasonably complete "kitchen guide" or nonencyclopedic reference work on the subject.

In this book you will discover where our numerous foods originated as well as various facts, historical and otherwise, about them, including the circumstances of their "migrations" from one area to another and information concerning their nutritional content. As complete data pertaining to the vitamin, mineral, and protein constituents of the entries in this handbook can be found in numerous works, it has not been thought necessary to duplicate such information.

The material has been brought together from a number of different sources, rewoven, enlarged upon, and presented from within the context of my own perspective, which is grounded on a broad base of knowledge and experience encompassing many diverse geographical areas and cultures. Although a native of California, I have traveled extensively abroad and have lived for varying periods of time in many different countries. I was also, for over ten years, a resident of Canada—a land which, despite its immediate proximity to the United States, is in so many ways different from the latter.

The concern here is chiefly with those Old and New World food plants that are commercially available in North America, the

British Isles, continental Europe, Latin America, and the Near East. Those that are *only* available in areas such as India, Africa, or the Far East are not included. Likewise, the many types of oriental "sea vegetables," all but one variety of wild mushroom, and plants used only in the production of beverages such as teas have been omitted. For readers with an interest in these particular subjects, each of which forms a separate category in itself, many studies by fully competent experts exist.

This book is neither a specialized botanical study, nor horticultural in its concerns. Similarly, certain information that is peripheral to the subject has not been included. For example, neither the numerous myths and legends that exist concerning our food plants nor a speculative etymological analysis of their names—both matters being more indicative of the folk imagination than of reality— are to be found here, because it is felt that they do not properly fall within the scope of this work, which is, after all, a very matter-of-fact handbook.

Although this book contains no recipes as such, you will find simple recommendations concerning the preparation and use of each entry. These are based upon my own experience with dishes that I have either prepared myself or have encountered in diverse lands and places. They are intended to provide the creative cook with a workable framework that can be modified to suit individual circumstances. Common sense will dictate the quantity of any particular ingredient used.

Lastly, inasmuch as I am for reasons of both health and ethics, a vegetarian, no mention is made here of nonvegetarian dishes. My vegetarian orientation does not, however, make the book any less valuable as a source of information for nonvegetarians, particularly considering the subject matter involved. The concern here is, after all, with vegetables, fruits, grains, nuts, spices, and herbs. Indeed, this volume is not intended for any one segment of the reading public, but as an accessible guide for all who possess an interest in the foods they eat.

The Food Plants and Seasonings of Our Planet

An Alphabetical Guide

Allspice

Pimenta officinalis

Allspice is an aromatic seasoning derived from a tropical tree that grows to a height of about twelve meters (40 ft.). Its fruits, which resemble peppercorns, are harvested while still green, dried in the sun, and ground into a powder for culinary use. Allspice is native to the West Indies, particularly to Jamaica. At one time, it was even termed "jamaica pepper." It is also widely grown in various areas of South and Central America.

The only major "sweet spice" of the New World, allspice was first exported from the West Indies to Europe by the Spanish and the English in the sixteenth century. However, it did not become popular in the Old World until the Dutch and the Danes brought it back to northern Europe from their Caribbean island colonies. At that time, it became particularly popular in Denmark, Sweden, and Finland. It remains a major spice in these countries, even today.

The flavor of allspice is like an amalgam of nutmeg, cloves, juniper berries, and cinnamon. It greatly enhances fruit dishes, puddings, custards, pies, and fruit cakes. It is especially delicious in pumpkin pies, on yogurt, or added to crêpes and pancakes, particularly when these are eaten with peach preserves. Quite aside from its pleasing flavor, it is also considered to be an excellent aid to digestion.

Almond

Prunus amygdalus

The almond tree grows to a height of about nine meters (30 ft.). A close relative of the peach, the almond "nut" or seed kernel is almost identical to that within the peach stone. The "fruit" on the outside of the almond—hard, thin, green, and covered with fuzzlike down—is inedible as is the shell that encloses the almond seed itself. There are sweet and bitter varieties of almond. Sometimes, the same tree will yield both.

Indigenous to the eastern Mediterranean area (particularly to the Holy Land), the almond spread eastward into Persia and westward into Greece and North Africa. It was used as a decorative motif on the candlesticks of the Jewish Temple in Jerusalem to commemorate the miraculous flowering of Aaron's rod, and almond branches and blossoms continue to be utilized at certain Jewish festivals.

Widely cultivated in ancient Greece, the almond eventually spread to the Italian peninsula where it was popularly termed "the Greek nut." By the eighth century, almonds were grown in some regions of present-day France. Indeed, Charlemagne had a whole grove of them planted in his palace gardens.

Today, almonds are cultivated throughout much of the world, including such widely diverse areas as China and the Azores islands. Spain and Italy are the major producers while California, Israel, Lebanon, and Greece also grow fairly large quantities.

A high protein food, almonds are most often eaten simply by themselves. Both the Greeks and Italians are fond of them dipped in a hard sugar coating. Powdered almonds mixed with water and honey provide a delicious drink that is not uncommon in both the Balkans and the Near East. Ground or thinly sliced, almonds are added to cakes, pastries, and other confections as well as used as a garnish with noodles, rice, millet, or wheat. Ground into a paste or "butter" and combined with raisins, dates, or chopped dried apricots, almonds provide an exceptionally fine filling for sandwiches.

The well-known European confection, marzipan, consisting of almond paste mixed with rose water and sugar, is said to date from the time of the Thirty Years' War when the city of Lübeck, during an extraordinarily long seige, had nothing left among its food supplies but almonds and sugar. These were used to make the candylike "bread" that, by the end of the seige, was the population's only sustenance.

It is perhaps worth noting that there is a widespread belief that almonds inhibit the growth of cancer cells.

Amaranth

Amaranthus hypochondria, A. gangeticus viridis

Amaranth plants are tall and long-stemmed, with dark green leaves strongly infused with a reddish purple color. The largest type grows to a height of over 2.5 meters (8 ft.) and bears long trailing seed clusters. The seed grains themselves are extremely tiny, being somewhat smaller than millet. Leaf amaranth is similar in appearance, but considerably shorter.

Amaranthus hypochondria is the chief variety of the New World grain commonly known as amaranth. It is indigenous to Mexico and Guatemala. *Amaranthus gangeticus viridis* is the main type of amaranth used as a leaf vegetable. It is said to be native to India but spread at a very early date to China where it is known as "hinn choi." There are also many other varieties, a few of which are utilized as decorative garden plants.

Present in various parts of the world long before the advent of mankind, amaranth was unquestionably one of the first plants eaten by man. Adaptable to widely different soils and climates, it was grown by the Aztecs in pre-Hispanic Mexico as well as by various native peoples in what is today the southwestern United States. After the Spanish conquest in 1519, however, the cultivation of amaranth was, to a large degree, suppressed by the Spanish due to its widespread use in Aztec religious rituals.

Currently undergoing something of a revival, amaranth grain is widely available in organic food outlets throughout North America, and is also becoming known in western Europe. This grain contains more protein than wheat or even soybeans. It also has within its chemical composition a quantity of the amino acid, lysine. When eaten together with dried beans, peas, lentils, or corn, a "complete protein" is created. Amaranth can be utilized in all the same ways as millet, from which it differs when cooked only in that it does not become fluffy, but retains a somewhat chewy texture. In flavor, it is rather nutlike.

The leaves of the amaranth taste like chard mingled with beets. Unfortunately, this ancient leaf vegetable is still not widely available in North America and Europe.

A curd-type product, high in protein as well as calcium and vitamin A, has recently been perfected from a concentrate derived from amaranth leaves. Its texture is said to resemble dry cottage cheese or the firmer type of tofu. Its culinary uses are as varied as the latter. Yet to be popularized, it is not generally available in the markets.

Anise

Pimpinella anisum

Anise is native to the eastern Mediterranean area. It is found throughout the Holy Land as well as in Syria and Egypt. It has also been grown in Greece and the Italian peninsula from very ancient times. The anise plant is related to fennel, to which it is very similar in appearance except that it is considerably shorter, only growing to a height of about sixty centimeters (2 ft.).

The seeds have been used as a flavoring since prehistoric times. Traditionally, the Italians and the Greeks used anise in the preparation of various types of breads, breadsticks, and cakes. Although its use was far more widespread in the ancient world than it is today, anise remains popular with the Italians but not with most northern Europeans.

Anise is extremely penetrating in flavor and should always be used very sparingly. An aromatic oil distilled from anise seeds is utilized for various medicinal purposes. Over the centuries, this herb has been used in the making of several anise-flavored liqueurs, notably Greek ouzo and French anisette. Today, however, *Illicium verum*, a quite different plant of almost identical flavor, is often used in the production of these potent beverages. This plant is native to northwest China and is termed "star anise" or "badian."

Apple

Malus pumila, M. sylvestris, Pyrus pumila; many varieties

Malus pumila, M. sylvestris, and *Pyrus pumila* designate the basic wild species from which the different varieties of cultivated apples are derived. The wild apple of Europe is believed to have originated in central Asia just south of the Caucasus between the Black and Caspian seas in today's regions of Georgia (Gruzhia) and Armenia—an area where many other fruits originated. From there, the apple spread westward into Asia Minor and Europe.

Whether the regular apple is a separate fruit or developed from the crab apple is a matter of conjecture. We do know that since prehistoric times apples have been the most commonly grown and eaten fruit throughout a large portion of the Old World, particularly in the Northern Hemisphere. Thriving in any but tropical climates, they do well in the British Isles, Scandinavia, and northern Russia. Although some believe that the Romans introduced the apple to the British Isles and Gaul (France), it was in all probability already growing in both areas much earlier. It was, in any case, cultivated by the ancient Norse long before the Roman legions came to Britain.

Likewise, the apple was grown at a very early date in the more temperate climates of Greece and certain other lands of the eastern Mediterranean area, including Phoenicia (today, Lebanon). The ancient Greeks are said to have particularly esteemed a golden yellow variety. Cato mentions seven different types as being familiar to the Romans of his day. Throughout the Middle Ages and medieval period, apples were the major fruit crop in northern and central Europe. Other fruits of those times included pears, cherries, quinces, and plums. These, together with apples, were all brought to the New World by European colonists.

Today, there are approximately one thousand different varieties of apple. Among the many flavorful apples available in North America are the Gravenstein, MacIntosh, Jonathan, Pippin, Golden Delicious, and Rome Beauty. The last, which is a deep purplish red, is grown extensively in the Pacific Northwest. Those from British Columbia, Canada, are to be particularly recommended for their delectable flavor. In England, the Worcester Peramain is particularly valued.

Apples can be baked and eaten with cream, used as a fruit filling in pies or strudel, made into a sauce, or cooked into a thick brownish paste known as "apple butter" and used on bread. Cut in small pieces, raw apples blend very well with oranges, raisins, and other fruits. They also blend well in a cabbage and carrot salad. People who find raw apple skins indigestible or constipating should always peel apples before eating them.

Inasmuch as toxic sprays, insecticides, and alar are widely used by most U.S. apple growers, it is generally advisable to limit one's purchases to the more expensive organic apples. Fortunately, such fruits, both native-grown and imported from New Zealand and elsewhere, are increasingly available in markets throughout North America.

Although they contain small amounts of vitamins A and C, apples are considerably less nutritious than most other fruits, however pleasing to the palate they may be.

See also **Crab Apple.**

Apricot

Prunus armenica

L ike peaches and plums, the apricot is a "drupe" or "stone fruit" that develops from self-pollinating white flowers. The color of the fruit varies from a pale yellowish orange to a deep orange, sometimes with a tinge of red. Its seed stones are quite large but the fruit itself is considerably smaller than the peach. There are a number of varieties, although the differences are negligible.

The apricot apparently originated in China and spread westward, coming first to central Asia, Armenia, and the Caucasus, and then to the eastern Mediterranean. In *Cultivated Plants and Their Wild Relatives*, Zukovskij also mentions a small wild variety that grows in Siberia and can withstand very cold temperatures. While no word for the apricot exists in either ancient Hebrew or Sanskrit, a Chinese character designating the apricot appeared in written Chinese records just prior to 2000 B.C.

Alexander the Great is said to have been the first to bring the apricot to Europe, introducing it to Greece in the fourth century B.C. Pliny mentions in his *Natural History* that apricot cultivation began among the Romans around 100 B.C. During the millenium and a half that followed, the apricot became widely disseminated throughout southern Europe and North Africa, first through extension of the Roman Empire and later via direct trade with Armenia and central Asia. Apricots were a favorite fruit of the Arabs, whose expansion undoubtedly contributed to the apricot's increased cultivation and popularity. According to Zukovskij, the domestic apricot was developed in Tajikistan in central Asia and was spread by Arab traders.

By the sixteenth century, apricots were being cultivated well into central Europe. Even England proved to have a sufficiently temperate climate for apricot trees to survive and produce fruit. Apricots were, in fact, quite popular during the reign of Henry VIII. The Spanish brought them to their New World colonies, planting them first in Mexico and later in the gardens of their California missions. The English, too, attempted to grow apricots in the New World, introducing them to their colony in Virginia, but they did not do at all well there or anywhere else in eastern North America.

Today, apricots are extensively cultivated in California, Israel, Syria, Turkey, Iran, Spain, and Russian central Asia. They are even grown in British Columbia, Canada. Unfortunately, as with a number of other fruits, apricots grown in North America have far less flavor than those raised in the Near East where the climate and soil conditions combine to produce particularly flavorful fruit. In addition, such fruits are harvested only after they have started to ripen and are made available to the public immediately. The aromatic quality of these fruits, both fresh and dried, is not soon forgotten. In North America, on the other hand, most fruits are harvested while still green and then kept too long in cold storage.

An ancient Near Eastern method of preparing dried apricots consists of removing the pit from the whole apricot without cutting the fruit in half. The fruit is then dried for a short period of time at a moderate temperature. These delectable, aromatic, still quite soft, dried fruits are an important export of contemporary Turkey.

Ordinary halved dried apricots cooked with sugar, and flavored with lemon juice and a vanilla bean, are also to be recommended. This dish is best served with sweet or sour cream and a touch of cinnamon.

Dried or fresh apricots mix well with other fruits such as pears or prunes in fruit compote combinations. For an ultimate gourmet touch, dried apricots can be mixed with quince preserves and murillo cherries in a fruit compote dish fit for a king.

From Kabul to Damascus and Jerusalem, dried apricots are utilized in candies, confections, and sauces. A favorite preparation method involves cooking them into a kind of paste, which is pressed into paper-thin sheets and cut in strips. This is then eaten as a candy or used in the preparation of various sauces.

Apricot preserves are excellent served as a garnish on cream-based puddings, or used on toast, in sandwiches, or on pancakes. Cinnamon goes especially well with apricot preserves as does cream cheese. An unusually good sandwich consists of apricot preserves and slices of fresh banana on a quality raisin bread.

Fresh uncooked apricots are perhaps best simply halved and served with lemon juice and sugar. Canned apricots are quite satisfactory for use in pies and pastries.

Dried apricots are rich in vitamin A, iron, and even protein. Thus, they are of far greater nutritional value than fresh ones and, to many people, are more pleasing to the palate as well.

It is interesting to note that apricots, both dried and fresh (and even including the pit kernels), are a main food staple in the tiny principality of Hunza in the Himalayas—an area known for the extreme longevity, excellent health, and almost exclusively vegetarian diet of its inhabitants.

Artichoke
Cynara scolymus

There are two varieties of artichoke—the tight-headed globular, which is seldom seen in North America, and the more usual conical. Both forms originated in Italy and grow to a height of 1.5–2 meters (5–6 ft.). Silvery green leaves grow on the thick stems from which the artichoke heads emerge.

The artichoke is sometimes described as a cultivated form of the wild cardoon of Greece, the Italian peninsula, and North Africa. However, it is unclear if the artichoke with its edible flower-head actually existed in the ancient world as a mutant form of the cardoon. In any case, the contemporary artichoke first appeared in the region of Naples during the fifteenth century. From there, it spread to both Florence and Venice where it became a stylish delicacy among the aristocracy. Catherine de Medici introduced the artichoke to the French Court in 1633 when she married King Henry IV. By the end of that century it was being widely cultivated in Italy, Spain, and France. Although brought to England during the seventeenth century, the English did not find it much to their liking.

Today, the artichoke is extensively cultivated throughout southern Europe and is very much a part of the Mediterranean diet. It has also become very popular in the United States. There, it is chiefly grown on huge tracts of fog-shrouded land along the coast near Monterey, California, where it was originally introduced by the Spanish during the 1700s.

Artichokes thrive in moderate climates close to the sea where the soil has a high salt content. Seaweed is said to be the best possible fertilizer for artichoke plants. The artichoke head is composed of leaflike bracts. A portion of each of these is edible as is the pulpy base or "heart" from which the bracts emerge. If permitted to reach full maturity, a beautiful thistlelike flower, purple in color, emerges from the center of the artichoke head.

Artichokes must be cooked. They can be either cut in half lengthwise and steamed, or boiled whole. They are usually eaten plain with either oil and vinegar or butter and lemon. A favorite in all Mediterranean lands, artichoke hearts are excellent in thick

Italian-type omelettes or "pies" made with eggs, cheese, and garlic. They can also be preserved in oil, brine, or vinegar, with herbs and garlic, for use in salads or as hors d'oeuvres.

The artichoke is rich in iodine, calcium, and vitamin A.

See also **Cardoon.**

Asparagus

Asparagus officinalis

Asparagus thrives in notably damp areas near lakes, rivers, and swamps, as well as near the sea. Surprisingly, it even tolerates brackish water and somewhat salty soil. Asparagus spears or "shoots" grow out of the ground headfirst at the base of the asparagus plant. The plant itself, with its feathery leaves and tiny seed capsules, can grow 1.5–2 meters (5–6 ft.) in height and can remain productive for forty years or more, making it one of the longest-lived vegetable-producing plants in existence. There are two types—one a deep green color and the other a pale white with a touch of lavender shading, the latter being a variety grown almost exclusively in Belgium and the Netherlands.

Asparagus is indigenous to the eastern Mediterranean regions and is believed to have spread from Syria, Phoenicia, and Asia Minor to Greece, the Italian peninsula, and Egypt at a very early date. It also spread northward to the Crimean peninsula and the southern Russian steppes. The Phoenicians are credited with introducing asparagus throughout the entire Mediterranean world, and may also have brought it to Wales in early times.

Although the ancient Greeks gathered only wild specimens of asparagus, the Romans began to cultivate this vegetable around 200 B.C., the area around Ravenna sometime later becoming noted for an exceptionally large variety. Besides using fresh asparagus in their cuisine, the Romans also developed a method of drying it for out-of-season use—a practice that well might be revived today. Indeed, dried asparagus could be utilized in combination with herbs, spices, onion, and garlic in the making of a variety of sauces.

During the 1500-year existence of Byzantium, asparagus was esteemed and cultivated throughout the empire. In the distant British Isles it was eaten during Roman rule and possibly before, but its popularity seems to have flagged in post-Roman times. However, it was reintroduced by the French in the sixteenth century and became widely cultivated as a choice table vegetable.

By then, it was already popular in France and the Low Countries. In the seventeenth century both the French and the English brought asparagus to North America, where it has been grown commercially and privately ever since.

Asparagus is delicious steamed and eaten plain with butter, in baked dishes with cheese, in cream soups with dill weed, or eaten cold in salads with mayonnaise.

Asparagus is extremely rich in vitamin A.

Avocado
Persea americana, P. drymifolia

The word "avocado" is said to derive from the Aztec word "ahvactl." The avocado is indigenous to Mexico, Central America, Peru, Colombia, and Brazil. There are two main species. The *Persea americana* (of which the "haas avocado" is a primary example) has a somewhat thick blackish skin and is thought to have originated in Guatemala. There is also a West Indian subgroup of this type. The second main species is the *Persea drymifolia*, which has a smooth, thin, green skin and is native to Mexico. The "fuerte" is the leading example of this type in contemporary North America. There are also a number of varieties that are hybrids of the two. While these basic types are all essentially pear-shaped (and hence were termed "alligator pears" in the earlier part of this century), another type exists which is spherical in shape. This large hybrid type—which possesses a shiny, bright green, hard shell—is extensively raised in Hawaii. The pulp tends to be much softer in texture than other varieties.

The avocado has been a dietary staple of the native peoples of Central and South America for centuries, but was not cultivated in North America until 1833 when Henry Perrine established extensive avocado groves in Florida. In 1873, the first avocado orchards were planted in California, at Santa Barbara. In both cases, the thin-skinned Mexican variety was used. Avocado trees grow rapidly, but it takes considerable time for them to mature and bear fruit. Therefore, it was well after the beginning of the twentieth century before avocados became a popular food among North Americans.

Fernandez de Encisco was the first European to mention avocados, which he found thriving in Colombia in 1509. In continental Europe and the British Isles, the avocado remains an exotic and quite costly luxury food even today. In the United States and Canada, however, the avocado is both reasonably priced and extremely popular. California, Florida, and Hawaii are all major producers of the avocado today. It is also extensively cultivated in the lands of its origin as well as in Polynesia and much of Africa.

Mature avocados differ widely in size. While most are no larger than small or medium-sized pears, a few attain the dimensions of an eggplant. These enormous specimens are rarely seen in the United States, but appear now and then in the exotic produce markets of London, Paris, Dublin, or Montreal, where they are sold for extremely large sums.

The avocado is particularly rich in protein as well as in vitamins A and B. Consequently, it is an important staple for vegetarians. It is most often eaten in salads with chopped cabbage or lettuce and tomatoes seasoned with garlic. Grapefruit segments and grated carrots also combine surprisingly well with it. Some people prefer avocados eaten directly out of the shell with a little oil and lemon juice. They are at their best when still quite firm and only slightly soft. Over-ripe, they are inedible.

A beautiful and very decorative houseplant can be grown from avocado pits planted in moist soil (be sure to get the more pointed end right-side up). With proper care, such plants reach a height of two meters (6 ft.) or more.

Azuki Bean

Phaseolus angularis

The azuki is an Old World bush bean that grows to a height of sixty centimeters (2 ft.). Native to the Far East, it is extensively grown in both China and Japan, being a particular favorite of the Japanese. It is red in color, somewhat sweet in flavor, is exceptionally nutritious, and is most often used in dried form.

Dried azuki beans are extremely hard and are best when soaked for several days before cooking. They are excellent cooked in a miso sauce with a bit of sugar. In the Orient, they are often made into a delicious sweet bean paste for use in various dessert-type confections.

Large quantities of azuki beans are grown in Japan. In recent years, dried azuki beans have become increasingly available in North American organic food stores. They are also to be found in

Japanese specialty shops, but remain little known in continental Europe and the British Isles. Although the short green pods provide an excellent fresh vegetable dish, they are seldom encountered outside the Orient.

Banana

Musa sapientum

M*usa sapientum* is Latin for "the fruit of wise men." Bananas are native to India, the Malay Archipelago, and southeast Asia in general. They are also present in abundance on various Pacific islands, where they were probably brought by immigrants from southeast Asia who settled the islands around the first century A.D.

Precisely when the first traders from India or Africa brought the banana to the West is unknown. The troops of Alexander the Great encountered bananas in India in 327 B.C. By the beginning of the Christian era, the banana was cultivated in much of the eastern Mediterranean area. During the thousand-year history of the Byzantine Empire, bananas were favored as the chief ingredient of a dessert dish served with honey, nuts, and various fruits.

Bananas were already growing extensively in equatorial Africa when the Portuguese arrived in 1498, probably having been introduced many centuries before by Arab traders who had brought the plants from India. Banana plants were brought from the Canary Islands to the island of Hispanola in the West Indies by Tomas de Berlanga in 1516. Soon thereafter, they were also taken to Mexico and Central America.

In *Edible Plants of the World*, however, the nineteenth-century botanist, Sturtevant, states that bananas were already present in the New World at the time of the Spanish conquest. As proof of this, he cites Aztec tradition and also notes that banana leaves have been found in Incan tombs which predate the conquest. In addition, Las Casas, a member of Columbus's fourth expedition, mentions bananas growing in Costa Rica together with pineapples and coconuts in the year 1503. Thus, it is quite possible that banana plants had been brought to South America by migrants from the South Pacific sometime after the first century A.D. In any case, cultivation of the banana only became widespread in the New World after the coming of the Spanish.

The Spanish also introduced bananas to southern California,

and Captain George Vancouver found them thriving in the gardens of the Santa Barbara mission in 1793. Nevertheless, they have never been grown as a commercial crop in North America. First imported to the United States in the early 1800s, bananas became fairly common, although still quite costly, in the cities of the eastern seaboard by the year 1850. It was only after the beginning of the present century that bananas became affordable to the whole spectrum of North American society.

Today, huge banana plantations throughout Central America, northern South America, the West Indies, and Hawaii supply the large demand for bananas throughout the Western world. African bananas are seldom exported as they constitute a major food staple for millions of people on that continent.

Banana plants are propagated by replanting sections of the underground roots or budding stems. They grow very rapidly and in one year produce lovely red, yellow, and black flowers from which the fruits develop. Bananas contain vitamins A, B, and C, are rich in carbohydrates, and have a high zinc content.

The banana is unquestionably the most popular of all tropical fruits. It can be eaten by itself, mixed with other fruits, or added to puddings or cakes. Its richly aromatic flavor is greatly enhanced by the addition of coconut. An unusual and exceptionally nutritious dessert can be made by combining bananas with cooked millet, raisins, tahini (sesame seed butter), lemon juice, and honey. Bananas also go very well with cream cheese, yogurt, and sour or sweet cream.

Perhaps the most aromatically flavorful of all bananas is the ten-centimeter (4-in.) long *Musa nana,* variously termed the "dwarf" or "finger banana." Popular in North America some twenty years ago or more, it is available less frequently today and is often quite costly.

See also **Plantain.**

Banana Squash. *See* **Winter Squash.**

Barley

Hordeum, many varieties

Barley's place of origin is uncertain, although it most likely developed somewhere in the Near East. One of the major grains, barley was known as early as 5000 B.C. in Egypt and 3000 B.C. in the Mesopotamian region of the eastern Mediterranean. By 2000 B.C., it was cultivated in most of Europe as well as in China. Known to the Stone Age Neolithic lake dwellers of Switzerland, it was also a grain staple in ancient Israel, as well as among the ancient Greeks and Romans. Throughout much of Europe and the Near East, from prehistoric times well into the sixteenth century, the flour used in making bread was derived chiefly from barley mixed with varying amounts of wheat, rye, or pea flour.

Extremely adaptable climate-wise, barley can be grown in such totally different climates as those of northern Norway and central India. Canada, France, Turkey, India, and the United States are all major growers today.

Whole grain barley can be eaten in a variety of ways. It makes a very palatable dish when left to soak until it begins to sprout and then boiled in a pure vegetable "bouillon" until sufficiently soft. It can then be eaten as is or fried with chopped onions, garlic, and a generous portion of paprika. Fresh sliced mushrooms, added after the dish is prepared, are also to be recommended. Just about any steamed vegetable blends beautifully with fried barley and onions. Grated or melted cheese can transform fried barley and vegetables into yet a different dish. Chopped parsley is excellent as a garnish. The creative cook will find barley a notably versatile food that can be prepared in a vast number of ways. Some people enjoy barley eaten as a cereal with cream, honey, raisins, or prunes. Various other fruits—fresh, dried, or canned—can also be added.

Basil

Ocimum basilicum, O. minimum

Basil plants of the main variety, *Ocimum basilicum,* produce a number of branches and eventually reach a height of sixty centimeters (2 ft.) or more. *O. minimum* has smaller leaves and is much shorter, growing very close to the ground. Both are slow-growing and require considerable warmth.

Basil or "sweet basil" is called "tulsi" in India and "basilicus" by the Greeks. Thought to have originated in India, basil has been grown throughout much of the Near East, Greece, and the Italian peninsula from very early times. It remains an important culinary herb in all of these areas today.

Traditionally viewed as a "holy plant," basil was grown around shrines and temples in Greece and India, infusing the air with its clovelike fragrance.

Chopped, fresh basil leaves are frequently used in the varied cuisines of the Near East, providing a flavorful addition to cous cous, chopped wheat dishes, and many types of vegetables. In many areas, such as Jerusalem, it is often used instead of parsley as a chopped fresh garnish on felafel (deep-fried cakes of ground chick peas and garlic).

Basil is also a major herb of Italian cuisine. It is utilized in salads, sauces, and as a garnish on various vegetables and pastas. Chopped fresh basil is also a perfect garnish for noodles or new boiled potatoes with fried mushrooms.

Basil imparts a unique and delectable flavor to plain spinach as well as to spinach and cheese dishes. Combined with chopped garlic and either sliced tomatoes or tomato paste, it is excellent with sourdough or pita bread. Pesto, an Italian pasta sauce combining fresh basil, pine nuts, oil, garlic, and grated cheese has recently become very popular in North America. It originated in Genoa.

Fresh basil is available throughout southern Europe and the Near East as well as in British and North American cities with large Italian populations. The season for fresh basil is usually late summer and fall, but in warmer areas it can be grown year-round. Unfortunately, dried basil, which is available in most grocery stores, to a large degree loses its clovelike pungence in the process of drying.

Bay Leaf

Lauris noblis

In the Mediterranean area, bay or laurel trees often grow to a height of eighteen meters (60 ft.), but in cooler climates they seldom reach more than six meters (20 ft.). Elliptically-shaped, fresh bay leaves are a deep green, but as they dry, they become much paler.

Bay trees are common to a large portion of the Mediterranean world, but are particularly prevalent in Asia Minor and Greece. Bay leaves were used in ancient Greece not only to season food, but to crown victorious athletes and poets. They were also used as offerings to the gods, and were especially associated with the oracle at Delphi.

The bay tree spread throughout much of temperate Europe from the Mediterranean world and has even been grown in the British Isles since the sixteenth century. It is also found in various parts of North America, particularly in California where it was introduced by the Spanish and has thrived to the extent that today it seems like an indigenous tree. In fact, Californians can often find bay leaves of excellent quality growing practically in their back yards. The most aromatic bay leaves available, however, are generally considered to be those imported from Turkey. These derive from ancient laurel groves dating back to Byzantine times. They are essentially no better than those grown in Greece itself, but for some unexplained reason the Greeks apparently do not export their bay leaves.

The pungent aromatic quality of bay leaves greatly enhances the flavor of pea soup, lentils, dried beans cooked in tomato paste, and vegetable stews made with potatoes, onion, and celery. Unlike many seasonings, bay leaves are far more flavorful when dried.

Beans. *See* **Azuki Bean; Black Bean; Black-eyed Bean; Chinese Green Bean (Long Bean); Fava Bean (Broad Bean); Green Bean (French Bean); Kidney Bean; Lima Bean; Mung Bean; Navy Bean; Romano Bean (Italian Bean); Scarlet Runner Bean.**

Beet

Beta rubra

Beets (or beetroot as they are termed in the British Isles) are indigenous to a wide area surrounding the Mediterranean, including the coastal regions of North Africa and Asia Minor. They have also been grown in central Asia from very early times. The cultivated beets we are familiar with today are the result of selective breeding over the centuries, which has resulted in a considerably larger root than the wild beet originally possessed. While the ancient Greeks and Romans ate the leaves of the beet plant, they used the extremely small roots only for medicinal purposes. By the third century, the Romans had begun to eat the roots which, through careful cultivation, had greatly increased in size. Apicius, a third-century Roman with culinary interests, even gave several recipes for the preparation of beetroot.

Although known in the British Isles since the fourteenth century, the beet has been seriously cultivated there only since the sixteenth century, at which time the eating of beetroot also became fairly widespread in France and Germany. Considering its southern origins, the beet adapted surprisingly well to cool northern climates, even becoming an important vegetable staple in certain areas of northern Europe. In Russia and Poland, it became cherished as a primary soup ingredient, being used either in a thick borscht with potatoes and cabbage or as the basis of a clear magenta-colored beet broth eaten with sour cream and dill weed. The beet apparently became part of the northern Slavic cuisine about the same time that it became popular in western Europe. By the end of the eighteenth century, beets were also being cultivated in North America.

A close relative of chard, beets are valued, too, for their exceptionally nutritious stalks and leaves, which have been traditionally viewed as a blood purifier.

Beetroots are excellent in soups and are especially delicious served cold in mixed vegetable salads. Whereas larger beets are best cut up for soups, the smaller ones are delicious by themselves, either plain with butter or in a mild sweet mustard sauce with oil and dill weed. For an unusual and surprisingly pleasing entrée, try boiled beets and potatoes served with sour cream and fresh dill weed. A little sugar should always be added when boiling beets, which, it may be noted, are one of the few vegetables not ruined by boiling.

A yellowish beet is said to exist in parts of western Europe. It is related to the yellow-white "sugar beet," *Beta vulgaris*, which is used to produce sugar but not eaten as a vegetable.

Belgian Endive. *See* **Endive.**

Bell Pepper

Capsicum annuium

Also called "green peppers," bell peppers apparently derive their name from their vaguely bell-like shape. These same peppers ripen to a bright orange-red color and become somewhat sweet, but the tiny seeds within the partially hollow interior can be fairly "hot." Both the green and red forms are used in cooking.

All *Capsicum* peppers are native to both South and Central America. The bell pepper was cultivated by the Incas for thousands of years. In fact, dried specimens have been found in Incan tombs that date to some 2000 years ago. Various *Capsicum* peppers, including the bell pepper, were brought to Europe from the West Indies by Columbus. From Spain, their cultivation spread to much of southern Europe during the sixteenth century. Somewhat later, the Spanish also introduced them to California.

When green, bell peppers are crisp in texture, mild in flavor, and can be eaten either cooked, or raw in salads or sandwiches. Sliced green bell peppers are excellent with sautéed vegetables, particularly okra. They go exceptionally well with cheese and egg dishes, blend beautifully with onions and garlic, and add a gourmet touch to tomato sauces. Bell peppers can be baked whole and stuffed with cheese and mashed potatoes or grains such as wheat, rice, or millet. One of the most delicious sandwiches imaginable consists simply of good-quality rye bread with cream cheese and slices of green or red bell pepper.

Widely used in Latin American cuisine, bell peppers have also become very popular in North America, Spain, and the Balkans. They are not particularly popular in northern Europe or the British Isles.

Raw green bell peppers may be indigestible if eaten in quantity. As the green peppers ripen and turn a deep orange-red, their texture loses its crispness and the pepper becomes far more digestible. The ripe red bell peppers can be used in all the same ways as green peppers, and are especially good cut in small pieces and cooked with rice, millet, or barley. They also greatly enhance creamy mashed potatoes.

Bergamot
Citrus bergamia

The bergamot is an extremely rare type of citrus tree. It has the leaves and flowers of an orange tree, but is considerably smaller. The fruit of the bergamot citrus has a very thin, very smooth, bright yellow rind.

The bergamot is only found in Calabria in southern Italy. Whether it is a natural "sport" or was deliberately developed from some variety of orange or a mixture of orange and lemon is a matter of speculation. While Fitz-Gibbon states in *The Food of the Western World* that the fruit is pear-shaped, others describe it as round and close to eight centimeters (3 in.) in diameter. Perhaps there are variations in shape.

The marvelous fragrance of this rare citrus fruit's rind simply defies description. Although sometimes simply grated for use in gourmet puddings and confections, the rind is more commonly used in the form of a highly scented oil or essence that is extracted from it. This is, for instance, one of the ingredients in Earl Grey tea. Regardless of how bergamot is used, only the most minute quantity is needed. In Greece, a superb, layered phyllo-type pastry filled with thick sweet cream flavored with bergamot is sometimes available.

Needless to say, since bergamot is so rare it is also very expensive. It is all but unknown in North America and should not be confused with "false bergamot." Vaguely reminiscent of *Citrus bergamia* in fragrance, the falsely designated "bergamot" is derived from the plant *Monardia didyma*, which is a type of mint indigenous to the New World. It, too, is used to flavor certain types of tea.

Black Bean

a variety of *Phaseolus vulgaris*

Included in the very general *Phaseolus vulgaris* classification, the black bean is a small New World bean that is actually a deep purple color. It has been cultivated in South, Central, and North America from the remote past. In 1535, explorer Jacques Cartier noted that black, as well as red and white, beans were being cultivated by the native people living along the banks of the St. Lawrence River in Quebec.

Every type of bean is unique in flavor, and black beans are no exception. Many bean enthusiasts consider black beans to be the most delectable of all New World beans. Indeed, most people who have tasted properly prepared black beans or black bean soup acclaim them as among the finest foods known to man.

Black beans are exceptionally hard and should be soaked for twenty-four hours before cooking. Sugar, black peppercorns, onions, chopped garlic, and a few bay leaves should be added once the beans have been left to simmer. Oil should be added only when the beans are served. Chopped parsley or basil makes an excellent garnish. The same procedure can be used for black bean soup. In this case, purée the beans, add more water, and allow the soup to simmer for a while longer. Black bean soup can also be made with milk, in which case the bay leaves should be omitted.

Rather curiously, the black bean did not become as popular in

Europe as the white navy bean or the large red kidney bean. In China, however, it became extremely popular from the sixteenth century on, being used interchangeably with a native Chinese black soybean in many Chinese specialties. Black bean purée is the basis of various sauces used on vegetables, tofu, and noodles. A thick, sweet, black bean paste is also used as a filling for a delicious Chinese confection known as "black bean cake." These "cakes" are often available in North American cities with sizable Chinese communities.

Blackberry

Rubus, many varieties

Rubus canadensis (trailing) and *Rubus cunifolius* (upright) are two of the main blackberry types. A deep purple in color, blackberries are native to both the Old and New Worlds, but are found in particular profusion throughout North America where, for centuries, they have been an important item in the diet of the native Indian peoples.

The blackberry, which grows well even in areas where a cold winter climate prevails, remains a predominantly wild plant and in many areas is only infrequently cultivated commercially. A member of the rose family, it has extremely sharp barbs or thorns covering its stems. A seedless type has been developed, but is seldom encountered.

Frequently made into delicious preserves or jam for use on toast or pancakes, blackberries can also be eaten fresh with cream and sugar, or used in pies and pastries.

Blackberries are rich in vitamins A and C.

Black Currant

Ribes nigram

A deep purple in color, the black currant is native to northern and central Europe as well as to Siberia. It is particularly popular in Poland, Hungary, and Yugoslavia. Throughout eastern Europe, concentrated black currant juice is diluted with water for a popular and refreshing fruit drink.

Black currants, which are exceptionally high in vitamin C, are generally not grown commercially in southern Europe or in the New World. Nevertheless, North Americans can still enjoy this delectable fruit thanks to the excellent black currant jam imported from Hungary. It has a rich nutlike flavor that some people find reminiscent of blueberries. Occasionally, the juice or syrup is available, although this is far easier to find in Canada than in the United States.

See also **Red Currant.**

Black-eyed Bean or Black-eyed Pea

Vigna sinensis

Some authorities believe that the black-eyed bean is native to India while others are of the opinion that it originated in China as its Latin name would indicate. It is, in fact, closely related to the Chinese "long bean." Whatever its origins, cultivation of the black-eyed bean spread at a fairly early date to Africa, where it became a major food staple. Although the ancient Greeks and Romans apparently were not familiar with it, Sturtevant states, in *Edible Plants of the World*, that it was known to the Byzantine Greeks by the fourth century A.D., after which time its cultivation spread throughout Asia Minor and elsewhere in the Mediterranean world, including the Italian peninsula.

Black-eyed beans have long been a favorite in the southern United States, having been brought there by African slaves who introduced them to the West Indies, Virginia, and the Carolinas in the eighteenth century. This vegetable, both in dried form and as a fresh green bean, was popular among the slaves as a familiar food of their homeland.

Among the British colonists, black-eyed beans were used instead of the familiar green pea of northern Europe, which did not grow well in a climate as warm as the Carolinas. Hence, it came to be known as the "black-eyed pea," although it is, in fact, a bean. Attempts to grow the black-eyed bean in northern Europe failed as the brief warm summers do not last long enough for the beans to develop.

The pods of the black-eyed bean grow up to twenty-five centimeters (10 in.) long, and look like a longer variety of the regular green string bean. Before reaching full size, they are excellent eaten as fresh "whole pod" beans. Throughout North America, however, they are more commonly available as a dried legume, and should be prepared in the same ways as other dried beans—notably with onions, garlic, bay leaves, and other herbs such as oregano or basil.

Tomato paste or a generous amount of paprika can be added for variety and the beans can be served as a soup or as a thick "porridge" with rice, millet, cous cous, or noodles. Black-eyed beans also make an excellent cream or milk soup but, for this, dill weed, rather than bay leaves and oregano, should be used, and chopped parsley and butter should be added as a garnish before serving. Be aware that black-eyed beans—unlike other varieties of bean—become soft after soaking only one hour, and, therefore, should be cooked for no more than fifteen or twenty minutes.

The "crowder," a very similar type of bean but without the black spot, is also grown and eaten in some parts of the United States.

Black Pepper

Piper nigrum

Black pepper is undoubtedly the most heavily used spice in the Western world. It is available as whole dried unripened peppercorns as well as in ground or powdered form. So-called "white pepper," which is actually tannish gray in color, is derived from the same peppercorn after it has ripened and been dehusked. It is milder than black pepper and is quite popular in many areas of northern Europe. As for the rarely encountered green peppercorns, they differ from the black in that they are pickled rather than dried.

The trailing vines, which produce long "strings" of twenty or more fragrant peppercorns, grow to a length of 3–4 meters (10–12 ft.) and are native to southern India. They spread from India to the Malay Peninsula and the East Indies (today's Indonesia) at an early date.

Black pepper has been a major item of the spice trade with the East for millenia and for much of its history was a luxury item used only by the aristocracy. So great was their value that peppercorns were even used as currency during the Middle Ages and medieval period in certain areas. The Phoenicians were undoubtedly the first traders to introduce the use of pepper throughout southern Europe and North Africa, at least among those wealthy enough to purchase it. Pepper was known to the ancient Greeks and Romans, but its costliness prevented it from being widely used. During the thousand-year existence of the Byzantine Empire, however, peppercorns became more widely used in the Mediterranean world, and from the warehouses of Constantinople they were shipped to western Europe.

With the decline of Byzantium, the center of the spice trade shifted to Venice at the head of the Adriatic. Aside from pepper, other spices important in the commerce of the time included cloves, cinnamon, and ginger, all of which were imported from the East and disseminated throughout Europe.

Venetian domination of the spice trade ended with the rise of Portugal as a major European power. Later, the Portuguese were replaced by the Dutch who, from their colonies in the East Indies, established a total monopoly on southeast Asian spices through various methods of control and manipulation, including vast stockpiling and widespread destruction of certain spice-bearing trees. Thus, the Dutch merchants established a virtual stranglehold on the spice market, keeping prices extremely high and reaping outrageously high profits.

In the late 1700s, the French finally broke the Dutch monopoly on southeast Asian spices by means of competitive prices. From that time onward, the use of pepper and other spices became widespread among all classes of European society. Today, pepper is grown not only in Indonesia and India, but also in the Malagasy Republic (Madagascar) where it was introduced by the French, and in Brazil where the Portuguese began cultivating it on a small scale during the seventeenth century. The finest quality black peppercorns, however, are said to come from the Malabar region of India.

Black pepper can be used in innumerable nondessert dishes. A few black peppercorns, simmered with rice, millet, lentils, or dried beans greatly enhance the flavor.

In conclusion, it may be noted that, in a sense, pepper—together with cloves, cinnamon, and ginger—played a part in the discovery of the New World, for it was to facilitate the transport of peppercorns and other spices to Europe that a direct maritime route to the East was sought.

Blood Orange

a variety of *Citrus sinensis*

The blood orange is placed within the basic sweet orange classification *Citrus sinensis* and, somewhat surprisingly, considering how different it is from other oranges, is not designated by a secondary botanical name.

Also known as the maltese orange, the somewhat rare blood orange is exceptionally aromatic, its unique flavor resembling an admixture of oranges, raspberries, and concord grapes. Its pulp ranges from red to reddish purple, and its rind from a regular orange to an orange deeply suffused with red. The branches of the blood orange tree are covered with thorns.

Generally believed to have originated in Italy as a mutation, the blood orange has been cultivated there for centuries. It is also grown extensively in southern Spain and Malta, with the Maltese claiming its origin for themselves.

Exported from both Spain and Italy, blood oranges—when in season—can be found in the finer produce markets of many cosmopolitan cities throughout the world, ranging from London and Athens to Montreal and San Francisco. Although not unknown in North America some twenty years ago in sophisticated urban centers, the blood orange, quite inexplicably, all but disappeared from North American markets until quite recently. Indeed, the majority of North Americans have never seen a blood orange, let alone eaten one. Fortunately, blood oranges are now raised on a small scale in southern California and are appearing with increasing frequency in North American shops.

An aesthetically pleasing way of serving a blood orange is to place its segments, sprinkled with sugar, in a frosted glass dessert goblet. These can then be eaten with a fork.

Blueberry
Vaccinium angustifolium, V. coryboscum

Vaccinium angustifolium and *V. coryboscum* are the most important species, one growing close to the ground and the other considerably above it. Blueberries are native to North America, being found throughout much of Canada as well as the northern regions of the United States. Huckleberries are closely related, but not nearly as prevalent.

The French explorer, Samuel de Champlain, noted that the Huron Indians not only dried and pressed blueberries into cakes for later use, but also ate them raw and made a type of flour out of them. In the Arctic, they are an important item of the Inuit diet. It is interesting to note that, in *Edible Plants of the World*, Sturtevant mentions a related variety growing wild on the Kamchatka peninsula, where it was probably introduced via Inuit traders.

Although commercially available in the United States, blueberries are far more popular in Canada, where they comprise a major fruit crop. In both countries, they are obtained from both wild plants and cultivated hybrids, the latter yielding a far larger berry than the former. Maine and Minnesota in the eastern United States, and Oregon and Washington in the Pacific Northwest are important blueberry-producing centers.

Blueberries are used in pies, muffins, jams, and preserves. In Canada, they are very popular fresh or frozen and eaten with sugar and cream.

Blueberries contain vitamins A, B, and C, as well as calcium and iron.

Bok Choi

Brassica chinensis

The basic botanical category of *Brassica chinensis* is extremely broad in its application and is used to cover several quite different varieties of leaf vegetable that are native to China. Although designated a member of the cabbage-mustard-turnip family (*Brassica*), the most common types of bok choi, or pak choi, are, in fact, far more similar in appearance and flavor to the chard of the West, although they are not related to it.

Some botanists use the Latin name *Brassica pekinensis* for regular chinese cabbage and *Brassica chinensis* only for the various types of bok choi as well as for gai choi (mustard greens). Many people believe that Western botanists are very lax in their attitude towards Chinese leaf vegetables, and that a much clearer system of classification is needed. One might suggest classifications based upon those used by the Chinese themselves.

Bok choi in its most common form is a dark green, smooth-leaved vegetable with fairly thick white stems extending upwards into the leaves. It grows to a height of sixty centimeters (2 ft.) or more. This form of bok choi has for millenia been the most popular green leaf vegetable of the Chinese diet. Usually, it is steamed or sautéed and served with noodles, rice, or millet. It can also be stir-fried with onion and mushrooms in soy sauce, and eaten with bean curd.

Bok choi is widely available in North American markets today, but is difficult to come by in the British Isles and continental Europe.

See also **Shanghai Bok Choi; Cabbage,** paragraph on chinese cabbage.

Boletus Mushroom
Boletus edulis

The boletus or bolete mushroom is found in both the Old and New Worlds, growing throughout the temperate and northern areas of Europe and North America. Although there are a number of variant types, all possess certain common characteristics. Generally, they are found growing under or near pine trees or, more rarely, oaks. They differ from other edible and nonedible mushrooms in that they do not have "gills" on the undersides, but rather a yellowish, orangish, or yellowish green "sponge." The cap of the boletus mushroom is covered with a smooth brownish membrane. This is somewhat slimy or mucilaginous to the touch and should be removed before eating. Unless very young, the sponge, too, should be excised.

The boletus can reach an enormous size of close to twenty-five centimeters (10 in.) across, but is best eaten at about half this size. It can be eaten raw, cooked, or dried. It is excellent simply cut up raw and eaten with a little lemon juice and oil on sourdough bread. The flavor is extremely delicate, and this is one variety of mushroom that should not be used with strong-flavored herbs or seasonings. Boletus mushrooms are particularly delicious in a cream or milk soup made with potatoes and dill weed.

Although fresh boletus mushrooms are not available commercially in North America, they can often be found at the base of pine trees throughout much of the United States and Canada, just as they are in much of Europe, from Italy to Poland and Russia. In North America, the brown-capped yellow or yellow-green sponged boletus is always safe and cannot be mistaken for any poisonous mushroom varieties. Enormous quantities of boletus mushrooms are harvested in Italy and Switzerland and dried for export throughout Europe, where they are widely used in making both soups and sauces. Various European firms put out excellent dried soup packets containing dried boletus mushrooms. Occasionally, these are available in North America, although considerably less so today than previously.

See also **Mushrooms.**

Brazil Nut

Bertholletia excelsa

Brazil nuts are native to Brazil and Venezuela. Attempts to grow them elsewhere have not been successful. The trees grow to a height of forty-five meters (150 ft.), with branches starting about fifteen meters (50 ft.) above the ground. The trunk of the tree is generally about two meters (6 ft.) wide. Approximately twenty hard-shelled nuts are contained in each of the large coconut-type "fruits" that eventually fall from the trees with tremendous force, splitting open and releasing the hard-shelled nuts within them, many of which are driven into the earth by the force of the fall. Thus, brazil nuts are often still crusted with bits of earth when they appear in shops. Brazil nuts, which have a white, earthy tasting kernel, are generally eaten by themselves, although they are sometimes sliced or chopped for use in various cakes and confections.

Broad Bean. *See* **Fava Bean.**

Broccoli

Brassica oleracea botrytis cymosa, B. o. italica

There are several different types of broccoli and authorities differ as to their proper Latin names. *B. o. italica* is the name generally used to designate the thick broccoli clusters common in our markets today.

Although sometimes said to have originated on the Italian peninsula and to have spread from there to other areas of the Mediterranean world, broccoli is more often held to have been indigenous to Asia Minor. It was, in any case, held in highest esteem by the ancient Romans, who cooked it with particular care in many different ways. It is mentioned by Pliny, in his *Natural History*, under the name "cyma."

Broccoli is one of the many vegetables that Catherine de Medici introduced into France in the early sixteenth century. Although, in all probability, the Romans introduced broccoli to Britain and Gaul when the latter were distant outposts of the Roman Empire, the native populations apparently did not develop a fondness for the vegetable and simply let it die out after the departure of the Romans. It was reintroduced to the British Isles from France in 1720.

Although broccoli was first brought to North America during the eighteenth century, its use did not become widespread there until after World War I. Its increased popularity was chiefly due to the large number of Italian immigrants and the cosmopolitan influence that they came to exercise over North American cuisine. Today, broccoli is an important vegetable crop in both the United States and Canada, with perhaps the world's most flavorful broccoli being produced in British Columbia, Canada. This is no doubt due to the particular combination of soil and climate that prevails there.

Like most vegetables, broccoli should be steamed rather than boiled. It can be served in a cheese sauce or prepared with chopped garlic and oil. It can also be served cold with mayonnaise or oil and vinegar, either by itself or in combination with other salad vegetables and macaroni.

A slightly different species termed "broccoli raab" or "sparachetti" has long thin stalks with small end-heads. A similar variety, "gai-lon," is grown by the Chinese.

Broccoli of all types is rich in vitamins A and C.

Brussels Sprout

Brassica oleracea gemnifera

Brussels sprouts look like tiny hard-headed cabbages and are usually laid out in markets after having been removed from their stems. In their natural growing state, however, they present a delightfully unique sight to the viewer. Indeed, one could well picture them growing on some other planet. Imagine a thick one-meter (3-ft.) stem densely covered with clusters of walnut-sized cabbages, and you will form a fairly realistic picture of this very delectable and highly nutritious vegetable.

The brussels sprout is a northern European vegetable that originated during the sixteenth century in the Low Countries, which is to say Belgium and the Netherlands. In *The Origin of Cultivated Plants*, Schwanitz states that the ancient Romans had a primitive brussels sprout known as the "arician cabbage" but this variety of *Brassica* apparently became extinct, nothing more being heard of it after Roman times.

Whether the brussels sprout was an accidental mutation or was deliberately developed is unknown. It has been suggested that, either as a "sport" or as a developed species, the brussels sprout may have derived from the "jersey tree cabbage," which produces a cabbage head on the top of an extremely long thick stem.

The first description of the brussels sprout as we know it today occurred in 1587. By the end of that century, it was being grown throughout the Low Countries and exported to neighboring lands, becoming in a relatively short period of time popular in much of northern Europe, including the British Isles where its use became widespread among the aristocracy during the late Elizabethan period. Several centuries elapsed, however, before the general population could afford to purchase this costly imported vegetable. Somewhat astonishingly, the brussels sprout only began to be extensively cultivated in the British Isles during the 1850s. Since then, it has become a favorite vegetable there.

Although the brussels sprout may have been introduced to North America by Waloon Dutch settlers in the New York area during the seventeenth century, there is apparently no mention of it being raised in the New World until the early 1800s. In fact, it was not raised commercially in North America until after the beginning of the twentieth century. Today, it is chiefly grown in the coastal regions of central California as well as in New York state and British Columbia, Canada. It is a far more popular vegetable in Canada than in the United States. The frosts and the particular mineral composition of the soil give the British Columbian brussels sprouts a particularly delectable flavor.

Despite their small size, brussels sprouts are inedible raw. They should never be boiled, but rather always steamed. That way, both the unique flavor and the full nutritional value are preserved to a maximal degree. They are excellent eaten with mashed potatoes, millet, or noodles. They require no herbal additions and are best eaten with no seasonings other than a bit of sea salt, butter, and paprika. They are also delicious eaten cold with mayonnaise as a salad vegetable. Sliced, they make remarkably good sandwiches. Many people are fond of them in a cream sauce with new boiled potatoes.

Brussels sprouts are rich in vitamin A and contain exceptionally large quantities of pyridoxine, a B vitamin.

Buckwheat

Fagopyrum esculentum, F. sagittatum

In parts of western Europe buckwheat (from the Dutch "bokweit") is known as "groats," while among the Russians and other Slavic peoples of eastern Europe, where it is a major food staple, it is termed "kasha." It is also a favorite among Jewish people. Its place of origin is said to be central Asia. It gradually traveled westward and by the beginning of the Middle Ages was widely eaten throughout much of Europe.

Although, strictly speaking, not a grain cereal, buckwheat is prepared like a grain and has similar culinary uses. It can be obtained either roasted or unroasted and is cooked like rice or millet. The end result, however, is not the same inasmuch as buckwheat's texture is very different and its unique flavor much stronger than either rice or millet.

Buckwheat is best served mixed with various vegetables such as chard, green beans, or brussels sprouts. Butter or oil should be added to it. Dill weed goes exceptionally well with buckwheat, which, once cooked, is delicious fried with onions.

Buckwheat is rich in protein, iron, vitamin E, and several B vitamins.

Cabbage

Brassica oleracea capitata

There are many varieties of cabbage, most green in color, but some a purplish red. *Brassica oleracea capitata* designates the commonly available cabbage with which we are familiar today. Cabbage is of the same genus as broccoli, brussels sprouts, kale, cauliflower, and kohlrabi. It is perhaps the most ancient, widespread, and universally popular vegetable known to man.

Cabbage seeds have been found in numerous prehistoric excavations in widely separated areas of the Old World. In one form or another, cabbage is found from China to the British Isles and from Greece to the shores of the Baltic. According to some authorities it originated in Asia Minor and the southern Mediterranean area, but others claim that its actual place of origin is unknown. It is quite possible that it was native to a very wide area, even extending far into the north. Indeed, cabbage may have been indigenous to both Gaul and the British Isles as well as to Scandinavia and eastern Europe. The Latin word for the cabbage family, *Brassica*, is said to derive from the old Celtic "bresic." This fact in itself would seem to indicate that the Celts of Gaul (France) and the British Isles were familiar with the cabbage prior to the incorporation of these areas into the Roman Empire.

Eaten even by the ancient Egyptians and highly regarded by the ancient Greeks and Romans, cabbage was an important vegetable from the very beginnings of civilization and, for millenia, a major source of vitamin C among most Old World peoples. The great apostle of vegetarianism, Pythagoras, apparently wrote an entire treatise extolling its nutritional and medicinal properties. Not only did the ancients regard cabbage as a delicious food, but they emphasized its curative powers. Hippocrates recommended its use for numerous stomach ailments, and Cato declared that it was a remedy for practically any disease known to man, providing that it was eaten in sufficient quantity.

Cabbage was unquestionably the most widely eaten vegetable throughout Europe during the Middle Ages and well beyond. Indeed, it remained *the* major vegetable throughout the entire medieval period in the British Isles, the Low Countries, Scandinavia, eastern Europe, and the areas which today comprise France and Germany.

Until the ninth century the only kind of cabbage known was the loose-leaved type; hard-headed cabbage became widely cultivated only during the thirteenth century. It is the type best suited to a cool climate and consequently became popular among Scandinavians, northern Slavs, and Germans. In the seventeenth century, an oval, flat-topped, hard-headed variety appeared. It remains a favored type in northern and eastern Europe, but is seldom seen in North America. Yet another kind, the pointed or conical cabbage, was developed in the eighteenth century. It is often seen in North American markets today and is somewhat in-between hard-headed and loose-leaved.

Cabbage was first introduced into the New World in 1542 by the French in what is today Quebec, Canada. During the next century, the British began cultivating it throughout their North American colonies. By the late 1700s, cabbage was being grown by many of the native Indian peoples of North America, not only in French Canada but all the way from New England to the Carolinas. Today, it remains an important North American vegetable and is eaten both cooked and raw by the majority of the population, regardless of ethnic background.

Cabbage is particularly rich in calcium and vitamins A and C and was one of the foods consistently served in the British Royal Navy over the centuries. Together with whole dried peas and fresh limes, it was eaten as a preventive of scurvy as well as a means of ensuring general good health. Even today, doctors recommend cabbage and cabbage juice to alleviate and heal ulcer conditions as well as liver and kidney ailments.

Savoy cabbage, *B. o. bullata major*, is easily identified by its crinkly curly leaves and should be cooked rather than eaten raw. It is a loose-headed type and existed even among the ancient Romans, who called it "sabellic cabbage." Although available in North America, it is eaten in far greater quantity in southern Europe where it originated.

The reddish purple cabbage, *B. o. capitata rubra*, is said by Sturtevant, in *Edible Plants of the World*, to be "a very ancient type," yet most botanical authorities claim that it was not mentioned until the late sixteenth century. This generally spherical and hard-headed cabbage is said to derive from the regular green cabbage, which has genes that can cause anthocyanin to form in the plant, thus producing the red coloration of the leaves. It is esteemed by the Dutch and Germans among whom it probably originated. It makes an excellent sauerkraut, and although it is somewhat tough, many people use it in coleslaw.

Chinese cabbage, *B. o. pekinensis*, is a very pale, elongated, greenish white, loose-leaved cabbage. In parts of North America, a variety of chinese cabbage is known as "napa cabbage." This cabbage is especially delicious raw, either by itself or in salads. The texture and even the flavor is more like lettuce than cabbage! Like the other Chinese *Brassicas*, it remained unknown in the West until the late eighteenth century. It is widely available in North American markets, although not so easily found in Europe and the British Isles.

Regular cabbage, both hard-headed and loose-leaved, is excellent raw—chopped, sliced, or grated—and eaten either by itself or combined with other vegetables such as tomatoes and grated carrots in a salad. Diced apples and raisins also go well with it, as do avocados. Cabbage salads of all types are best served with oil and either wine vinegar or lemon. Dill weed, chopped parsley, and sea salt are to be recommended with all types of cabbage salad.

Germans, Dutch, northern Slavs, many Scandinavians, and even some British and North Americans are fond of sauerkraut, which consists of finely grated or cut cabbage pickled in vinegar, with or without the addition of sugar and various spices such as cloves.

Plain sliced cabbage is excellent steamed very lightly and eaten together with potatoes or noodles and oil or butter. Cabbage should never be boiled, except when used in soups. A fine, thick, all-vegetable borscht can be made by combining shredded cabbage, beets, turnips, onions, and potatoes.

Eastern Europeans—ranging from Czechs and Poles to Russians and Hungarians—fry chopped or grated cabbage with onions and, with or without the addition of tomato paste seasoned with dill weed, serve it with noodles or potatoes.

Cantaloupe

Cucumis melo reticulatus

In English, "cantaloupe" refers to the popular muskmelon, *Cucumis melo reticulatus*, with its fragrant orange pulp and "netted" or "ribbed" outer rind. Like other melons, it is indigenous to the area encompassing Persia, Georgia (Gruzhia), and Armenia in the region of the Caucasus. Well known in the ancient world, it was cultivated in Greece by the third century B.C., and by the first century A.D. had become a popular but costly item which graced the tables of wealthy Romans.

A quite different melon, scarcely larger than an orange and with a scaly rather than netted rind, was known as a "cantaloupe" in the ancient world. This type, *Cucumis melo cantaloupsis*, sometimes termed the "true" cantaloupe, is said to have originated in the area of Lake Van in Armenia and to have been later transported to Italy where it is still found today. It has, over the centuries, gained something in size, although it remains considerably smaller than the muskmelon cantaloupe so familiar to North Americans. The flavor of both types is similar, and is greatly enhanced by the addition of lemon juice and sugar. Both are also outstandingly rich in vitamin A. The regular muskmelon cantaloupe, *C. m. reticulatus*, is extensively grown today in California.

Caper

Caparis spinosa

Capers are the unripened buds of a shrub that is native to most areas surrounding the Mediterranean. They thrive particularly in ancient ruins. Capers still grow wild in Israel, on the island of Cyprus, and throughout much of North Africa, even extending down into the Sahara Desert where the leaves of the bush turn sideways to protect themselves from the sun.

In Italy, Spain, Algeria, and southern France, capers are raised for commercial marketing. In England, they have been grown in private hothouses for several centuries. Capers are like green peppercorns in appearance and, to some degree, in flavor. They generally come in small jars and are immersed in brine or vinegar.

Capers offer the creative cook innumerable possibilities. Combined with chopped parsley, they are delicious as a garnish on buttered cauliflower or potatoes. Capers are also excellent on hot toast, with cous cous or millet, and in sauces used to enhance vegetable dishes. Widely eaten in much of the Near East and Mediterranean Europe where they are sold in bulk, capers are also used in English, Scandinavian, and German cooking—particularly in sauces. In North America, where they are not especially popular, they are fairly expensive.

Caraway Seed

Carum carvi

From very ancient times, the caraway plant has grown in both northern and southern Europe. It is found from North Africa to Siberia and even has the distinction of growing wild in Iceland. Of the same family as dill and fennel, the caraway plant is cultivated for its seeds in such diverse places as Finland, Morocco, and Holland. Not only was it known to the ancient Romans and mentioned by Pliny in his *Natural History*, but it is considered to be among the oldest of European seasonings. Caraway seeds have even been found in the excavations of ancient Swiss lake dwellings.

Throughout northern and eastern Europe, caraway seeds are used in the making of rye bread. They are also added to such dishes as mashed turnips or potatoes, cooked cabbage, and coleslaw. Scandinavians and Germans are today the largest consumers of caraway seeds.

The entire caraway plant is edible. People who have had the good fortune to obtain the roots of the plant praise them as one of the finest root vegetables in existence. The leaves of the plant, which somewhat resemble those of dill but are more sparse, are excellent as a seasoning while they are young. Both the roots and leaves, which taste like a mixture of dill and parsley, were eaten as vegetable dishes and in soups during the medieval period and long before throughout much of northern Europe.

For centuries, "seed cake," which utilized caraway seeds as a main ingredient, was a favorite in England. Likewise, the usual English manner of eating baked or roasted apples was with caraway seeds. In Shakespeare's *Henry IV*, Part II, reference is made to "a pippin and a dish of caraways." English fondness for caraway seeds, however, has declined considerably since Elizabethan times.

Cardamom

Eletteria cardamomum

Cardamoms are the dried seeds of a shrub or small tree that grows to a height of three meters (10 ft.) and bears lovely purple flowers. These flowers produce pods containing the clusters of tiny black seeds which are used as a spice.

Cardamoms are indigenous to southern India, East Africa, and Zanzibar. Today, they are also cultivated in Indonesia. Extremely aromatic, cardamoms are widely used in various Near Eastern confections and sauces as well as in making Greek-style coffee on festive occasions. In Pakistan and various parts of India, cardamom is used in certain types of curries. Rather surprisingly, it is also extremely popular in Sweden, Denmark, and northern Germany, where it is often used as a spice in cookies, cakes, and pastries.

The flavor of cardamom is greatly enhanced by the addition of sugar or honey and it makes an interesting addition to fruit compotes. It is also delicious with segmented fresh oranges and sugar. Immersed in warm milk or cream, whole cardamom seeds create an unusually pleasing drink.

Powdered cardamom tastes entirely unlike the whole seed. In

fact, many people who enthusiastically utilize the whole, some-what sticky cardamom seeds as a seasoning do not care for the powdered cardamom at all.

Cardoon
Cynara cardunculus

Native to the Mediterranean area, the cardoon is closely related to the regular artichoke. In fact, the leaves and branch foliage of the two plants are nearly identical. The thistlelike flower-heads of the cardoon, however, are much smaller than those of the artichoke. They are also extremely spiky and are inedible. The edible parts of the cardoon are the younger leaves and stalk as well as the roots. Although sometimes encountered as an ornamental garden plant today, the cardoon was traditionally grown in filtered light to keep its edible parts tender.

In the ancient world the cardoon was a vegetable staple culti-vated in Greece, Sicily, the Italian peninsula, and even in the area of Carthage on the North African coast. The ancient Romans were, in fact, unable to produce sufficient amounts of it to meet their needs. Consequently, they imported it in enormous quantities from what is today Libya in North Africa. During the Middle Ages and medieval period, the cardoon spread over an even wider area including both Spain and southern France.

While the cardoon is still a favorite vegetable of the Italians and is frequently eaten in much of the Mediterranean world, it is all but unknown elsewhere. It does, however, occasionally appear in North America in areas with large Italian populations.

Cardoons can be simply steamed briefly and eaten with oil, lemon, and chopped garlic. They are also excellent fried and served with chopped parsley, or baked in a casserole with cheese.

The dried flowers of the cardoon, once harvested in some quan-tity in Spain, can facilitate the hardening of cheese, having exactly the same effect as rennet. Rennet is an animal product, the use of which renders many cheeses unacceptable to vegetarians as well as to Jewish followers of a strictly kosher diet.

Carob

Ceratonia siliqua

The glossy-leaved carob tree is native to the eastern Mediterranean. It grows to a height of about fifteen meters (50 ft.) and bears red and yellow flowers. From these flowers, pods develop which contain up to fifteen brownish red seeds that are approximately 50 percent sugar. These seeds or "beans" are utilized as a food and seasoning. They are also known as "locust beans" and "St. John's bread," from the tradition that the "locusts" mentioned in the New Testament as the only food of John in the wilderness were actually carob seeds.

Today, carob seeds are most often roasted and ground to a powder. The powder has the aroma of chocolate and it is often used as a substitute by people who are allergic to chocolate. Carob is also extensively used as a food for cows.

Carrot

Daucus carota

Cultivated throughout the world today, the carrot is an Old World root vegetable indigenous to Mediterranean Europe, Asia Minor, and the Near East. Some authorities claim that it originated in that area today known as Afghanistan, from where it made its way westward at a very early date.

Known to Pliny, the carrot was generally taken in its wild state in the ancient world. Very much smaller than today's carrot, it was very seldom used as a food in either the ancient world or the Middle Ages. The carrots which we eat today derive from those developed by the French and Germans during the sixteenth century. Early cultivated specimens were frequently red or purplish in color, although some were orange or yellow. Eventually the deep orange type became dominant, although, to this day, regular orange carrots occasionally have a trace of red or purple around the top.

The carrot became a popular dietary item in much of the European world during the second half of the sixteenth century, enjoying a particular vogue in England during the reign of Elizabeth I. Introduced by the British to their North American colonies, the carrot was soon adopted by native American Indians. Today, it remains a favorite vegetable in North America, northern Europe, and the British Isles.

There are many varieties of carrot cultivated today, ranging in shape from long and thin to short and thick. The most frequently seen type in North America is the long, pointed, somewhat thin variety which is also grown throughout the Mediterranean area. A short, thick, stubby variety, however, has been developed and has become increasingly popular during the last decade. In Japan, there is a variety that grows to a length of sixty centimeters (2 ft.)!

Carrots are excellent eaten raw, especially when grated. They are a welcome addition to almost any salad and are surprisingly good eaten with chopped apples or grapefruit segments and a little sugar. Raw or cooked, they go especially well with dill weed. Cooked, they are excellent in a cream sauce with dill or simply sautéed in oil and served with chopped garlic and parsley. They blend beautifully with the Japanese seaweed, "arame," after the latter has been soaked in water. Both are then sautéed with onion. Carrots are also a flavorful dish simply broiled in a little oil with potatoes and onions. In many parts of the world, carrot juice is a popular drink. In the United States, however, carrot juice has never really "caught on."

Carrots are the richest vegetable source of vitamin A.

Casaba Melon

a variety of *Cucumis melo*

The casaba shares with a number of other melons the general botanical classification of *Cucumis melo*. It is sometimes identified as *Cucumis melo inodorus*, although, in the United States, botanical suffixes are not generally used for the different varieties of melon, all of which derive from those native to Persia, Armenia, and elsewhere in the general area of the Caucasus. In *Cultivated Plants and Their Wild Relatives*, however, the Russian botanist, Zukovskij, uses *Melo* for the genus and consequently classifies the casaba as *Melo cassaba*. He also informs us that this variety of melon is native to the western part of Asia Minor. It was undoubtedly a favorite in Constantinople during the existence of the Byzantine Empire.

The pulp of the casaba melon is a whitish cream color verging on pale green, and the somewhat ridged rind is a brilliant yellow. Categorized as a "winter muskmelon," the casaba and similar melons store well, retaining their freshness well into the winter months.

Like other melons, the delicately flavored casaba is greatly enhanced by the addition of lemon juice. Cut in small pieces and sprinkled with sugar and lemon juice, it blends exceptionally well with blackberries. Some people find the flavor of the casaba mildly reminiscent of a mixture of vanilla and honey.

The casaba should not be confused with the "canary" or "juan canary" melon, which has the same brilliant yellow color and ridged skin. This melon, which is oblong in shape and considerably smaller than the casaba, is occasionally available in North American markets today.

The Spanish brought melons to California in the eighteenth century. Today, melons of all varieties constitute a major fruit crop there. The large Armenian community around Fresno has contributed much to melon and other fruit farming in California.

Cashew Nut

Anacardium occidentale

In its natural state the cashew nut dangles from the bottom of an inedible, orange-colored, pear-shaped fruit. In other words, the nut is an appendage of the fruit. The oily shell of the nut is extremely toxic and is removed by being burned off. Then the nut is boiled and a second shell removed before the delicious inner kernel is revealed. How anyone ever discovered the delectable cashew is a mystery when it is necessary to go through so many steps to remove the toxic outer shells and arrive at the edible inner kernel.

The cashew nut is native to South America, notably to Brazil and Peru. The Portuguese introduced it to India and Mozambique in the sixteenth and seventeenth centuries. All of these countries, together with Tanzania, are now major producers of cashew nuts.

Rich in protein and vitamin A, cashews have a distinctive, slightly sweet flavor, and are generally eaten plain with a little salt. An excellent "butter" can be made from pulverized cashews, but unfortunately the cost prevents it from becoming a popular food item.

Cassava Plant

Manihot esculenta, M. aipi

There are several hundred varieties of cassava. More important in Brazil than elsewhere, the cassava (also known as manioc or yuca) plant is native to South and Central

America. It can also be found growing wild in the West Indies and Florida. It remains an important food staple in much of South America and the West Indies as well as in Africa where it was introduced three centuries ago. Today, it is also grown in southeast Asia and the Philippines.

Toxic if eaten raw, cassava tubers are always cooked, most often being boiled. Dried, the tubers are processed to produce tapioca, the granules of which are cooked in milk to make a delicious pudding.

Cassia. *See* **Cinnamon**.

Cauliflower
Brassica oleracea botrytis caulifloris

Cauliflower may have originated among the Greeks of Cyprus and spread from there to the eastern and western shores of the Mediterranean. Or, it may have spread to Cyprus and the West from Syria, where it had been cultivated since prehistoric times. In any case, the cauliflower was known to the ancient Greeks and Romans as well as to the Syrians and other peoples of the Near East, and was a vegetable staple throughout much of the Constantinople-based Byzantine Empire. In the twelfth century, it was introduced into Spain, and by the sixteenth century it was well known in much of western Europe and was being extensively grown in France and Holland. In 1586, cauliflower was introduced into England directly from Cyprus, a major cultivation and distribution center right up through the Middle Ages and medieval period. In England, it proved to be quite appealing to the more affluent segment of the population, and by 1619 it was available at high prices in the produce markets of London where it was known as "cyprus colewart." Only during the nineteenth century did cauliflower come into general use among all classes in the British Isles.

Cauliflower thrives in temperate climates, but as it spread to northern Europe the Mediterranean variety gradually adapted itself to the cooler weather of the north. Although closely related to broccoli, cauliflower consists of a fairly solid rounded head of undeveloped white "flowers." The leaves that surround the head are often tied together by the growers to protect the head from the sun. Direct sunlight tends to discolor the head and destroy the delicacy of the flavor.

A greenish yellow type, sometimes called "romanesco," has recently appeared in many North American markets. While this delectable vegetable is considered more of a broccoli than a cauliflower, it looks more like a chartreuse-colored cauliflower. One irregularly shaped type resembles an exotic coral growth, its beauty being such that one hesitates to eat it. The flavor is something of a cross between broccoli and regular cauliflower.

Cauliflower can be served either raw or cooked in salads. This versatile vegetable is delicious in a cream or cheese sauce, or broiled in a little oil with onions and carrots. A favorite Eastern European dish consists of small pieces of cauliflower, flavored with garlic, dipped in flour, fried, and served with chopped parsley. Many purists prefer cauliflower simply steamed and served with butter, capers, and chopped parsley.

Cayenne Pepper

Capsicum frutescens longum

Cayenne pepper, which is the hottest spice known, is the extremely fine powder derived from the dried pods of the red chili pepper, *Capsicum frutescens longum*. Indigenous to South America, these peppers have been used as a seasoning by the native peoples of that continent from very ancient times. Cayenne pepper itself was particularly important in the cuisine of the Cayenne region of French Guiana.

The red chili pepper has pointed leaves and bears white flowers that, on occasion, show traces of purple or green. It was introduced to India by sixteenth-century Portuguese traders soon after the Spanish conquest of South America. There, the spice derived from the ground peppers met with instant popularity, quite as though the entire Indian subcontinent had been waiting for it throughout its entire existence! Almost immediately, it became second only to cumin in frequency of culinary use. Cayenne is also much utilized in the cuisine of the entire Caribbean area. Most Europeans and North Americans, however, find its fierce hotness somewhat excessive and can only tolerate minute amounts of it. It has, during the last several decades, become more known in North America thanks to the immigration of large numbers of East Indians and the popularization of their cuisine.

Although cayenne can be used in place of regular black pepper, one cannot by any means use it in the same quantity! As it is very high in vitamin C content, cayenne is extremely nutritious.

Celery

Apium graveolens dulce

Celery as we know it today derives from "smallage," a form of wild celery indigenous to the Mediterranean area and well beyond. Smallage was used as a seasoning and as a medicinal herb by the ancient Romans.

It was only in the seventeenth century, after Italian botanists succeeded in developing a much larger strain which was not bitter, that celery began to be used as a vegetable food, first by the Italians and the French, and eventually by northern Europeans. By 1750, it had become a fashionable and rather costly winter vegetable on the tables of the Swedish aristocracy. Only during the nineteenth century did the use of celery become fairly widespread in the British Isles and North America.

The white or "blanched" variety, which was developed in Belgium and is the most popular type in Europe, is grown in sheltered trenches to protect the stalks from the sun. It has a much finer flavor than the very green, strong-tasting type that is commonly available in North America. The superior "blanched" or Belgian type is occasionally available in Canada, but rare in the United States.

Cooked, celery is used chiefly as a soup ingredient, served in a cream sauce, or broiled with other vegetables. Chopped up raw, it is an excellent salad ingredient that blends well with numerous other vegetables as well as with fruits such as apples and raisins. Raw celery goes exceptionally well with cheese and is often served that way in mixed platters of hors d'oeuvres.

Unfortunately, in North America one seldom encounters succulent young celery plants as the tendency among producers is to harvest the vegetable only when it has reached its full size and, consequently, is rather tough and unwieldy.

Celery Root

Apium graveolens rapaceum

Most people erroneously assume that celery root or celeriac is simply the root portion of regular stalk celery. It is, in fact, a totally different, though closely related plant, also ultimately deriving from "smallage." The stalk and the leaves of the celeriac are quite small and insignificant, while the root grows to enormous proportions, sometimes even becoming as large as a coconut. Although such specimens are somewhat inconvenient to use, rather surprisingly neither the flavor nor the texture are negatively affected.

The origins of the celeriac are shrouded in mystery. There are no references to it until about 1600 when it suddenly appeared in Switzerland, Italy, and France. By 1700, it had also become popular among the Germans and Scandinavians. As it does well in cooler climates, it soon became an important vegetable crop in much of northern Europe. Although grown in North America, it is not a popular vegetable there.

This delicious root can be prepared in various ways. It is very appetizing simply sliced, steamed, and eaten either by itself or with other vegetables in a salad with the addition of oil and lemon juice. It also can be sliced and lightly fried in flour or served in a cream sauce with fresh dill weed, Icelandic style.

Chard

Beta vulgaris cicla

Chard or swiss chard is closely related to the beet, but it is the stalks and thick, somewhat curly leaves that are eaten, rather than the root. Some find the flavor similar to that of spinach.

Chard is indigenous to the entire Mediterranean area from Asia Minor all the way to France. Today, it is cultivated throughout most of Europe and North America, doing as well in colder northern climates as it does in warm southern ones.

It has been suggested that chard is one of the earliest vegetables known to man, although it was not very popular in ancient Greece. Aristotle mentions it in the fourth century B.C., but arrogantly declares that it is a food proper only to peasants! The ancient Romans, however, were fond of it and it still remains a favorite vegetable of the Italians. Near Eastern Arabs have always enjoyed chard and, for centuries, it has been an important vegetable staple on the Iberian Peninsula.

During the medieval period, its cultivation spread from the Mediterranean to northern Europe where it became a favorite of both the Swiss and Germans. Quite inexplicably, it never became particularly popular in the British Isles. Its use in North America comes via French, Italian, and Swiss immigrants.

Unlike spinach, chard must be cooked. It is best simply steamed and served with lemon and oil or butter, either with or without the addition of chopped garlic. It can be used instead of spinach in Greek- and Italian-type pies or stuffed phyllo pastries. Chard stalks can be dipped in flour and lightly fried.

Chard is rich in vitamin A and contains small amounts of vitamin C and iron.

Chard is a delicious vegetable that deserves to be more popular. A red-veined variety seems to be undergoing a revival today and is more and more frequently encountered in markets.

Chayote

Sechium edule

Sometimes termed "chayote squash," this interesting vegetable, which grows on a vine, is botanically classified as a member of the gourd family. The pale green avocado-shaped chayote has a very firm texture, seems extremely heavy for its size, and contains only one seed!

Native to Central America and the West Indies, the chayote today also is cultivated in Brazil, North Africa, Australia, southern California, and Florida.

The chayote is somewhat sweet and very delicate in flavor. Raw, it is perhaps more like a melon than a squash, its texture being quite firm. Cooked, it is more like a summer squash. It can be broiled, fried, or steamed like any squash and served with chopped parsley and lemon, with or without garlic. It can also be sliced and eaten raw with lemon juice and sugar. In some areas it is used in a custard-type pudding.

This somewhat exotic squash has become increasingly available in North American markets during the last decade.

Cherimoya

Annona cherimola

The cherimoya is native to the highlands of South America, notably to Ecuador, Peru, and Chile. Today, it is also grown in Brazil, parts of Mexico, and even in Spain.

The pale green cherimoya is avocado-shaped. Patterns of indentation on the surface make it aesthetically very appealing. Its whitish cream-colored pulp is reminiscent of a sherbet or cream pudding that "melts" in the mouth, the unique flavor being like a delicately blended mixture of pineapple, banana, white peach, and cream! The well-known writer, Samuel Clements (Mark Twain), who died in 1910, described the cherimoya as "deliciousness itself."

Perhaps the most delectable fruit in existence, the cherimoya was among the first fruits imported to the United States from South America. There can be no question that around the turn of the century it was better known in the United States than it is now. Up until twenty years ago, cherimoyas were regularly available during their September to January season in many North American cities, although even then they were expensive, selling for up to two dollars each. During the last few decades, however, they seem to have all but disappeared from North American markets. Inquiries as to why cherimoyas are not available meet only with the response that "the distributors don't carry them" and "the importers don't import them." Hopefully, this situation will change in the near future.

This marvelous fruit can be propagated by either its bean-sized seeds or by grafting. It requires a warm climate, and will only grow at elevations of between 900 and 2000 meters (3000–6000 ft.). Furthermore, each tree requires 8–9 meters (25–30 ft.) of space around it in order to be productive. A mature tree can take up to five years before producing fruit. Although cherimoyas are not overly delicate, they do require reasonably careful handling in order to avoid bruising.

Some related fruits of the same family (Annonaceae) are also found in various parts of the Latin American tropics. One of them, the guanabana, *Annona muricata*, is popular in Cuba where it is used in ice cream and as a fruit drink ingredient. All fruits of this family are sometimes referred to as "custard apples."

Cherry

Prunus avium, P. cerasus; many varieties

P*runus avium* is the "sweet cherry" and *Prunus cerasus,* the "sour" or "sweet-sour" cherry. In *Cultivated Plants and Their Wild Relatives,* the Russian botanist, Zukovskij, uses *Cerasus* as the genus; thus, he speaks of *Cerasus avium.* There are over one hundred varieties of cherry in the world today—some sour, some sweet, and some a mixture of both.

Exceptionally productive, a single cherry tree is capable of producing up to nine hundred kilograms (2000 lb.) of fruit annually. One of the most ancient and universal of fruits, the cherry was spread over vast areas by birds (as indicated by the Latin *avium*). Its pits have even been found in various sites dating from the Stone Age.

Cherries were an important dietary staple in prehistoric Scandinavia, Switzerland, China, North America, and many other areas. Their place of origin is unknown, although one theory is that they spread to the Far East and the West from central Asia and the Caucasus region, eventually reaching Greece, Italy, the Balkans, and northern Europe. As to how they came to exist in the New World prior to the European colonization, it is quite possible that they were brought by early migrants from Asia.

Theophrastes, the Greek "father of botany" referred to the cherry in 300 B.C. The Romans were already grafting cherry trees before the Christian era, and Pliny, in his *Natural History,* refers to ten different varieties which grew on the Italian peninsula in the first century A.D. The Romans brought several varieties to the British Isles, and during the sixteenth century, Henry VIII's gardener introduced some new cherry stock from Flanders. Today, England is noted for the sharp-flavored Montmorency cherry used in preserves, jams, pies, and various confections. The well-known Queen Anne cherry is perhaps the most flavorful type for eating fresh. It is a very light red with a yellowish pulp.

English colonists brought cherries to the New World, as did the Spanish who brought the large, "black," sweet-sour Morello cherry to the gardens of their California missions. This variety is popular in jams and preserves, particularly in continental Europe.

Many of the cherries grown throughout North America today are Old and New World hybrids. One of the most frequently encountered is the Bing, a sweet dark cherry that was developed in Oregon in 1875 by a Chinese horticulturist. Unfortunately, in North America, cherries are often picked before they are sufficiently ripe and left in cold storage for too long before being sold, thus resulting in considerable loss of both flavor and vitamins.

Cherries, both cooked and fresh, are delicious mixed with other fruits in a fruit compote. They are excellent cooked with quince, shredded coconut, and dried apricots or pears. Preserved cherries with a little fresh lemon added are delicious served in a very small quantity and eaten while drinking tea. And, of course, cherries are very popular in plum puddings, fruit cakes, and pies. In the Near East and the Balkans, a "spice" called "mahleb" is prepared from finely ground cherry pits and is widely used in various confections.

Chestnut

Castenea sativa, C. dentata

Chestnut trees live to an immense age. Some in Sicily are said to be over 2000 years old! The nut is harvested from a spiny pod or burr that bursts open when the nut is ripe.

Castenea sativa designates the European or Old World chestnut and *Castenea dentata*, the North American. There are many variant types of each. Termed the "marron" by the French and other Europeans, the chestnut is indigenous to both the Old and the New Worlds. Once an important food staple of the poor in many areas of Europe, the chestnut is today rather expensive.

From ancient times, the chestnut was a major food of the Mediterranean peoples, being indigenous to a wide area including Asia Minor, Greece, much of the Italian peninsula, Sicily, Sardinia, Corsica, North Africa, Spain, and southern France. The smaller, sweeter, New World variety found throughout the northeastern region of North America constituted an important element in the diet of the native Indians. Most chestnuts grown in contemporary North America are hybrids derived from both Old and New World stock.

Chestnuts are most frequently roasted—a time-honored method that has been in use for millenia. Roasted chestnuts are fairly sweet and resemble the sweet potato in both taste and texture. The Romans also made a flour of them and used them in elaborate sauces. These sauces apparently survived well into medieval times, but today seem to have passed into the realm of "lost foods."

The Italians and Greeks also used chestnuts in porridges, puddings, and breads well into this century, but such usage has apparently all but died out. Plain roasted chestnuts remain popular in both lands as well as in France. Travelers will recall encountering vendors selling freshly roasted chestnuts in many continental European cities as well as in London, New York, and Vancouver, B.C.

Chick Pea. *See* **Garbanzo Bean.**

Chicory
Cichorium intybus

Originally from the Mediterranean region, chicory spread throughout most of Europe and is considered to be one of the most ancient salad vegetables in existence. It grows to a height of one meter (3 ft.) and has an exceptionally long root. The tooth-edged, somewhat curly leaves extend from the base of the stem. If allowed to grow to full maturity, the chicory plant bears bright blue flowers.

Chicory is cultivated chiefly in France, Belgium, Holland, and, on a smaller scale, in most other European countries as well as in North America, where it was introduced in the nineteenth century. In the United States, it is sometimes termed "endive," although endive is actually a different and quite separate "phase" of the chicory plant (*see* **Endive**). Strictly speaking, the fully mature plant should be called chicory.

The slightly bitter leaves are an excellent addition to any vegetable salad. Dried and ground, the roots are sometimes mixed with coffee to produce a bitterness or sharpness of flavor.

Up until twenty-five years ago, chicory was available in nearly every quality market in North America. Today, however, it is infrequently available in the United States, although it remains popular and widely available in Canada, where it is a favorite French-Canadian salad vegetable.

Chicory is said to possess exceptional healing properties, particularly in regard to the bladder and kidneys.

See also **Endive.**

Chili Peppers

Capsicum, many varieties

There are hundreds of different types of chili peppers native to South and Central America. Three of the most commonly used varieties are *Capsicum frutescens longum* (the long thin type from which cayenne pepper is produced), *C. f. abbreviatum* (small bush peppers, including those grown as ornamental plants), and *C. f. conoides* (the tabasco pepper used in making tabasco sauce). While some varieties are up to thirty centimeters (1 ft.) long, others are very small. Most are extremely "hot." They come in colors ranging from orange, red, or yellow to deep purple or green. Some varieties change color as they mature. Chili peppers are most frequently used in dried form to season a vast variety of dishes. As Anderson points out in *Plants, Man, and Life*, a thorough study of chili peppers is needed to properly identify the large number of *Capsicum* varieties.

Unripe green chili peppers—both hot and mild types—are eaten fresh in India, the West Indies, Mexico, and throughout Central America. The peppers are usually combined with tomatillo, cilantro, and garlic to make salsa.

Bush chilies are often available in North America as decorative potted plants. This plant produces extremely "hot," brightly colored chili peppers. Most North Americans find them inedible.

The "chili powder" so widely used in Mexican cuisine is composed of a number of different ingredients. While powder or paste from chili peppers forms the basis, powdered cumin and even chocolate are also added, together with oregano and, in some cases, other herbs and seasonings in varying amounts and combinations to create many different types of "chili powders" and sauces. Chili powders are often used in the preparation of dried beans.

See also **Cayenne Pepper.**

Chinese Green Bean

Vigna sesquipedalis

Also known as the long bean or yard-long bean, the chinese green bean (or "dow gauk") is more or less pencil-shaped, and may exceed sixty centimeters (2 ft.) in length. It is best eaten, however, when it is somewhat shorter than its full size.

Native to southern China and southeast Asia, the chinese green bean thrives even in temperatures as high as 38°C (100°F)! In such warmth, chinese green beans grow with astonishing rapidity, each plant producing a prodigious quantity of beans. They like to climb up poles, tripods, or even trees.

Although said to have been known in ancient Rome, this bean remained a rarity in the West for nearly two millenia. Fortunately, this excellent vegetable is now available in North America, particularly in areas with sizable Chinese populations. Although one encounters it far more frequently in Canada than in the United States, it does grow quite well in Florida, Hawaii, and other areas of the United States that have sufficiently long hot summers.

Chinese green beans are excellent very lightly steamed and served with oil and chopped garlic. They are also very good in a black bean sauce with rice or millet.

Chinese Onion

Allium fistulosum

The chinese, or welsh, onion is similar in appearance to the regular green salad onion, differing only in that it is milder in flavor and always grows in bunches or clusters of four or five. It is said to have first come to Europe in the thirteenth century. It became especially popular in the British Isles where it has been cultivated extensively for centuries. It is widely used in Chinese cuisine, particularly as a finely sliced garnish on various dishes such as noodles and bean curd.

Chinese Snow Pea. *See* **Snow Pea.**

Chive

Allium schoenoprasium

Chives, unlike regular onions, do not have underground bulbs, but are valued for the mild distinctive flavor of their thin grasslike leaves.

Found throughout the Mediterranean world even in antiquity, chives spread to northern Europe and the British Isles at an early date. Those specimens occasionally found growing wild in North America today are undoubtedly "escapes" from cultivated plants introduced after the European colonization.

Chives grow in small clumps and are perhaps the most popular of all "pot herbs." They can withstand frequent cutting, replenishing themselves constantly. They are particularly popular in France, Germany, Switzerland, Scandinavia, and England. In China, a variant type exists.

Chopped chives are particularly good as a garnish on various cheese dishes, cous cous, boiled potatoes or pasta, avocado salads, and fried tofu or tempeh.

Chocolate

Theobroma cacao

Chocolate and cocoa are derived from the fermented, roasted seeds or "beans" of the cacao tree, which is native to Mexico, Central America, and northern South America. Today, it is also cultivated in Ghana, Sri Lanka, and the West Indies. The trees grow to about seven meters (25 ft.), have large dark green leaves, and produce pointed "ribbed" fruits that turn colors ranging from orange-red to purple when they are ripe. In the center of the large oblong fruit are almond-sized seeds. After being allowed to ferment, these purplish seeds are roasted and crushed for use in the making of chocolate, which is generally flavored with sugar and vanilla.

Cocoa was first encountered by Europeans when it was served to Cortez and his officers at the court of the Aztec king, Montezuma. Cortez brought this delicious drink to Spain when he returned there in 1520, and it quickly became popular among the Spanish aristocracy. It was not introduced into France, England, or elsewhere in Europe until the second half of the seventeenth century, after which time it became one of the major imports from the New World. A "chocolate house" was founded in London in 1657, but chocolate only became affordable among the general population in the late nineteenth century.

Today, both cocoa and chocolate remain popular throughout Europe, with much of the finest-quality chocolate being processed in Switzerland and the Netherlands. There are two main types: the lighter-colored milk chocolate and the almost black, milk-free chocolate. Chocolate is particularly popular in the United States, where vast quantities are consumed in candies, cakes, pastries, and puddings. In Mexico, chocolate is even used as an ingredient in certain types of chili sauce.

The most subtle and refined type of chocolate is white chocolate, or "narcisse" as it is known in continental Europe. This delectable chocolate has only been introduced to the North American public-at-large within the last decade, although imported Swiss "narcisse" has been known to North American gourmets for some time.

Chocolate is said to aid in the lowering of high blood pressure as well as to have a positive effect on the nervous system.

Cilantro. *See* **Coriander.**

Cinnamon

Cinnamomum zeylanicum

Cinnamon, the most popular of all dessert spices, is derived from the inner bark of an evergreen tree that is native to Sri Lanka (Ceylon). In their wild state, cinnamon trees grow to a height of ten meters (30 ft.), but in cultivated cinnamon groves they seldom exceed three meters (10 ft.). They bear clusters of small yellow flowers.

In ancient Judaism, cinnamon was used in the holy oil made for anointing the vessels of the Temple. The ancient Greeks and Romans used cinnamon as a seasoning as well as in incense employed in religious ceremonials.

Throughout the Near East and the entirety of Europe from Italy to Sweden, cinnamon has for centuries been esteemed as a dessert spice. Until quite recent times, however, it was something of a luxury item. Together with ginger and black peppercorns, cinnamon was a major item in the spice trade with the Orient. Due to its presence on the island of Ceylon (today, Sri Lanka), the Portuguese occupied that land in the sixteenth century as did the Dutch in the latter part of the 1700s. Falling to the British in 1796, Ceylon continued to be highly valued as the center of the cinnamon trade, which became monopolized by the British East India Company. Even today, Sri Lanka remains the world's major producer of cinnamon, although it is also grown in the Seychelles and throughout much of southern India.

Highly aromatic, cinnamon is used primarily with fruits, puddings, and baked goods. It goes especially well with apples, quinces, and apricots. It is also an excellent addition to sweet or sour cream as well as to puddings and Icelandic "skyr"—a kind of yogurt with sweet cream poured over it, and served with sugar or honey.

Cinnamon is delicious with blintzes or mixed with sugar and sprinkled on toast.

Cassia, *Cinnamomum cassia* or *C. cassia lignae*, is a slightly different type of cinnamon that is found in China. It is derived from the bark of a tree that is indigenous to Burma and very closely related to the cinnamon tree of Sri Lanka. The flavor is essentially the same, although cassia is generally viewed as being somewhat sharper. It is first mentioned in Chinese annals dating to 2500 B.C. and was exported to Egypt as early as 1700 B.C. It is also mentioned in the Old Testament as a spice separate from regular cinnamon. The ancient Greeks are said to have first obtained it from Phoenician traders. Although rare in the United States today, Chinese cassia is widely available in Canada, where it is generally marketed as "hunan cinnamon" and is of impeccably fine quality.

Citron

Citrus medica

The citron is a somewhat elongated citrus fruit weighing up to two kilograms (5 lb.). It consists almost entirely of a thick, coarse-textured, yellowish green rind that has a particularly rich, somewhat resinous aroma. This rind is candied for use in fruitcakes and other confections. The inner fruit is very small, bitter, and inedible. The tree itself is both smaller and thornier than other citrus trees. When in full bloom or covered with fruit, the citron tree is exceptionally decorative and infuses the air with its aromatic odor.

Believed to be native to southeast Asia and India, where it was still growing wild even during the last century, the citron is said to have existed in the famed Hanging Gardens of Babylon. It was also widely cultivated in the ancient kingdom of Israel. Although familiar to the ancient Greeks and Romans, citron was apparently not cultivated in the European regions of the Mediterranean until the second century A.D., when it first appeared on the Italian peninsula. By the eleventh century, the citron groves of the Naples area were well known.

Today, citron is grown throughout much of southern Europe, that from Sicily and Corsica being regarded as the finest. It is available commercially throughout Europe and can be found in various specialty shops in North America.

Clove

Eugenia caryophyllata, E. aromatica

Cloves are the dried flower buds of the two trees named above, both being varieties of tropical myrtle. These trees thrive only in coastal areas and it is said that their fragrance permeates the air and is carried by the winds far out to sea. The trees can reach a height of twelve meters (40 ft.) and bear, if allowed to, clusters of brilliant scarlet flowers, the greenish pink buds of which are gathered and dried to become the reddish brown cloves available commercially throughout the world in both whole and ground form.

Clove trees are native to the southeast Asian islands that comprise Indonesia. In previous centuries, these islands were known as the "East Indies" or the "Spice Islands." They include Sumatra, Java, the Celebes, the Lesser Sundas, and the Moluccas. Today, the Malagasy Republic and Zanzibar are also major producers of cloves.

Long used as a seasoning in southeast Asia and India, cloves first became known in the West during the seventh century. By the medieval period, they were an important item of trade and were a luxury spice of the European aristocracy. The Dutch, who came to dominate the spice trade in the early 1600s, tried to increase the value of cloves by creating a "shortage" through the destruction of clove trees on all but two small islands of the East Indies. Continuing such a policy for well over a century, the Dutch reaped huge profits. Meanwhile, they stockpiled a vast supply of cloves in their Batavia warehouses, strictly controlling the quantity of this spice allowed on the world market. It is said that, in 1768, they had enough cloves on hand to supply all of Europe for ten years! Shortly thereafter, the French succeeded in destroying this Dutch monopoly by establishing their own clove plantations in Madagascar and Mauritius. It was only then that cloves ceased being a luxury item and permeated all elements of European society.

Used very sparingly, cloves are an excellent addition to puddings, fruit compotes, cakes, cookies, and pastries. They go particularly well with apples, oranges, and pears.

Clove oil possesses strongly antiseptic qualities and has long been used for various medical purposes.

Coconut

Cocos nucifera

The coconut is the seed of the coconut palm and is, in fact, the largest seed of any plant on earth. The trees, which can reach a height of thirty meters (100 ft.), produce as many as two hundred coconuts per year. The large white seed-nut is contained within a hard brown shell. The center of the nut is hollow and contains a delicious sweet milklike substance. The pulp of the nut is used as a food in itself as well as a seasoning and a source of oil.

The coconut palm is native to southeast Asia and may have originated in the Malay Archipelago. It was already growing on numerous South Pacific islands and even in South America when Europeans first came in contact with these areas. Thus, it was one of the few food plants common to both the Old and New Worlds (although unknown to Europe) at the time of European expansion. In all probability, it spread from southeast Asia via peoples migrating eastward. Arab traders are said to have introduced it to coastal Africa at a fairly early date. Today, both Florida and the West Indies are also major producers.

The coconut palms in the Key West area of Florida are descended from coconuts washed ashore from a shipwreck in 1840. It is possible that they also came to various Pacific islands and to South America in the same way. Pizarro found them growing along the coasts of Peru in 1524.

Coconut is delicious fresh, although you should be prepared for a rather arduous task in breaking open the extremely hard outer shell—an action that requires the use of a heavy hammer or even an axe. A hole should be made in the coconut shell prior to this operation in order to extract the juice or "milk." Fortunately, dried coconut, which is considerably richer in protein than the fresh, is widely available in thin-sliced or finely-shredded form. It is used in dessert dishes ranging from cakes to puddings. Grated coconut is particularly good with cream cheese, dates, yogurt, and fruit compotes.

Coriander

Coriandrum sativum

The coriander plant grows to a height of about sixty centimeters (2 ft.). Its leaves vaguely resemble parsley. The clusters of pinkish-colored flowers eventually produce groups of tiny fruits or seeds, which, in both whole and powdered form, have been used as a seasoning throughout the Old World for thousands of years.

While it is generally held that coriander is native to a vast area ranging from southern Europe through the Near East all the way to India, it is quite possible that it originated in southern Europe and spread eastward.

Powdered coriander is an important ingredient of East Indian curries and is also used in certain chutneys eaten with chapattis (East Indian pita bread) or papadoms (a type of thin, dry, pea-flour pancake). Coriander, often mixed with cumin, is also used in various vegetable dishes in North Africa, the Near East, and Greece.

Fresh coriander leaves, known as cilantro, are used as a garnish in Chinese and Mexican cuisines. Although coriander leaves do not taste even remotely like parsley, they are sometimes termed "chinese parsley" or "mexican parsley." Their flavor is also very different from that of the powdered seeds. People in the West are generally unaware that these leaves are, in fact, coriander leaves. Neither the leaves nor the seeds are particularly popular among people of northern European antecedents.

Fresh cilantro is frequently available in North American markets, particularly in California and the southwest where it is extensively used by people of Mexican background. In Canada, it can usually be found in urban areas with large Chinese populations.

Corn

Zea mays, Z. m. saacharata, Z. m. indentata, and other varieties

Zea mays is "indian corn"; *Z. m. saacharata* is the "sweet corn" widely eaten as a vegetable in North America; *Z. m. indentata* is the corn used in making the flour used in tortillas.

At one time the term "corn" designated grains in general, including wheat, barley, and even oats. Since the discovery of New World corn, however, the term has come to designate this plant and its grains alone.

The earliest type of corn is said to have originated in the Andean regions of northern South America in what is today Peru and Bolivia. The Incas believed that it was from another world. Gradually, this Andean corn traveled northward to Central America and Mexico where it is said to have hybridized with a type of maize called *Tripsacum* and eventually developed into the various types of corn known today. Corn was cultivated in the Tehuacan Valley of Mexico as early as 5000 B.C.

Long before the European colonization of the New World, the native Indians throughout much of North America were cultivating corn. It was an especially important food for the Hopi tribe as well as the native peoples of Virginia. Many North American Indians never harmed the crow, believing that it was responsible for bringing corn to them from afar. *Sweet* corn, an important strain in the Andes, was unknown among most North American native peoples.

Corn was brought to Europe from the Caribbean islands in the last decade of the fifteenth century, and from Spain it was introduced to other European countries, but most Europeans simply did not care for it and grew it solely as a food for farm animals. In Italy, however, its use was adopted in the form of the coarse-ground corn flour used in making "polenta." The Portuguese, who little utilized corn themselves, introduced it to East Africa where it became an important food over a large area.

Corn comes in a variety of colors—red, yellow, white, and bluish purple. The yellow, which is of greater nutritional value than the others, is the most popular. The white sometimes is available in North American markets and, during the last several decades, the bluish purple type has been raised on a small scale, chiefly as a novelty item. For some reason, red corn is a rarity and is usually only seen in the extremely attractive multicolored hybrid varieties of "indian corn" widely used for decorative purposes. The familiar large-eared yellow sweet corn that became the main type of corn grown and eaten in North America was only developed in the early nineteenth century.

While continuing to be largely ignored by most Europeans, corn remains extremely popular in North America where it is one of the more important crops. Corn is most often eaten directly off of briefly-boiled cobs, but a far more satisfactory method is simply to slice the kernels off the cob and eat them, buttered and peppered, from a dish. Eaten in combination with other foods, corn has considerable nutritional value. For instance, a native Indian dish known as "succotash," which consists of corn and fresh beans, is not only delicious, but provides a complete vegetable protein. Another native Indian dish, consisting of corn mixed with wild rice, is also to be recommended. Corn is, in fact, pleasing in combination with nearly any type of grain or with sautéed dried beans. Even by itself, corn is rich in vitamin A.

Corn flour provides the basis for the corn tortilla, an ancient food of Mexico that has become increasingly popular in North America. It is, in effect, the pita bread or chapatti of the New World and can be used in many of the same ways. Rolled up, after being covered with cream cheese and jam, it can even become a crêpe substitute.

Cos Lettuce. *See* **Lettuce.**

Crab Apple

Pyrus baccata

The crab apple is thought to have originated in Siberia and northern China, and to have spread at a very early date to a considerable portion of the Old World. According to Sturtevant in *Edible Plants of the World*, there are also native North American crab apples. *Pyrus rivularis*, for example, is found in the Pacific Northwest from Alaska to northern California and was, at one time, an important food source for the native peoples of this region. Another type, *Pyrus coronaria*, first observed by Verazzano in 1524 along the New England coast, is said to have been excessively tart.

The crab apple is one of the most ancient foods used by man. Its remains have been found even in Stone Age caves. Most crab apples are about the size of a walnut and while some are virtually inedible, others are remarkably aromatic and succulent. In all probability, the regular apple developed out of the smaller, tarter crab apple.

Crab apples of the more desirable type are delicious eaten raw with sugar, cooked as preserves, or used as an ingredient in fruit compotes. In the United States, crab apples sometimes can be found in the remains of Victorian gardens and orchards dating to the last century, but are only very rarely encountered in public markets.

Cranberry

Vaccinium macrocarpon, V. oxycoccus

Vaccinium macrocarpon is the North American cranberry and *V. oxycoccus* is the British cranberry. The cranberry is closely related to the English fenberry, the Irish bogberry, and the Swedish lingonberry. The native North American cranberry is more extensively eaten than are its Old World counterparts. For centuries the native peoples of North America used the cranberry both medicinally and as a food. In 1677, English colonists in Massachusetts sent ten bushels of cranberries as a gift to King Charles II, terming them "the choicest product of the colony." Throughout the nineteenth century, cranberries were eaten by North American seamen as a scurvy preventive.

Cranberries grow on a shrub that thrives in swampy ground or bogs. They prefer cool winters and warm summers. Wild cranberries grow from Nova Scotia to North Carolina, and by the 1850s were being raised commercially in New England and the Canadian Maritime Provinces as well as being harvested from wild plants. During the twentieth century, the Pacific Northwest also became a major area of cranberry cultivation. Cultivated cranberries are not grown outside of Canada and the United States.

Cranberry sauce and jelly are delicious with brussels sprouts and other vegetables. They transform boiled or mashed potatoes into a special treat and are especially delectable eaten with sour cream or mixed with other fruits such as pineapple or oranges. The juice, too, is both nutritious and refreshing.

Cranshaw Melon

a variety of *Cucumis melo*

Like other melons within the "muskmelon" category, the cranshaw is the fruit of a trailing Old World vine which originated in Persia and the Caucasus. The cranshaw melon is pale green infused with yellow, and the pulp is orange-pink. Cranshaws, like the closely related casabas, are considered to be winter muskmelons. As with other melons, the flavor is improved by the addition of lemon juice and sugar. Fresh raspberries and blackberries also go well with it.

Cucumber

There are many varieties of cucumber:

1. *Cucumis sativas* or *Cucumis vulgaris,* the common cucumber.
2. *Cucumis longus,* the long cucumber, thus classified in the sixteenth century. This category includes the "english," the "armenian," and the "chinese" types.
3. *Cucumis anguria,* the very small "warty" variety known as the gherkin.
4. A small, round, pale yellow variety known as the lemon cucumber. There would seem to be no information whatever concerning this variety in any botanical or horticultural manual. It may be related to another type, the so-called "russian cucumber," which is also round, but is described as being brownish and "netted."
5. Various others which are only rarely encountered.

Both the common cucumber and the long cucumber are believed to have originated in northern India, and have been cultivated for 3000 years. Numerous variations have either developed naturally as mutations or have been deliberately developed from the two basic types. For example, the chinese, armenian, and english varieties all developed from an original long type indigenous to India.

The cucumber made its way to Egypt at a very early date and became a favorite of the Jewish people during their captivity in Egypt. It was also popular in ancient Greece, Rome, and throughout North Africa. Mentioned by Pliny in his *Natural History,* it is said to have been among the favorite foods of Tiberius Caesar. It gradually penetrated the whole of Europe, and as early as the ninth century was being grown in Charlemagne's royal gardens. Although the cucumber had been introduced into the British Isles by the Romans, it had become a rarity by 1573 when it was reintroduced to England, this time directly from India. The cucumber was first planted in the New World on the island of Haiti in 1494, the seeds having been brought by members of a Columbus expedition. It was not long before its cultivation spread to the native peoples of mainland North America along the entire Atlantic seaboard, extending even as far north as Quebec.

The common cucumber and the english cucumber are both deep green in color, with a pale greenish white pulp. The long thin english type can reach over thirty centimeters (1 ft.) in length. Generally raised in hothouses, it is produced in considerable quantity in Canada where it is an important vegetable export. It is almost seedless and is generally considered to have a more delicate flavor than the common cucumber. The latter, however, is the main type eaten in the United States. It is much thicker than the english type and is best eaten when not more than fifteen centimeters (6 in.) long. Larger specimens are inevitably tough, bitter, filled with large hard seeds, and extremely indigestible. Cucumbers that have been coated with wax and refrigerated for a long period of time are all but flavorless and should be avoided.

The armenian cucumber was developed in Armenia centuries ago and is still cultivated there and in much of the Near East. It is now occasionally available in U.S. markets thanks to the efforts of Armenian farmers in southern California. Inasmuch as armenian cucumbers are "crook-necked" and either yellow or a very pale green, they are easily recognizable. The flavor is unique. As for the chinese cucumber, it is similar to the english, but is seldom seen in the West.

The small, round, yellow lemon cucumber is considered by many to be the finest of all cucumbers. Due to the tiny gray-black protuberances on its pale yellow skin, it is sometimes called the "salt and pepper cucumber." It may have developed from a variety known in previous centuries as the "russian cucumber," which was described as being round and "brownish." The lemon cucumber, unfortunately, is not easy to find, although it does turn up in U.S. markets occasionally. It should only be purchased when absolutely fresh.

Cucumbers contain very small amounts of vitamins A and C, but are usually eaten more for their flavor than for any possible nutritional value. A favorite salad vegetable, cucumbers are often sliced and served with lettuce, tomatoes, and green onions. The addition of dill weed or chopped parsley greatly enhances the whole. Cucumbers are also excellent in sandwiches with the addition of a little parsley, onion, and mustard sauce. In East Indian cuisine, they are grated into yogurt to create a refreshing pale green dish. Cucumbers have also been pickled for centuries. The small, warty, pickling type, known as the gherkin, was developed in the West Indies.

Cucumbers are popular not only in England, North America, India, and throughout the Near East, but also in northern Europe where they are an ever-present part of the Scandinavian, Polish, and Russian cuisines. In Iceland, they are a major vegetable crop grown in extensive natural-steam hothouses.

Cumin
Cuminum cyminum

Indigenous to the eastern Mediterranean area, cumin was introduced to India in prehistoric times. It was known to the ancient Romans who, rather surprisingly—as modern Italians do not use it in their cuisine at all—made a paste of ground cumin for use on bread. It is the pulverized seeds of the cumin plant that are used as a seasoning, rather than the leaves. Cumin is grown commercially and used extensively in India and the Near East, and is also an important part of North African and Maltese cuisines. It is not, however, a popular seasoning in most of Europe, although during the medieval period it was highly regarded as a medicinal herb.

Many westerners find the pungent, acrid flavor of cumin decidely unpleasant and unquestionably more medicinal than culinary in quality. For those who like the flavor of cumin, it is widely available in East Indian and Near Eastern specialty shops, both by itself and in various combinations with other herbs and spices. It is an ingredient in many East Indian curries and has been adopted by the Mexicans as an integral part of their chili sauces.

Currants

The term "currants" is widely, but incorrectly, used in English to designate dried corinth or zante grapes. These exceptionally small grapes are used in dried form only, in confections, bakery products, and puddings. They are not true currants at all. For true currants, *see* **Black Currant** and **Red Currant**.

Custard Marrow. *See* **Scalloped Squash.**

Daikon

Raphanus sativas longipinnatus

Daikon is a Japanese term designating a number of large, white-rooted radishes that are native to China and Japan. Although some varieties are round, most are shaped like large, thick carrots. They are generally about 30–45 centimeters (1–1.5 ft.) long. Over 25 percent of Japan's total vegetable crop consists of daikons.

Daikons are often shredded and used raw as a relish with rice, bean curd, and deep-fried vegetables. Grated daikon can also be mixed with grated carrot and eaten with a little lemon juice and sugar, pickled in vinegar, or sliced into vegetarian soups. Fried, it is excellent served with chopped parsley and noodles. The leaves can also be eaten, but they are seldom available in North America.

Although the flavor of the daikon is similar to that of the Western radish, it can be considerably stronger. The "sakurejima," for instance, which grows to a size of twenty-two kilograms (50 lb.), is so sharp in flavor that it cannot be eaten raw! Daikons of a more usual sort have become widely available in North American markets during the last decade. They are much less frequently encountered in the British Isles and continental Europe.

Dandelion

Taraxacum officinale, T. erythrospermum, and other varieties

Nearly everyone is familiar with the dandelion—its bright yellow flowers, its oblong leaves, and its soft white globe-shaped seed heads that blow apart and are borne by the winds to settle and thrive even in the least productive soil.

The dandelion with its flavorful, slightly bitter, "tooth-edged" leaves has for millenia grown in much of Europe and central Asia. Probably native to the Mediterranean area, it spread to the north and east in very remote antiquity. Today, it also grows throughout most of North America. Some authorities claim that it is no less indigenous to the New World than to the Old.

Unfortunately, inasmuch as dandelions grow in such profusion and with no care whatever, many people, particularly in North America, regard them as nothing more than weeds to be mercilessly expunged from gardens. Europeans are wiser and in many

European home gardens dandelions are carefully preserved and even cultivated. Sometimes, they are "blanched" by tying the outside leaves over the central core of new ones or by placing them under an upside-down flower pot. One need not go to such lengths, however, to enjoy the dandelion as a salad vegetable, for it is just as delicious in its natural state.

Ordinary dandelion leaves, particularly the younger ones up to fifteen centimeters (6 in.) in length, provide an excellent and nutritious salad vegetable. Somewhat resembling chicory in flavor, they can be used in mixed salads, or eaten by themselves with chopped garlic, oil, lemon juice, and possibly a pinch of oregano. Although the bitterness increases when dandelion leaves are cooked, some people enjoy them steamed and served with millet, rice, or bulgar wheat. Dandelion leaves are particularly popular in Greece, Albania, Italy, France, and Spain. In all of these areas, they are viewed as beneficial to the liver, and are also used as a general "tonic" for the blood and the entire system.

The dandelion is unquestionably one of the greatest untapped vegetable resources of our planet and should be accorded the respect that it deserves. Although occasionally available commercially, even in North America, it is always available from wild plants growing in fields, vacant lots, gardens, lawns, and along roads and lanes everywhere. Dandelion leaves are harvested by cutting them from the plant, never by taking the whole plant. They are, in fact, very fast-growing and replenish themselves with remarkable rapidity. Today, particularly in North America, one should be careful to avoid all specimens that may have been exposed to toxic sprays or excessive automotive exhaust.

Dandelion leaves are a favorite food of pet geese and are highly recommended for them. As for the beautiful bright yellow flowers of the dandelion plant, they are not only extremely attractive in mixed bouquets, but are sometimes used in making wine.

Danish Squash. *See* **Winter Squash.**

Date

Phoenix dactylefera

Date trees bear clusters of lovely white flowers that eventually turn into heavy clusters of ripe dates. Living to an immense age, date palms perpetuate themselves both by seeds and by offshoots from the base of the tree. Their branches are traditionally a symbol of triumph and majesty and are used in religious ceremonies and processions by all of the Near Eastern religions.

Date palms are indigenous to an area ranging from the Persian Gulf and the Arabian peninsula to Iraq (ancient Babylon), Israel, Egypt, and a considerable portion of North Africa. Some botanical authorities believe that the date palm spread to all of these areas from the Persian Gulf.

The date may have been the first fruit cultivated by man. Its seeds have been found in ancient excavated sites in Egypt. A food staple throughout the Near East, the date's importance to the nomadic desert peoples cannot be overemphasized. Thriving in the intense heat of the desert sun, date palms thrust their roots deep into cool underground water sources, thus indicating the presence of water. They also provide shade to weary desert travelers.

With the exception of southern Spain, date palms do not produce fruit in Europe. Dried dates, however, did make their way to Europe at an early date, probably via the Phoenician traders traveling throughout the Mediterranean. Later, during the Middle Ages, dates were an important trading commodity throughout the Byzantine Empire. Returning crusaders helped popularize dates in western Europe. In consequence, this fruit became a prominent luxury food import. In Elizabethan England, dates were popular as an ingredient of puddings and sauces. No doubt they were used in cakes and baked products as well.

Date trees were first introduced to North America—in New Mexico—in the sixteenth century by the Spanish. Later, they were also planted in southern California. Today, dates are an important crop in both Arizona and the inland desert areas of southern California. Date palms will grow, but not bear fruit, as far north as Eureka, California.

In recent years, several of the rarer varieties of dates, faced with extinction in their own natural habitats, have been successfully grown in southern California. These include the "medjool" or moroccan date and the "deglet noor" or "golden finger" date, which is indigenous to Algeria. Unfortunately, in North Africa these exceptionally fine dates are being decimated by an incurable disease.

Each variety of date has a distinct flavor of its own. Even the sizes, shapes, and textures can be quite different. One of the most delectable imported types is the "barhi." Although only available in dried form in Europe and America, dates are often eaten fresh in the Near East. Fresh dates unquestionably are one of the finest fruits in existence. Unfortunately, they are not available to the North American public in that form.

Dates are often eaten by themselves, although they can, of course, be combined with other foods or used in puddings, cakes, and confections. They go particularly well with yogurt, cream cheese, cottage cheese, or thick sweet cream. Cream cheese and date sandwiches are to be highly recommended. Dates are also excellent in a dessert dish combined with coconut, honey, millet, and tahini.

Dates contain vitamins A and B as well as sugar and protein.

Dill

Anethum graveolens

Dill or "dill weed" is a delicious, green, feathery herb. Although almost identical to fennel in appearance, dill is decidely different in flavor.

Dill's particular place of origin is unknown. From ancient times, it grew wild over a wide area of the European continent, ranging from the Mediterranean area and the Iberian Peninsula to Scandinavia and the Baltic. Some theorize that it spread to northern Europe from the south. It was known to the ancient Greeks, and was a popular seasoning among the Byzantine Greeks of Asia Minor, from whom it was adopted by the Turks.

Today, among Swedes, Finns, Danes, Estonians, Poles, and Russians, fondness for dill amounts almost to a passion. Dill is popular in Jewish cuisine, and is also used to a lesser degree by the Dutch and Germans. Although at one time said to have been widely used in England, today its use there is very limited.

Dill is still used by Greeks and Turks, but other Mediterranean peoples do not care for it. The French are said to dislike it intensely. In Spain and Portugal, where dill grows wild as a "field weed," it is never eaten. The reasons for this antipathy to dill among most Latin peoples remain a mystery.

If fresh dill is unavailable, dried dill is quite satisfactory for most culinary purposes. Dill is especially good in "pease porridge" or pea soup, with boiled or mashed potatoes, in cabbage salads, cream sauces, beet soup, and vegetable stews. It is an excellent garnish for sautéed carrots, parsnips, kohlrabi, or beets. Although dill blends well with garlic, black pepper, or paprika, it does not blend well with other herbs such as basil, bay leaves, or oregano.

During spring and summer, many people grow their own dill. It is not difficult to raise although the seeds take a fairly long period of time to germinate. Fresh dill is always available, in season, in northern and eastern Europe, and has, in recent years, also become available in U.S. produce markets. Dill is, in any case, always available in dried form throughout North America and northern Europe.

Dulse

Rhodymenia palmata

Dulse is an edible reddish purple seaweed growing on both sides of the North Atlantic on undersea rocks and even on other seaweeds. Many people consider it to be the most delectable of all sea vegetables. *Dilsea carnosa* is another type of edible seaweed, unrelated to regular dulse but almost identical to it in taste, appearance, and nutritional value.

Dried dulse is a popular food in Canada, where much of the world's supply is harvested, the gathering and processing of dulse being an important industry in the provinces of New Brunswick and Nova Scotia. From there, this high-quality product is exported to Scotland, Ireland, and the United States. Recently, dulse has also begun to be processed in Maine, but, so far, has proved to be inferior in quality to the Canadian dulse.

The peoples of Ireland, Scotland, and Iceland have been using dulse for centuries. Scottish people call it "dillosk" and collect it, with considerable effort, off the coasts of Scotland. In both Scotland and Ireland, it is most frequently eaten with boiled potatoes. It is also excellent simmered in milk, put in soups or salads, or even used as a main ingredient in sandwiches.

Strong-flavored herbs or seasonings can overpower the delicate sea flavor of dulse. Dill, however, goes very well with it as do black pepper and paprika. Ground or powdered dulse is also available and can be used in the same ways as the whole-leaf product. Powdered dulse is excellent as a garnish with fried tempeh and oriental pasta products.

Dulse is extremely rich in iodine, phosphorous, calcium, and potassium. In fact, it contains a larger quantity of potassium than any other food.

In Canada, dulse is available in most major food outlets across the country; in the United States, however, it can be rather difficult to obtain as it is not a popular food there. This is perhaps due to the fact that many people in the United States seem to have an almost "psychopathic" horror of seaweeds! Fortunately, this flavorful product of the sea, although still unfamiliar to most inhabitants of the United States, is available there in many natural and organic food shops.

Eggplant

Solanum melongena

The eggplant is said to have originated in India or Burma and to have spread throughout Asia at an early date. It has a thin shiny skin and is usually a deep purple, although white and yellow varieties also exist. It comes in several sizes and shapes, ranging from gourdlike to almost spherical. In China, a dwarf variety has been popular for millenia.

The eggplant was unknown in ancient Greece and Rome. It did, however, become a favorite Arab and North African vegetable between A.D. 900 and A.D. 1200, and probably became known throughout the Byzantine Empire during the same period. The Moors introduced it to Spain sometime prior to the thirteenth century, and by the fifteenth century it was known in much of the Italian peninsula.

For many centuries, most Europeans cultivated the eggplant only as an ornamental garden curiosity. A notion that it was poisonous was widespread. It was only during the sixteenth century that eggplant began to be eaten without fear in western Europe, although for some time prior to this it had been enjoyed by both the Greeks and Turks in stuffed, baked, or fried form.

Today, the eggplant is a favorite vegetable among the Italians, who bake it sliced in a casserole with tomato paste, cheese, garlic, and basil. Another Italian method involves inserting pieces of garlic into sliced eggplant, dipping it in flour, and lightly frying it. Both dishes are extremely appetizing. Although the Spanish introduced the eggplant to the New World in the sixteenth century, in contemporary North America, it is, by and large, eaten only by people coming from those Old World lands where it is popular. The same may be said of northern Europe. In the eastern Mediterranean world, cooked eggplant is combined with onions, peppers, tomato, garlic, and herbs as a pâte for bread or for use as a relish with millet, cous cous, rice, or pasta.

Egyptian Onion
Allium cepa viviparum

In *Edible Plants of the World*, the nineteenth century botanist, Sturtevant, classifies egyptian onion as *Allium canadense*. Also known as the "greek" or "tree" onion, the egyptian onion is a bushlike plant with a trailing network of stalks that can exceed a height of 1.2 meters (4 ft.). It differs from other onions in that it does not produce seed, but rather small bulbs, first greenish in color and then somewhat purple, on the tips of its stalks! The first cluster of bulbs appear when the stalks are about one meter (3 ft.) long, and are followed by second and even third clusters growing out of the first one. As these become larger and heavier, the hollow stalks crack and fall over, allowing the clusters of small onions to reach the earth and take root as new plants.

As egyptian onions were unknown in England until brought there in 1820 from what is today Canada, it was assumed that they were indigenous to the New World. The fact that they can withstand heavy snowfalls and prolonged periods of freezing temperatures would seem to substantiate such a view. On the other hand, they can *also* sustain temperatures up to 43°C (110°F) in humid climates, a fact which would seem to suggest an origin in keeping with their name. Egyptian onions are, in fact, widely cultivated in Egypt, Greece, and elsewhere in the eastern Mediterranean region, and are viewed by the local peoples as indigenous to these areas. Unfortunately, botanical literature is of no help in tracing the history of these remarkable onions. If they do, in fact, owe their origins to Egypt, it is certainly a mystery as to how they came to the New World, especially to the wilds of Canada—unless, of course, Phoenician explorers brought them in prehistoric times! It is also possible that the egyptian onion is indigenous to both the Old and New Worlds.

The young leaves of the egyptian onion can be used like chives as a garnish, while the older stalks are excellent in vegetable soups and sautées. The small lightweight bulbs are delicious sliced in salads, sauces, and sandwiches.

Egyptian onions are commercially available in most lands of the eastern Mediterranean, but very seldom appear in North American shops. They can, however, be raised in home gardens.

Endive
Cichorium endiva

Endive is native to the Mediterranean area and was eaten by the ancient Egyptians as well as by the Greeks and Romans. Although several varieties of endive exist, the "belgian" is the type most often available today. Resembling a miniature chinese cabbage, it is usually only about ten centimeters (4 in.) long. Kraft, in *Exotic Vegetables,* states that belgian endive is actually a "phase" of "witloof" chicory, deriving from the latter's roots.

Growers subject endives to a blanching process that prevents their exposure to the sunlight. This is sometimes done by placing "blanching pots" over the plants or, more frequently, by raising them in barrels of sawdust.

The endive has been extremely popular in France, the Low Countries, and elsewhere in Europe for centuries. It was first introduced into England in the sixteenth century and has been grown on a small scale in North America since the last century. Tending to be rather expensive, endive is generally viewed as something of a delicacy. Although its tender leaves are sometimes eaten raw in salads, it is more frequently cooked. It is well to remember that it only takes several minutes to steam endives. Some people prefer steamed endives with an oil and caper sauce, while others like them in a cream sauce with chopped chives.

Fava Bean
Vigna faba

Fava bean plants grow to a height of two meters (6 ft.). Their foliage and general appearance is strikingly different from that of New World beans.

Some botanical authorities designate the fava bean *Faba vulgaris* or *Faba pliniana.* Popularly known as the broad bean, the fava is native to the Mediterranean area and was the chief type of cultivated bean in southern Europe and the Near East prior to the introduction of New World beans from Mexico and the Andean regions of South America.

Cultivated from prehistoric times, the fava bean was a favorite vegetable in ancient Egypt, Israel, Greece, and Rome. It also became a staple in North Africa and, to this day, can be found growing wild in Algeria. Fava beans have been found in ancient Egyptian tombs as well as at Bronze Age excavation sites in Switzerland, thus indicating the wide distribution of this vegetable and its importance in the diet of ancient man.

In ancient Greece, fava beans were consecrated to the dead as well as used as offerings to the gods, particularly to Apollo. Such rites are mentioned by Homer in the *Iliad*. They were also a basic food staple of the common people.

Throughout the Middle Ages and the medieval period, fava beans remained a widely consumed vegetable, not only in the lands of their origin but well beyond, Roman soldiers having introduced them to both Gaul (France) and the British Isles.

Fava beans are most frequently eaten shelled, but can be eaten "whole pod" before they have reached their full size. They are excellent sautéed "whole pod" in tomato paste with garlic and mushrooms, and served with cous cous, rice, or pasta. They are also good simply steamed and eaten with oil, wine vinegar, and chopped parsley, either hot or in a salad.

In North America, the fava bean is not widely available commercially except in areas with large Italian or Arab populations. However, it can always be grown in home gardens. It remains a popular vegetable in Italy, North Africa, and throughout the Balkans and the Near East.

Fennel

Foeniculum vulgaris

Fennel is a feathery-leaved perennial plant that bears clusters of bright yellow flowers and can grow to a height of nearly three meters (10 ft.). It is related to both dill, which it counterfeits in appearance, and anise, which it counterfeits in flavor.

Originally native to southern Europe, particularly the Italian peninsula, fennel now grows wild throughout a large portion of both the Old and New Worlds. It thrives on the island of Cyprus in the eastern Mediterranean as well as along the coasts of Wales in Great Britain; it grows in profusion in northern California and in British Columbia as well as in Egypt and throughout Italy.

Fennel was used by the ancient Egyptians, Greeks, and Romans both medicinally and as a seasoning. An Italian variety, florence fennel, has a bulbous base that is used as a vegetable. Eaten by some Greeks as well as Italians, it is occasionally seen in North American markets. Fennel is sometimes used as a flavoring in breads or confections. Some people—particularly those who are fond of dill—do not care for the pungent penetrating flavor of fennel.

Fenugreek

Trigonella foenum graceum

Fenugreek is of the same legume family as peas and beans. Although said to have originated in India, fenugreek has grown wild throughout Asia Minor, Greece, Egypt, and elsewhere in the Mediterranean world for centuries. It has pealike flowers and its leaves resemble clover. The narrow pods contain a quantity of tiny yellowish brown seeds.

The dried seeds, in ground or powdered form, are an important ingredient in many East Indian curries as well as in certain Greek and Egyptian dishes. The somewhat bitter seeds are usually roasted before being ground. In Egypt, the seeds are also let to sprout and then eaten with honey. Various Arab peoples make the seeds into a conserve and use this as a condiment. Throughout the Near East and Greece, fenugreek is sometimes used in halva—a delectable confection composed of solidified sesame "butter" and honey.

Fresh fenugreek leaves make a unique salad when served with oil and lemon juice. In India, the leaves are sometimes added to vegetable "dahls" or legume porridges, and served with rice. Fenugreek is said to be particularly esteemed among the Parsees.

In North America and the British Isles, fenugreek seeds, whole or ground, can be found in East Indian and other specialty shops. In the eastern Mediterranean area and in India, both seeds and leaves are commonly available.

Fig

Ficus carica

There are many types of fig, the fruit ranging in color from blackish purple to golden yellow and pale green. The inner pulp is either reddish pink or yellow. The fig is native to the entire Mediterranean area—from the Holy Land and Syria to Asia Minor, Greece, the Italian peninsula, and Spain. The finest figs are considered to be those grown since early Byzantine times in the Smyrna region of Asia Minor. Today exported from Turkey, they are esteemed by gourmets everywhere. Figs grown in Sicily are also highly regarded.

Said to have been under cultivation since 3000 B.C., figs were grown in the famed gardens of Alcinous, king of Phoenicia. In India, the tree under which Gautama Buddha was sitting at the time of his Enlightenment is believed to have been a species of fig. Among the ancient Egyptians, the sepulchral cases used to house mummies were made of fig wood. Much later, in the Middle Ages, the fig was among the fruits cultivated in the palace gardens of Charlemagne.

Fig trees were brought to the British Isles from Italy by Cardinal Pole in 1548, but the climate did not prove conducive to their productivity. During the sixteenth century, the Spanish introduced the fig to Mexico, Peru, and Florida. The black or "mission" fig, available fresh in North American markets when in season, derives from a variety planted by the Spanish during the 1700s at their California missions.

The fig tree fruits in a most curious manner. Rather than bearing external flowers out of which the fruits develop, the fig fruit develops first, enclosing the flower within it. Some varieties require pollination for the fruit to develop, others do not. Certain types, including the smyrna, are pollinated by the "blastophaga" wasp that lives inside a very hard, inedible species of fig known as the "capri." The capri figs (with the wasps inside) are always grown close to groves of smyrna figs. The capri figs are picked and hung in bags on the smyrna fig trees. The wasps emerge and attempt to enter the smyrna figs to deposit their eggs. Pollen from the capri fig adhering to the wasps thereupon brushes off and fertilizes the interior blossoms of the smyrna figs. Without these wasps, the latter would remain unfertilized and inedible.

The calimyrna, a golden yellow hybrid fig that is part smyrna, is one of the varieties raised in California. It, too, is pollinated by wasps in the manner described above. Another variety, the kadota, also a golden yellow, is used chiefly for canning, the end product being of excellent quality.

Fresh, dried, or canned figs are all exceptionally delicious eaten with thick sweet cream or cream cheese. Dried figs are often used in puddings, cakes, and various confections.

Garbanzo Bean or Chick Pea

Cicer arietinum, C. judaicum, C. pinnatifidum, and many others

The garbanzo bean is a legume, but is quite distinct from both peas and beans. Differences between the various species of the *Cicer* genus are very slight.

An important food for thousands of years throughout the Mediterranean world, the garbanzo bean was extensively cultivated by the ancient Egyptians, Jews, and Greeks. The Greeks introduced it to Sicily and the Italian peninsula and from there it spread to both Spain and France. According to some botanical authorities, it originated in Asia Minor. The Spanish brought it to Latin America and what is today the southwestern United States.

Most frequently, dried garbanzo beans are soaked, boiled with onions and garlic, and then eaten with oil, lemon, and chopped parsley or basil. The Italians and the Spanish are fond of cooked whole garbanzo beans either in tomato paste or served with other vegetables in a salad. Essentially unknown in much of northern Europe, the garbanzo bean is widely used in the United States by the large Latino or Spanish-speaking population as well as by Greeks, Italians, and peoples of Near Eastern origin.

Garbanzo flour is used as the main ingredient of deep-fried "felafel" cakes often sold by street vendors in Israel and elsewhere in the Near East. Variations on "felafel" involving the addition of wheat germ as well as vegetables such as grated carrots or chopped zucchini and garlic to the basic garbanzo flour can provide the creative cook with a wide range of possibilities. Mixed with a little water, garbanzo flour is also an excellent substitute for egg batter.

The high protein content of the garbanzo bean makes it a very desirable food, and it is widely available in both dried and canned forms throughout North America. It should be noted that dried garbanzo beans can be very time-consuming to cook even after having been soaked for a considerable period of time.

Garlic
Allium sativim

Garlic has been used from the very dawn of mankind, being esteemed for its superb flavor as well as its undisputed medicinal properties. There are many varieties. The size of the bulb clusters differs greatly as do the colors of the tissuelike skins, which vary from pure white to purple or pink. The latter types are generally viewed as having the finest flavor.

Garlic is variously held to be indigenous to the Mediterranean world, southwestern Siberia, or China. In any case, garlic was extensively used in the ancient world by the Jews, Egyptians, Greeks, Romans, and Chinese.

Today, garlic is cultivated throughout the world. Many peoples, including the Greeks, Italians, Spanish, French, Chinese, and Slavs, use it extensively in their respective cuisines.

In spite of its popularity in much of the world, the Irish, the various Scandinavian peoples, and, until quite recently, most Japanese rarely use garlic, and even view it with some degree of hostility and dislike. Although the English are not in the antigarlic camp, they nevertheless use it quite sparingly.

In North America, garlic is universally available and is widely used by a fairly large proportion of the population. In the larger urban centers, through exposure to diverse Mediterranean, Chinese, and Slavic cuisines, many North Americans of other ethnic backgrounds have learned how splendidly garlic enhances the flavor of a vast variety of foods. There are, nevertheless, many North Americans particularly in the Midwest, who loathe garlic and never use it.

All of the peoples who traditionally use garlic in their cuisines also possess a strong sense of its medicinal qualities. Throughout the Middle Ages and medieval period right up into the contemporary world, garlic has been known for its antiseptic properties which purify the blood and destroy disease-causing bacteria in the intestines, lungs, and elsewhere in the body. Its use is said to have saved countless lives during the terrible plagues of the medieval period. Thus, it is not without reason that, from very ancient times, garlic has been believed to counteract evil and put demons to flight!

Quite aside from its medicinal qualities, garlic is a marvelously pungent seasoning capable of enhancing the flavor of an immense variety of dishes. It is delicious both cooked and raw. Chopped raw garlic is an asset both in salads and with nearly every cooked vegetable in existence. It is excellent with bread and in cheese dishes, soups, and sauces. Garlic also can be combined with a finely-chopped herb such as basil, parsley, dill, marjoram, or oregano to produce a highly recommended garnish for innumerable vegetarian dishes. In fact, just about any nonfruit or nondessert dish, however simple, can be transformed into a gourmet's delight simply by adding chopped garlic and *one* of the above herbs.

Elephant garlic, *Allium scorodoprasum*, is much larger than regular garlic, rendering it inconvenient for use as a seasoning. Many westerners do not find its peculiar flavor to their taste, although it is often eaten whole as a vegetable in its native India. Elephant garlic is sometimes available in organic food stores.

Ginger
Zingiber officinale

The ginger plant has reedlike stems with long pointed green leaves. It attains a height of about one meter (3 ft.) and bears exceptionally lovely yellow and purple flowers. From its bulbous base just beneath the soil surface extend networks of thick, creeping, irregularly-shaped rhizomes that somewhat resemble jerusalem artichokes. They are the edible part of the ginger plant.

Native to a wide area of Asia, ginger came to Europe via Arab traders and was, for centuries, erroneously believed to be native to the Arabian peninsula. Today, the generally accepted view is that it originated in southeast Asia. It has been cultivated in southern China and India for millenia. Today, it is also grown in various parts of the African continent and on the island of Madagascar. It was introduced into the West Indies soon after the discovery of the New World and continues to thrive there. According to some people, the finest quality ginger comes from Jamaica where it has been grown since the 1500s. For the last century, it has also been cultivated in Hawaii.

A favorite seasoning among the Chinese for millenia, ginger was also known to the ancient Greeks and Romans. Indeed, it very early became a major item in the East-West trade. For many centuries, ginger was a luxury item in Europe, its use relegated to the more affluent classes, who, during the medieval period, developed a fondness for it in cakes, cookies, and pastries. By the middle of the

1700s it was also being used by the general populations of England, the various German principalities, and Scandinavia.

Ginger frequently has a very "hot," almost peppery quality and should be used with discretion. Thin slivers of fresh ginger are especially good in a variety of oriental dishes, particularly with different types of oriental pasta served with green vegetables, bean curd (tofu), and moderately sweet "mizo" or soy sauce. It is also delicious preserved or crystallized in sugar in the Chinese fashion. In the Near East, it is sometimes used in Greek-style coffee, as well as added in small thin slivers to fresh oranges and other fruits after they have been sliced and sugared. Its use in gingerbread and cake among northern Europeans is, of course, well known. Today, fresh ginger is widely available in North American markets as well as in those of the larger urban centers of the British Isles and continental Europe.

Gooseberry

Ribes grossularia, R. hertellum

R*ibes grossularia* is the Old World variety that grows in profusion in the British Isles, and *Ribes hertellum*, the North American variety. Gooseberries are closely related to currants and, in fact, grow in many of the same northern areas. Although there is a red variety, most gooseberries are a light greenish color. They are used in various dessert dishes and are made into jam or preserves. Gooseberries are not particularly popular anywhere except in the British Isles, where a rather unusual dessert called "gooseberry fool" is highly regarded.

Grape

Vitis vinifera, V. rotundifolia; many varieties

V*itis vinifera* is the general term designating various Old World grapes of Europe and the Near East, while *Vitis rotundifolia* is used to indicate a major New World species. Today, there are, in fact, over one thousand varieties of grape.

Grapevines are trailing plants that are often grown on trellises and in arbors. The fruits may be red, purple (sometimes called "black"), or green (often termed "white"). Although from antiquity most grapes have been cultivated for wine-making, many types have also been developed for use as table grapes, raisins, or for making grape juice.

The Old World grapevine is native to an area stretching from the shores of the Mediterranean all the way to the Caspian Sea. Grape seeds have been found in ancient Egyptian tombs and in Swiss excavations dating to the Bronze Age. The New World grape was particularly prevalent in the eastern seaboard regions of North America.

For many peoples, the grape took on various religious associations. Among the ancient Egyptians, it was associated with Osiris, and in ancient Greece, wine played an important part in Dionysiac rites. Wine, of course, also has a place in both Judaic and Christian rituals, and, on the east wall of the Temple in Jerusalem a grapevine of gold with grapes made of gemstones was a major decorative motif.

The cultivation of grapes spread at a very early date from both the Near East and the Greco-Roman world, first via the Phoenicians and then via the Romans. Both brought grapevines to Iberia (Spain and Portugal), Gaul (France), and even the British Isles. The Romans also planted grapes along the Rhine in what is, today, Germany. Britain's climate proved unsuitable for grapegrowing, but the extent and importance of viticulture in southern France and along the Rhine in Germany cannot be overestimated, with many gourmet wines being produced in both areas.

The Vikings found such an abundance of grapevines growing wild along the northeastern coast of North America that they called it "Vinland." Later, the English encountered a type of wild grape in Virginia, but it was smaller, more tart, and less flavorful than European types. Old World varieties were brought in, but were soon ravaged by insects and fungoid diseases to which the native New World grapes were immune. Consequently, most European grapes grown in California and elsewhere in North America today have been grafted onto New World roots.

Viticulture was introduced to California by the Spanish in the 1700s. Since then, many different types of Old World grape as well as various New World species from eastern North America have been brought to California where they have been crossed and grafted to produce new and unique strains. Grapes are a major crop in the United States with over 90 percent of the total being grown in California. Grapes are also grown in British Columbia as well as in eastern Canada.

Unfortunately, toxic pesticides are used on many of the grapes destined to be sold in North American markets. Consequently, an increasing number of consumers buy only "organic" grapes that have been cultivated without the use of any toxic, chemically-based pesticides.

Fresh grapes are most frequently eaten by themselves, but they also mix very well with other fruits and are especially good with cottage cheese or served with thick sweet cream and sprinkled with sugar and allspice. Concord grapes, which were developed from a native New World variety, are exceptionally fragrant and quite unique in flavor. They are, perhaps, the most delectable of all table grapes and should be purchased whenever the opportunity arises as they are not available with any great degree of frequency.

A large number of grapes are dried for use as raisins. Golden raisins are to be particularly recommended. Canadians are fortunate to always have available the delectable aromatic sultana raisin which is imported from Australia, but remains essentially unknown in the United States. Raisins are used in puddings, cakes, cookies, and other confections. They are also used in raisin bread and are excellent combined with honey and cinnamon in yogurt.

Grapefruit

Citrus paradisi

Grapefruit trees, with their marvelously fragrant white flowers, grow up to eight meters (25 ft.) high, a single tree producing 680 kilograms (1500 lb.) of fruit per year! The pulp of the fruit is either yellowish, pink, or red. Originally, grapefruits had a core of one hundred or more seeds, but over the last century "seedless" types have been developed. In these, only a very few seeds exist.

For many years, the French word "pamplemousse" was used for this fruit. The English term, "grapefruit," apparently derives from the fact that the fruits grow in almost grapelike clusters of forty or more on a single stem! The origins of the grapefruit remain something of a mystery. There is simply no mention of it in any known written records until the year 1750 when a British traveler and naturalist, Griffith Hughes, in his *Natural History of the Barbados*, notes its extensive cultivation in that area of the world. Somewhat later, in 1814, the botanist, John Leenan, mentions the grapefruit as being "native to Jamaica" in a book dealing with the plants of that island.

In all probability, the grapefruit originated either as a "sport" or as a deliberate horticultural development of the southeast Asian pomelo, which had, in fact, been widely planted on many of the Caribbean islands. There is no evidence whatever that the grapefruit existed either in southeast Asia or as an indigenous New World species prior to the European colonization. Thus, the mystery of the grapefruit's precise origins remains unsolved.

Commercial cultivation of the grapefruit only began in the United States around 1880, and by the early 1900s it was being produced in Florida in relatively small quantities. It was, at that time, an expensive luxury item. As the quantity of grapefruits being produced increased, however, they became affordable for all. Today, grapefruit is a major crop in the United States, notably in Arizona, Texas, California, and Florida. It is also cultivated extensively in the West Indies and Central and South America as well as in Israel and Jordan. For many years, grapefruits were extremely costly imports in continental Europe and the British Isles. Today, they are available there at far more reasonable prices than they were in the past.

The grapefruit, which is high in vitamin C, is extremely popular in North America. Both the fruit itself and the delicious juice it produces are widely consumed. A grapefruit is best eaten in a bowl after having been peeled, segmented, and sprinkled with sugar. Pieces of grapefruit also go remarkably well with other fresh fruits as well as with avocados and grated carrots.

Green Bean

Phaseolus vulgaris, many varieties

Without becoming bogged down in a futile discussion pertaining to a theoretical definition of the term "green bean," suffice it to say that the term is used to signify many different varieties of New World bean that are eaten cooked as a *fresh* vegetable, either "whole pod" or sliced. The "french bean," so termed because of its popularity in France, is the main variety of green bean commonly found in our produce markets. Its inner seed-beans are very small. It has largely replaced the string bean that essentially differs from the french bean only in that it has a long, tough, stringy fiber along its "seam." The so-called "haricot beans," which are allowed to mature and then are dried for later use, would also qualify as green beans when used in immature form as a fresh vegetable.

Although native to Central America and the Andean regions of South America, green beans of various types had spread throughout much of North America and were widely cultivated by numerous native Indian peoples long before the coming of the Europeans. Cartier encountered what was to become known as the "french bean," together with other varieties intended for drying, growing near the St. Lawrence River in Quebec in 1535. Most were introduced to France shortly thereafter. The small-seeded green bean that was eaten as a fresh vegetable was an immediate success not only in France but in much of continental Europe and the British Isles as well. Everywhere, it became known as the french bean. At first limited to the tables of the affluent, green beans had, within a century, become a popular vegetable among the general population as well. They also proved to be a favorite of both the French and English colonists in the New World. Today, green beans remain one of the most widely eaten vegetables in North America.

Green beans are exceptionally good steamed briefly and eaten with chopped garlic and oil. Cooked with onion and garlic in tomato paste, green beans go well on pasta, millet, cous cous, or rice. The same combination, puréed and partially dried out, makes a delicious "spread" on bread or toast. Steamed green beans are excellent with cubed bean curd and fresh chopped parsley in a sweet miso sauce.

There are also yellow and purple varieties of the conventional french bean. The purple bean has been available in North American markets for about a decade. When cooked, it turns a pale green. In choosing green beans, it is well to remember that young pods, picked considerably before they have reached maturity are inevitably more flavorful.

See also **Romano Bean.**

Green Onion

Allium cepa

Green onions, also known as spring onions or salad onions, are the very young specimens of regular white onions of the *Allium cepa* type. Harvested before the bulb has reached maturity, they are the familiar salad onions with long green leaves and small, oblong, white bulbs. They are usually eaten raw. One popular variety is the White Lisbon.

Green onions have been a favorite food for millenia throughout the Near East and most of the Mediterranean world, being native to that entire area. In some places, such as Israel, Lebanon, Turkey, Greece, and the Balkans, these onions are sold by street vendors to passing workmen and pedestrians. Green onions are also popular in North America, in salads and as hors d'oeuvres.

Although always sold in bunches, green onions grow separately rather than clustered in a group. They are, nevertheless, similar in appearance to the milder chinese or welsh onion, which always grows in clusters. Both types are sometimes referred to as "scallions."

See also **Chinese Onion; Chive; Egyptian Onion; Onion; Shallot.**

Guava

Psidium guajava, P. lucidum, P. catteiamum

P*sidium guajava* is the common guava; *P. lucidum* is the yellow guava; and *P. catteiamum* is the popular reddish guava with a strawberry flavor.

Guavas, New World fruits of the myrtle family, are native to a wide area of Latin America and the Caribbean, ranging from Brazil to Cuba and Mexico. Today, the trees, which require a warm climate with no severe frosts, are also cultivated in southern Florida and China, both for their fruits and as ornamental garden plants.

Guavas grow on low-branched shrubs and small trees, some of which reach a height of six meters (20 ft.). The leaves are oblong and the small fruits, which develop from fragrant four-petaled white flowers, are most frequently spherical. The seed-laden inner fruit varies from cream-colored to pale pink.

The sweet-sour pulp is quite acidic and very juicy. Although guavas can be eaten raw, they are far more frequently made into jelly or preserves. They must be eaten when they have just become ripe. If allowed to overripen, they emit an extremely unpleasant odor. They are particularly important fruits in Cuba and Costa Rica.

Today, guavas are only very rarely available in North American markets and remain essentially unknown in Europe as fresh fruits, although guava jelly is sometimes available in gourmet shops. Guavas are particularly high in vitamins A and C.

Hazelnut

Corylus avellana, C. americana

The hazelnut is a relatively small nut that grows on a tree which seldom exceeds six meters (20 ft.) in height. Hazelnut trees are common to both the Old and New Worlds. *Corylus avellana* designates the European variety and *C. americana*, the notably smaller North American variety.

The Old World hazelnut is said to have originated around Damascus in the eastern Mediterranean and to have spread from there to Asia Minor, the shores of the Black Sea, Greece, and the Italian peninsula. The hazelnut is mentioned by Pliny in his *Natural History*, and may have been introduced to the British Isles by the Romans. Today, it is the main type of nut tree grown in the British Isles. Spain and Turkey are the major world suppliers. At the turn of the century, hazelnuts were also produced in considerable quantity around the city of Kazan in southern Russia.

Hazelnuts are excellent eaten plain, and, ground or chopped, they make an appetizing filling for pastries and confections.

Honeydew Melon

a variety of *Cucumis melo*

According to some authorities, the honeydew was originally called the "white antibes winter" and derived from a type of melon developed in France. Other authorities claim that the honeydew is an ancient type of muskmelon that, like all muskmelons, originated in the region of Persia and the Caucasus. Many types of melon in the general "muskmelon" category were known to the ancient Greeks, but according to Pliny, in his *Natural History*, they only became widely cultivated by the Romans in the first century A.D., the same century in which he was writing.

The honeydew melon has a pale yellow exterior. The inner pulp is pale green. Very refreshing in warm weather, this melon is quite popular throughout North America. As with other melons, its flavor is greatly enhanced by the addition of lemon juice and sugar.

Horseradish

Cochleania amoracia, Amoracia lapthifolia, A. rusticana

A member of the mustard family, horseradish is native to a wide area of northern and eastern Europe. A number of different botanical names designate the same plant, which grows to a height of 1.5 meters (5 ft.). The leaves extend separately from the top of its whitish tan root together with clusters of small white flowers. Its use goes back to prehistoric times and continued throughout the Middle Ages and medieval period. Today, it is still popular in many parts of the world.

The root of the horseradish plant is made into a paste for use as a garnish. As such, it is a favorite European condiment that is used in a variety of dishes. Extremely sharp and peppery, horseradish should always be used with discretion. There are various ways of preparing it, some of which include adding sugar. Said to possess powerful antiseptic qualities, horseradish was used medicinally in former times.

Horseradish is used extensively in sauces and is particularly good in a cream sauce with cauliflower, noodles, or boiled potatoes. Chopped parsley or dill sprinkled over the whole enhances the flavor. Horseradish is chiefly used by Swedes, Germans, Russians, Poles, and Baltic peoples, as well as by the English and Dutch. It is also a Jewish favorite.

Hubbard Squash. *See* **Winter Squash.**

Husk Tomato. *See* **Tomatillo.**

Irish Moss

Chondrus crispus

Irish moss (also called carageen or iberian moss) is actually a seaweed, not a moss. It is found along the coasts of the North Atlantic in both Europe and North America, and can be either reddish purple or green in color. In many parts of Ireland, irish moss is steamed and eaten with potatoes or cabbage. Ireland remains a major source of the world's supply.

Its most common use outside of Ireland is in making a natural, rennet-free gelatin, which is of utmost importance to vegetarians throughout the world. This gelatin is extensively used in making cream cheese, cottage cheese, ice cream, aspics, and jellies. A "tea" made from irish moss is sometimes used as a "tonic." In North America, irish moss is available in most health food stores.

Italian Bean. *See* **Romano Bean.**

Italian Marrow. *See* **Zucchini.**

Jerusalem Artichoke
Helianthus tuberosis

The jerusalem artichoke—a relative of the sunflower—is a New World tuber indigenous to the Atlantic seaboard area of North America, extending from Quebec to the Carolinas. Jerusalem artichokes resemble ginger root in appearance, are slightly sweet, and possess a mildly nutlike flavor that is said to be enhanced by the first frost. They are usually a whitish cream color, although this can be infused with shades of red or pink. They are neither related to nor bear any resemblance to the actual artichoke, except, perhaps, very mildly, in flavor. In addition, they have no connection whatever with Jerusalem.

An important food staple of the Huron Indians, the jerusalem artichoke was first brought to Europe from the Quebec area by French explorers returning to France in 1607. The French proved to be the chief enthusiasts and cultivators of this New World food. Over the centuries that followed, they developed a variety of different types. From France, the jerusalem artichoke was introduced into Italy, Holland, and eventually England. Although Sir Walter Raleigh's expedition observed jerusalem artichokes in Virginia in 1585, apparently no attempt was made to introduce the plant to England at that time. It was not until the early seventeenth century, by way of France and Holland, that it finally came to be cultivated in England. There, it was regarded as a delicacy for a brief period of time, but, by the middle of the century, the novelty had worn off. As it turned out, even the common people of Britain did not care for this New World tuber. Thus, its cultivation in England ceased until the nineteenth century when the jerusalem artichoke was reintroduced into the British cuisine, once again via France.

Jerusalem artichokes can be cooked in a number of ways and

are excellent simply steamed and eaten with butter, lemon, and parsley. Although a native North American food, jerusalem artichokes have never been popular in either the United States or Canada except, to some degree, among the French people of Quebec. They are, nevertheless, increasingly available in organic food shops during the winter season. On the other hand, in western Europe they are highly regarded and widely used.

The jerusalem artichoke contains a natural sugar that diabetics can eat without any ill effects.

Jicama

Pachyrrhizus erosus, P. tuberosus

The green-leaved vines of the jicama plant can exceed six meters (20 ft.) in length and bear fragrant white or purple flowers. The pods, seeds, and flowers of the jicama are extremely toxic and are, in fact, used in the production of certain pesticides. **Only the brownish tan tubers of the plant can be eaten.**

Jicama tubers are native to Mexico and to Central and South America. Today, they are also grown in many other tropical parts of the world including India, the Malay Archipelago, and the Fiji Islands.

The jicama is reminiscent of the chinese water chestnut in flavor and texture, and can be used in the same ways. It is also eaten sliced and fried, as well as in salads. During the last decade, jicama has become widely available in many North American markets. It remains all but unknown in Europe.

Kale

Brassica oleracea acephala

The term "kale" designates several closely related plants of the cabbage family which have curly or crinkly leaves and do not form compact heads. An extremely hardy plant with grayish green leaves, kale can withstand frost and freezing temperatures. In fact, a severe frost enhances the flavor of kale. Its curly-leaved branches, which grow to a height of about sixty centimeters (2 ft.) from a central stalk, are harvested a few at a time, never "whole plant." A purplish variety exists, but is more often used as an ornamental garden plant than as a food.

Kale grows wild in many areas of Europe and is one of the most ancient vegetables known to European man. Thought to have originated in Asia Minor, it has, for millenia, been grown in an area ranging from the Mediterranean to the British Isles. In *The Origin of Cultivated Plants*, Schwanitz states that the ancient Greeks were familiar with two types of kale. A favorite vegetable of the ancient Romans, kale has also been a particularly popular vegetable in Scotland and Ireland for many centuries. In fact, kale was the chief and sometimes the *only* green vegetable of the Scottish diet, and as such was essential to the health of the entire population.

Kale is very popular in Hungary, Czechoslovakia, Holland, and Belgium. Although cultivated in small quantities in North America, kale has, unfortunately, never become a popular vegetable there.

While too tough to be eaten raw like cabbage, kale is prepared in a variety of ways. Cut or chopped, it is excellent steamed and eaten with butter, pepper, and lemon juice. "Colecannon," a dish that combines creamy mashed potatoes with cooked chopped kale, is popular in Scotland and Ireland. Kale is also delicious eaten with boiled new potatoes in a cream sauce to which dill weed has been added. Kale and potato soup can be made in the Portuguese way with oil, or the Scottish way, with milk. Onions can be added to either type.

Kale is exceptionally rich in vitamins A, B, and C, as well as in various minerals. Indeed, some people assert that kale is the most nutritious of all vegetables!

Kidney Bean

a variety of *Phaseolus vulgaris*

Phaseolus vulgaris is the general "catch-all" botanical classification used to designate many different varieties of New World beans, including the kidney bean. Most people would agree with Anderson who states, in *Plants, Man, and Life*, that a comprehensive system of classification needs to be developed for the many varieties of *Phaseolus vulgaris*.

In North America, the term "kidney bean" is used almost exclusively to designate the large red kidney-shaped bean. In the British Isles and various other areas, the term "kidney bean" is generally used in a much broader sense to include all kidney-shaped New

World beans that, regardless of size or color, grow in clusters in groups of three.

Found throughout North, South, and Central America as well as in the Caribbean islands, New World beans of various types, probably including the large red kidney bean, were first encountered by Europeans in 1492 when members of the Columbus expedition came across them in what is today Cuba. Somewhat later, in 1535, the French explorer, Cartier, observed "kidney beans—black, red, white, and spotted"—being cultivated by the native peoples residing around the mouth of the St. Lawrence River in Quebec.

Not long after its discovery in the New World, the large red kidney bean was introduced for cultivation in southern Europe. Today, it is particularly popular among Greeks, Italians, and Spaniards, as well as among North Americans.

Like other types of dried bean, kidney beans are delicious sautéed with garlic and onion, with or without the addition of tomato paste. Cooked corn can be added just prior to serving the beans. Kidney beans combined with chopped parsley and celery, wine vinegar, and oil also make a very appetizing salad. Eaten with rice, cous cous, millet, or pasta, kidney beans provide a complete protein.

Kiwi Fruit

Actinidia chinensis

Technically a berry, the kiwi fruit grows on a tropical treelike vine indigenous to the Yangtze Valley in China. Externally covered with a thick brown fuzz, the inner fruit is a beautiful pale green with a center of tiny black seeds. The unique flavor is reminiscent of strawberries and bananas.

The kiwi fruit as we know it today was developed by careful selection in the early 1900s by Alexander Allison in New Zealand where, by the thirties, it had become an important commercial crop. Kiwi fruit was exported from New Zealand in the fifties, and became a popular fruit in western Europe and Canada before it was known in the United States where it did not become widely available until the seventies and eighties.

Although New Zealand remains the major producer of the kiwi fruit in the contemporary world, today this exotic fruit is also cultivated in the United States, France, and Japan. In China, it still grows wild in certain areas and can often be found in open-air rural markets under the name "mihoutao." A mutant type of kiwi fruit with a bright red pulp is presently being developed by Chinese horticulturists.

Kiwi fruit can be eaten plain, in combination with other fresh fruits, with cottage cheese, or in cakes and confections. It is available fresh or canned in public markets everywhere. In New Zealand, a certain amount of it is also dried.

The kiwi fruit is high in vitamin C and iron.

Kohlrabi

Brassica oleracea gongylodes or *B. o. caulorapa*

The kohlrabi is a globe-shaped vegetable with sparsely-distributed gray-green leaves growing out of it on stems. The pale green globe remains on the surface of the earth, its small root extending into the ground. Its unusual appearance is very pleasing aesthetically, and it is, in fact, grown by the French as an ornamental garden plant. Rather curiously, they have never been much interested in it as a food!

In the middle of the sixteenth century, the kohlrabi suddenly appeared in parts of northern Europe without explanation, as though from the experimental gardens of some horticultural "alchemist." Although several very primitive forms of *Brassica* vaguely resembling the kohlrabi may have been known in earlier periods, there is no evidence whatever for the existence of the kohlrabi as we know it before 1554.

Some botanical authorities believe that the kohlrabi is the result of a hybridization between the cabbage and the turnip, while others claim that it is a "sport" of the "marrow cabbage," a little-known variety of *Brassica oleracea*. Its place of origin is believed to have been either the Low Countries or one of the German principalities. By the end of the seventeenth century, it was being cultivated not only in the presumed areas of its origin, but also in Poland and Sweden.

Kohlrabi tastes like a combination of turnip, cabbage, and mustard greens. The cool, succulent, slightly sweet globe is extremely refreshing simply sliced and eaten raw with oil, lemon juice, and fresh dill weed. Cooked, kohlrabi should be sliced and steamed. It can then be eaten plain with oil or prepared in a cream sauce flavored with dill *or* capers, and served with boiled potatoes.

Sliced steamed kohlrabi can also be dipped in flour, briefly fried, and served with chopped chives. The creative cook will find numerous other ways of preparing it.

While the kohlrabi is highly regarded as a desirable vegetable throughout most of northern and central Europe, in North America it is primarily used to feed farm animals and remains little known to the majority of the population. Nevertheless, it is sometimes available in North American markets where it is purchased chiefly by those European ethnic groups who have valued it as a healthful and delicious food ever since its mysterious appearance in the sixteenth century.

Laver

Porphyra laciniata

Laver is a reddish purple, crinkly seaweed that is gathered off the shores of the British Isles. This ancient food has been esteemed for centuries by the Scots, Welsh, and Irish.

When cooked, laver turns a green-brown color. In Scotland, it is dipped in oatmeal and fried, or made into a purée. The Welsh marinate it in oil and lemon juice, and serve it with black pepper on toast. The water in which laver is cooked turns into a thick jelly, rich with a sealike flavor. This broth can be combined with diced potatoes and kale or mustard greens to make a delicious and healthful soup.

Laver is not generally available outside Great Britain and Ireland, but with the increased interest today in seaweeds, or "sea vegetables" as they are more aptly termed, it is to be hoped that laver will become available in North America as well. A start in this direction has been made in the Canadian Maritimes, where some effort is being put into harvesting and processing a type of laver called "wild nort."

Leek

Allium porrum

The leek, a member of the onion family, has a white, hourglass-shaped root or bulb which has a much milder flavor than other onions. The wide green leaves can exceed sixty centimeters (2 ft.) in length.

The leek is native to the Mediterranean area, and may have originated in Egypt. According to some botanical authorities, however, its place of origin was further west in the region of Algeria—an area where leeks still grew wild at the turn of the century.

Like the onion, the leek is one of the most ancient food plants of mankind. It was held in great esteem by the ancient Egyptians and became a favorite of the Jews during their long sojourn in Egypt.

In his *Natural History*, Pliny notes that the finest leeks were imported from Egypt for the tables of wealthy Romans. The mad emperor, Nero, was known as "the leekeater" because of the large quantity of leeks that he consumed.

The Romans apparently introduced leeks into the British Isles where they thrived. Eventually, in Wales and Scotland, they became an important vegetable staple, frequently eaten in a porridge with dried peas.

The leek is still popular in the British Isles as well as in France, Switzerland, and elsewhere on the continent. A particularly good dish from the British Isles is a thick milk soup made with leeks, potatoes, black peppercorns, and butter simmered slowly for a considerable period of time and served with croutons and chopped fresh parsley on top. Leeks are also excellent served with steamed cauliflower or cabbage or added to a pot of lentils.

Leeks are widely available in North American markets. They can also be grown in home gardens but require twenty-five centimeters (10 in.) between each plant. Insects of all types are said to be repelled by leeks.

Lemon

Citrus limonium

Like all citrus trees, lemons thrive in warm climates. The lemon tree grows to a height of six meters (20 ft.) and has marvelously fragrant white and purple flowers.

Believed to be native to Burma, India, or elsewhere in southeast Asia, the lemon was apparently unknown to the ancient Greeks and Romans. Nevertheless, by A.D. 1000 it was being cultivated in the Near East and the Byzantine Empire. By A.D. 1200, it was being grown in North Africa and Spain. Lemons were probably introduced to the southern part of the Italian peninsula via Byzantium, not by way of returning crusaders, as is popularly believed.

Columbus is said to have brought lemon seeds to the West

Indies. During the next several centuries, the Spanish introduced lemons to Mexico, South America, Florida, and southern California. Today, while California produces half of the world's supply, Italian lemons are the main type used in Europe. Those from Cyprus are particularly prized. They are sometimes exported in small numbers.

Today, more lemons per capita are used in Greece than any other country. Anyone who has been to Greece will recall that lemons are an integral part of the Greek cuisine. They are, of course, also utilized throughout the Western world in a variety of ways. Lemon juice enhances tea, jams, fruit preserves, fresh fruits, and green vegetables such as spinach, chard, kohlrabi, and mustard greens. Lemonade, made with water, sugar, and lemon juice, is perhaps the most delicious drink known to man. For a delectable treat, lemons can be cut in thick slices, peeled, and dipped in sugar.

Like other citrus fruits, lemons are high in vitamin C. They are best used within one or two days of being picked from the tree. Unfortunately, in North America, they are often stale by the time they reach the consumer.

Grated lemon peel can be used as a flavoring, but due to the widespread use of toxic sprays, any use of the peel should be strictly avoided unless "organic" lemons are available.

Lentil

Lens escuelenta, L. nigricans, L. culinaris, and others

The lentil plant is a climbing vine similar to the pea, but with only two lentils in each pod. The two main types are the orange or "egyptian" lentil, which is very small and generally available only in split form with the skin removed; and the brown-colored "french" type, which is at least twice as large and is marketed whole with the skin intact. This lentil, which is preferred among Europeans, can also be used as a sprout.

Grown since Neolithic times, the lentil is native to a large area stretching from Egypt and Israel all the way to India. It very early made its way to Greece, the Italian peninsula, and even further west to Gaul (France). Lentils have been found in Egyptian tombs dating to 2400 B.C. where they were left as food offerings for the dead. They have also turned up as far north as Switzerland in the excavation of Bronze Age dwellings at Lake Bienne. They are said to have been the primary food of the ancient Egyptians and they were certainly a food staple of the ancient Greeks, Sumerians, and Jews.

Like barley and wheat, lentils were used for making "puls," a term designating both grain and legume porridges or pastes in much of the southern European world right up into the medieval period. The ancient Greeks simmered various grains as well as lentils—often sprouted—in water and oil with herbs and spices to produce these ancient porridge-pastes of Neolithic culinary tradition. The Romans, too, ate lentils in a "puls," although, unlike the Greeks, they never sprouted them beforehand. Lentils are still used today in thick vegetable soups popular in many areas of Europe.

Lentils, rye bread, and cabbage are said to have constituted the main items of the eighteenth-century German peasant's diet. The orange or egyptian type continues to be the most frequently used legume in the making of East Indian "dahls" (the "puls" of India), without which no Indian meal is complete. Orange lentils continue to be a major food staple in Egypt and have spread to many other areas of the African continent.

Lentils are over 25 percent protein, making them one of the most nourishing foods available. Soaked sprouted lentils are delicious raw, particularly when sprinkled with a bit of sugar. Cooked lentils are best after they have been soaked for several days and have begun to sprout. Cooked in a "porridge" with onions, garlic, and peppercorns, with the addition of corn and green peppers, they are excellent served with pasta. Cooked, drained lentils, fresh chopped parsley, and garlic can be mashed into a paste for use on pita or sourdough breads.

Lettuce

Latuca sativa

Many varieties of lettuce are cultivated in both the Old and New Worlds. The oblong-shaped "romaine," an ancient lettuce developed by the Romans, is the most popular type in most of Europe. It is known as "cos" lettuce in the British Isles. North Americans seem to prefer the solid-headed round "iceberg" or "imperial" lettuce. Also popular in North America is the small loose-leaved "butter" lettuce.

Lettuce is native to the eastern shores of the Mediterranean, including Asia Minor, and spread throughout the entire Mediterranean world at a very early date.

The ancient Greeks ate lettuce salad at the *end* of meals, a custom which also became notable among the French. The Romans, however, like North Americans, ate it at the beginning of their repasts. The Romans favored a dish consisting of lettuce served with hard-boiled eggs, olives, and some sort of dressing. Although the Romans had over ten varieties of lettuce, the predominant and most popular type was the same romaine lettuce that we know today.

Like so many other vegetables, lettuce spread with the extension of the Roman Empire. The Romans may have introduced it to the British Isles, but there is no evidence to support this theory. In fact, it was not until the reign of Henry VIII that there are any references at all to lettuce existing in the British Isles. Henry VIII, himself, enjoyed lettuce from the royal gardens mixed with fresh cherries.

Minute amounts of laudanum in the milklike juice of lettuce stems cause this vegetable to have mild sedative powers. Actually, one need have no fears on this account. Lettuce is widely eaten as a salad vegetable in continental Europe, the British Isles, and North America. It is usually served with sliced tomatoes and cucumbers, although it blends well with almost every vegetable imaginable. Fresh basil and chives, or dill and garlic, are excellent additions to any lettuce salad.

Lima Bean
Phaseolus limatus, P. limensis

Native to Central America and the Andean regions of South America where it has been cultivated for centuries, the lima bean spread to Brazil where it still grows wild in the area around the Amazon basin. The Spanish first encountered the lima bean in Peru and introduced it to continental Europe shortly thereafter. It was also brought to Africa where it thrived, particularly on the island of Malagasy (Madagascar), where an especially large variety was developed.

Long before the coming of the Europeans, the lima bean had spread to North America where it was cultivated by the native peoples of the southwest, as well as by those living along the eastern seaboard. The native North American Indian dish called "succotash" usually consists of corn and lima beans mixed together, although on occasion other types of bean are used. A popular dish throughout much of North America prior to the European colonization, "succotash" was also adopted by many of the European settlers.

The lima bean is one bean that is much better fresh than it is dried. In most areas of North America, frozen lima beans are available. Whenever possible, purchase the full-sized frozen limas, as they are much more flavorful than the very small ones. Twenty years ago, fresh lima beans were available in many North American markets, but they are rarely encountered today. Of course, since lima beans thrive in almost any climate, people with their own gardens can grow and enjoy this delicious bean as a fresh vegetable. The young ones are quite good "wholepod." While the older pods tend to be tough and stringy, the shelled fresh beans are delectable.

Fresh or frozen lima beans are excellent by themselves served with a little butter or oil. They can also be eaten, Indian fashion, mixed with corn, or together with millet, rice, or noodles—either plain or sautéed with onions in tomato paste. Served cold, with oil and vinegar, they are a welcome addition to almost any kind of vegetable salad. Some people are fond of dried lima beans sautéed with onion and garlic.

Lima beans are especially rich in vitamin A.

Lime

Citrus aurantifolia

Lime trees are quite small, averaging about 2.5 meters (9 ft.) in height, and grow best in humid tropical climates. The trees are generally covered with small sharp thorns. The round, green or greenish yellow fruits develop from clusters of fragrant white flowers. The skin of the lime is very thin and adheres tightly to the firm-textured pulp.

The lime is indigenous to Burma and eastern India. Arab traders brought the lime from India to the Near East and Africa sometime prior to the eleventh century. Gradually, its cultivation spread further westward, and by the twelfth century it was known throughout the Byzantine Empire, from which it was introduced to the Italian peninsula in the early 1200s. Columbus brought lime seeds to the New World on his second expedition to the West Indies. Somewhat later, the Portuguese introduced the lime to Brazil and the Spanish began its cultivation in Mexico and elsewhere in their New World colonies. In the eighteenth century, Spanish Franciscans planted lime trees in the gardens of their California missions. During the 1600s, large quantities of limes were imported from the West Indies to Britain where they were used by sailors as a deterrent against scurvy. This was, of course, due to the lime's high vitamin C content, although studies now show that lemons contain more.

Egypt, Mexico, Tahiti, and the West Indies are the main producers of this fruit today. The Tahitian type is shaped more like a lemon and may be a lime-lemon hybrid. The limes available in North America are usually from Mexico, although a few are grown in Florida. Egypt and the West Indies supply most of the limes for the markets of Europe and the British Isles.

Lime juice is delicious by itself in water or added to sautéed vegetables and tomato paste. A fresh slice of lime will also enhance fresh fruits and fruit preserves. Some people enjoy occasionally substituting lime for lemon in tea.

Loganberry

Rubus loganobaccus

Very rarely seen today, the delicious loganberry is a cross between the raspberry and the Pacific trailing blackberry. Its origins in 1881 can be traced to a certain Judge Logan in Santa Cruz, California. It is exceptionally rich in vitamin A and the flavor reminds some people of pomegranate. It is a mystery why this marvelous berry is so rarely encountered today. One might have expected it to become the most popular berry in existence.

Loquat

Eriobotrya japonica

The loquat is a medlar, a little-known family of small fruits. The pale yellowish orange plum-sized fruit is quite sweet and, for many people, quite bland in flavor. The addition of lemon juice considerably enhances the taste.

Indigenous to Japan, China, and the northern regions of India, the loquat has also been cultivated throughout the Mediterranean world for centuries.

Although the loquat can sometimes be found in U.S. gardens dating from the Victorian era when it briefly enjoyed a certain vogue, it is only very rarely available commercially in North America.

Lotus

Nelumbium nelumbo

Native to India, the lotus or water lily spread to China at a very early date. With the emergence of Buddhism, the exquisitely beautiful flower of this aquatic plant, viewed as a symbol of rebirth and enlightenment, became widely utilized as an art motif. Indeed, it became a veritable symbol of that religion throughout the Orient.

Its spiritual significance, however, did not prevent the lotus plant from being used as a food. The whitish tan root, which has spongelike holes throughout, is used extensively in the Chinese and Japanese cuisines. It is usually steamed or sautéed, and eaten with rice, millet, and green vegetables. It can also be cut into very thin slices and marinated in a sweet soy sauce to make a flavorful condiment or relish that is eaten in very small quantities with deep fried vegetables and rice. Lotus root also enhances many other vegetarian dishes. Dried or preserved lotus root is usually available in the Western world in oriental markets.

The true lotus or water lily of the Orient should not be confused with a totally different plant, *Zizyphus lotus*, which was sometimes eaten in the ancient Mediterranean world and produced a state of mildly euphoric forgetfulness.

Lychee

Nephelium litchi

The lychee is the fruit of a tree native to China, and also cultivated in India and Florida. The fresh fruit has a brilliant scarlet, rough-textured exterior skin. The fruit inside is a translucent white and has a sweet, delicate flavor.

Fresh, canned, and dried lychees are available wherever large communities of Chinese exist in North America. In dried form, they are often referred to as "lychee nuts."

Dried lychees in their round, brittle, cinnamon-brown shells are often served as a dessert in Chinese restaurants. The pulp resembles a small shrunken prune both in appearance and flavor.

Macadamia Nut
Macadamia integrifolia

The trees on which macadamia nuts, also called queensland nuts, grow reach about eight meters (25 ft.) in height and have rectangular-shaped leaves extending perpendicularly from their branches. The hard-shelled nuts grow in clusters and are harvested when they fall to the ground.

The macadamia nut is native to Australia where, over the centuries, it was one of the main food staples of the native people. Today, it is chiefly cultivated in Hawaii. Although commercially available in North America, Europe, and Britain, macadamia nuts remain an expensive luxury food. Many people claim that it is the most delectable of all nuts.

Mace. *See last paragraph under* **Nutmeg.**

Mango
Mangifera indica

There are over five hundred varieties of the mango in different shapes, sizes, and colors. Some mangoes weigh up to two kilograms (5 lb.). The smaller type most commonly seen in North American markets is more or less oblong in shape. Most mangoes are ripe when they turn a golden yellow suffused with a deep red. Others remain greenish with only a slight trace of red. In southeast Asia, mangoes are also planted as "shade trees." As free-growing outdoor trees in tropical areas, mango trees grow to enormous heights, reaching thirty-eight meters (125 ft.) or more and producing an extremely dense foliage.

The mango is native to the southern part of the Indian subcontinent and is also found in much of the Malay Archipelago. Today, it is cultivated in nearly all parts of the world with a tropical climate. The mango, which is often referred to in the *Mahabarata* and *Ramayana*, has been cultivated and eaten in India for 5000 years. It is a major fruit staple there and although chiefly eaten as a fresh ripe fruit, is also used in dried or powdered form in chutneys and curries. Today, India produces 5 million tons of mangoes annually.

The Portuguese introduced the mango to Brazil and to certain areas of Africa. Today, it thrives in both of these places as well as in the Philippines, Mexico, and the West Indies. In the United States, it can be grown only in Hawaii and in southern Florida. Some mango groves are also found in Puerto Rico.

The orangish pulp of the fruit tends to cling very stubbornly to the large pit. It is easier to cut the fruit away from the pit, rather than trying to remove the pit itself. The mango, which can be eaten only when it is fully ripe, is pleasantly aromatic with a mild peachlike flavor that is enhanced by the addition of lemon or lime juice. It also combines well with other fresh fruits, especially with pomelo segments or slices of banana.

Mangoes are extremely rich in vitamin A.

Mangoes are widely available in North America. In the British Isles, they can be found in urban centers with sizable East Indian communities, but in many areas of continental Europe, mangoes remain all but unknown.

The pit of the mango can be planted indoors to produce a very attractive reddish-leaved plant. One should allow about six weeks for it to begin to grow. Temperatures should not fall below 15°C (60°F). The greater the warmth, the more the plant will thrive.

Marjoram

Origanum marjorana

Marjoram or sweet marjoram is of the same genus as regular oregano but tastes like a wholly different herb with its sweet, uniquely aromatic flavor.

Native to much of the Mediterranean area, marjoram had by the Middle Ages spread throughout western Europe. There it became especially esteemed by the French.

Marjoram is seldom used in the United States. In Canada, however, marjoram imported from France is a popular seasoning among both French and English Canadians. The French use marjoram in a variety of dishes, particularly in puréed spinach. Marjoram is also widely used in Great Britain and Germany. It has been used in the British Isles since its introduction from France in the 1500s. Today, a type of marjoram is said to grow wild on the "chalk downs." Although occasionally found in Victorian herb gardens in the United States during the last century, it is seldom seen or used there today.

Millet
Panicum mileaceum, P. molissimum, Setaria chaetochia, Penisetum glauchim, and many others

The term "millet" includes many diverse small seed grains produced by similar grasses, some growing to a height of one meter (4 ft.), some considerably shorter.

Panicum mileaceum, corn millet, which is believed to have originated in India, is one of the most common types. Other varieties include *P. molissimum,* native to Sudan; *Setaria chaetochia,* "foxtail" millet, a type grown in China; *Penisetum glauchim,* "bajri" millet, also native to India; and *Setaria ketchevelli,* found in both Mongolia and Georgia (Gruzhia).

When we purchase dried millet, it is in the form of thousands of very tiny separate grains. In its natural state, certain varieties of millet grow on what are very like tiny ears of corn. Indeed, long before the discovery of *Zea mays* or New World corn, millet was often referred to as "corn."

Millet has been cultivated as a food staple for millenia, and is indigenous to widely separated areas of the planet, being found throughout the entire Mediterranean area as well as in India, China, Africa, and the Caucasus.

Although millet is little used by North Americans, it remains a basic food staple for the northern Chinese, the Africans, and the notably healthy, long-lived, and almost totally vegetarian Hunzas of northern India. Millet is extensively cultivated in African areas near the Sahara where neither wheat nor barley grow due to the intense heat. The famous "cous cous" of Morocco and elsewhere in North Africa is frequently produced from millet.

In ancient China, foxtail millet was more important than rice. Indeed, for much of China's history, millet and soybeans constituted the two most important crops. Even today, millet remains an important food staple in many areas of China, India, the Near East, and much of Africa. It may be observed that the very dark brown "teff," *Eragrostis abyssinia,* (the major cereal grain of Ethiopia) is generally regarded as an "ethiopian millet." *Andropogon sorghum,* "kaoling," is an important Chinese crop that came to China from

India and is also sometimes classified as a variety of millet.

Millet should be soaked in water for at least twenty-four hours before cooking. Many people prefer to let it soak for several days until it is somewhat sour. This is a very ancient mode of preparation that greatly enhances the flavor of millet. Millet is cooked and eaten like rice, but is considerably more flavorful than the latter.

Millet is particularly good as a main entrée with steamed brussels sprouts, fried cabbage, or green peas. It is also delicious eaten by itself with a little paprika, butter, and chopped parsley, or it can be combined with raisins, chopped pitted dates, fresh fruits, cinnamon, and honey for a dessert dish. An especially delicious way to prepare millet is to combine it with sesame tahini, lemon juice, sugar, and fresh fruits, especially peaches or strawberries.

Millet is rich in iron and has a higher protein content (9 percent) than any other grain except amaranth. It is one of those highly nutritious foods that offers the creative cook a wide field for culinary experimentation. Hopefully it will, in the future, become far more important in the North American diet. It is widely available in health food stores and organic food shops throughout the continent. For vegetarians, it is an extremely important dietary staple.

Mint and Peppermint

Mentha viridis, M. longifolia, M. rotundafolia, M. piperata, M. spirata, M. citrata, and many others

Mint is indigenous to the regions surrounding the Mediterranean, including North Africa. Today, many consider the finest quality mint to be that produced in England where it was introduced by the ancient Romans.

People tend to be either extremely fond of mint or to dislike it intensely. While the English use it extensively in various sauces as well as in jelly, the French are notably unenthusiastic about it, except for use in certain candies. As for North Americans, they seem to possess an absolute passion for chocolate-covered peppermint candy. North Africans and Near Eastern Arabs use mint extensively as a "tea" which is served with the addition of a considerable amount of sugar. During the last few decades, mint "tea," albeit unsweetened, has become a popular herbal beverage in North America.

M. citrata—variously termed orange flower, lemon, or bergamot mint—may be singled out as possessing a delicate fragrance and flavor that is pleasing even to those who detest regular mint. It is excellent eaten with fresh fruits or added in the form of several crushed leaves to a regular cup of tea. In North Africa and the Near East, it is also used, fresh or dried, as a flavoring in cooked crushed wheat or rice. *M. rotundafolia*, pineapple mint, with its cream-dappled leaves, is also noted for its fruitlike flavor. Unfortunately, it is seldom obtainable.

Mung Bean

Phaseolus aureus or *P. mungo*

Some botanical authorities place the mung bean within the genus *Vigna*. Native to India, this green, peppercorn-sized bean is widely available today in dried form throughout Canada and the United States. Extensively used in making "dahl" in East Indian cuisine, the mung bean is also favored in North America for that increasingly popular food item—bean sprouts.

To many non-East Indians, cooked mung beans seem flavorless compared to nearly any other variety of bean. East Indian cuisine, of course, relies very heavily on curries and spices, so the blandness of the mung bean itself hardly presents a problem.

Mung beans are exceptionally high in protein.

Mushroom

Agaricus bisporus

Agaricus bisporus is the most frequently encountered common edible mushroom raised commercially and sold throughout North America, continental Europe, and the British Isles.

Mushrooms are parasitic fungi that live on decaying matter. They reproduce by minute spores that, like dust, are carried by the air. They grow throughout the Old and New Worlds and while many are edible, others are toxic to the point of being lethal. Edible mushrooms were prized even in ancient Egypt where they were reserved solely for the consumption of the "god-kings" or Pharaohs. Among the ancient Romans, mushrooms were used in a wide variety of gourmet dishes. In India, however, the consumption of mushrooms was proscribed by Hinduism for both the highest castes and for yogic aspirants. Nor was the mushroom particularly esteemed by most Near Eastern peoples or by the Scandinavians. On the other hand, mushrooms have always been highly valued as a food by the Latin, Slavic, and Chinese peoples.

Commercial cultivation of mushrooms in the West began in eighteenth-century France in caves outside Paris, during the reign of Louis XIV. Not long thereafter, mushroom cultivation spread to Italy and elsewhere in continental Europe. Only during the late nineteenth century did mushroom cultivation begin in the United States.

Full- or at least half-grown specimens of commercially-grown edible mushrooms are far more flavorful than the very young "button mushrooms" that some people mistake for a separate species. Fortunately, the more mature but still unopened specimens are frequently available in North American markets. In Europe, they have always been the preferred type.

The regular, commercially available mushroom can be prepared in many different ways. Suffice it to say that mushrooms are delicious raw—whole or sliced—in salads or simply eaten by themselves with a bit of garlic, oil, and pepper. They are also a very desirable addition to numerous vegetarian entrées—sautéed, baked, broiled, or fried. In nearly every case, garlic enhances the flavor of mushrooms. Fried with onions, mushrooms are excellent served with boiled or mashed potatoes and fresh dill weed. Among eastern Europeans, chopped mushrooms—often with the addition of potatoes, cabbage, and onion—are frequently used as the main ingredient of pies or deep-fried pastries.

An ancient, commercially cultivated oriental mushroom, the shitoke ("leong gou" in Chinese), *Lentines exodes*, has become increasingly available in North American markets. It has been grown on logs in China and Japan for millenia. Its flavor is quite different from that of the *Agaricus bisporus*, and for many westerners is something of an acquired taste.

Numerous guidebooks dedicated to the study of mycology or the science of mushrooms are available. No one should undertake the gathering of wild mushrooms without having acquired a thorough knowledge of the subject.

Mustard

Brassica juncea, B. alba, B. nigra, and others

There are many different varieties of mustard growing throughout the Old World, from the shores of the Mediterranean to China in the east and Poland in the north. Mustard was widely used in ancient Israel, Greece, and Rome. Today, diverse mustards also grow wild throughout much of North America. Whether such plants derive from Old World stock or are indigenous to the New World as well as the Old is a matter of conjecture.

Tremendously rich in vitamins A and C, mustard leaves make an excellent green vegetable. *Brassica juncea,* the main type grown for greens, is said to have developed from an East Indian strain. Often neglected in North America, mustard greens remain popular in much of Europe where they have been a vegetable staple from prehistoric times through the medieval period right up to the present. A form of Chinese mustard greens called "gai choi" resembles western spinach in appearance rather than mustard. Mustard greens of all types go particularly well with noodles and pasta, rice, millet, or barley. The Chinese often serve mustard greens with pieces of tofu or bean curd which have been fried or sautéed in soy sauce.

Mustard as a condiment is processed from the powdered seeds of the mustard plant and prepared in various ways with a wide range of additives ranging from vinegar to sugar and from dill weed to ginger. Turmeric, the major ingredient of many types of processed mustard, accounts for the brilliant yellow-gold color we have come to associate with many types of mustard.

In England, for centuries, mustard sauce was prepared simply by adding vinegar and honey to powdered mustard. This mixture was then rolled into small balls and stored until needed, at which time it was diluted with vinegar. Later, more elaborate methods evolved. Using *Brassica alba* as their main source of mustard seed, Tewkesbury, Durham, and Norwich successively became the important centers of mustard production in England. The use of mustard seeds in a condiment is said to have been brought to both the British Isles and to Gaul (France) by the ancient Romans who used it extensively in their own cuisine.

Brassica nigra is the variety of mustard most cultivated for its seeds in continental Europe where France remains a major center of mustard production. In the area of Dijon, several varieties are still produced according to an early seventeenth-century formula. A considerable amount of mustard is also produced in both Germany and Sweden. The dark brown Swedish mustard is very sweet and contains a small amount of powdered cloves or nutmeg.

French and other continental mustards are made with a variety of seasonings added to the powdered mustard in different combinations. Making a mustard to suit one's individual taste can offer a wide variety of possibilities to the creative cook.

Mustard sauce is excellent, when used sparingly, in many types of salad and goes especially well with cooked beets, cauliflower, and peas.

Navy Bean

a variety of *Phaseolus vulgaris*

The navy bean is among the many varieties of bean included within the extremely broad botanical classification, *Phaseolus vulgaris*. Like other beans within this category, the navy bean is indigenous to the New World.

This small white bean was extensively cultivated by the native Indian peoples of New England and elsewhere in North America at the time of British and French colonization. It was brought to the Old World and spread throughout much of Europe during the sixteenth and seventeenth centuries. In England, the navy bean became extremely popular among the poor. In British North America, it soon became a major culinary item among all classes of colonial society, particularly in the New England area. Indeed, "New England baked beans" remain a basic North American favorite even today. In this dish, already-cooked dried navy beans are slowly baked with sugar, honey, or syrup, and, sometimes, tomato sauce. This nutritious legume was a staple among sailors on British and U.S. ships, hence the name "navy" bean.

Navy beans have always been inexpensive, providing healthy, flavorful, and filling meals for millions of poor people in North America, the British Isles, and continental Europe. Europeans frequently sautée navy beans with garlic and onions in tomato paste and serve them with chopped parsley. Sugar greatly enhances the flavor. They are also often used in vegetable soups and go especially well with kale, mustard greens, or chard. When eaten with grains such as rice or millet, dried beans of all varieties provide a complete vegetable protein.

The larger great northern bean is grown extensively in Canada and is prepared in the same ways as the navy bean. No doubt, the great northern was among the beans which, in 1605, Champlain observed under cultivation by the native people of the Quebec area.

Other popular, closely related dried beans include the tannish cream-colored pinto bean, which is dappled with red speckles, and the common small red bean of the same size and shape as the navy bean. Both types of bean are popular in Mexico and the southwestern United States.

All dried beans should be soaked, even up to the sprouting stage, before cooking.

Nectarine

Prunus persica nectarina

Although the nectarine tree appears to be indistinguishable from that of the peach, the fruit differs from the peach in that it has a smooth, not fuzzy, skin. Nectarines can be either freestone or clingstone. Like the peach, the pulp of the fruit varies from white to yellow or orange. Many types are infused with a pink or reddish hue, particularly close to the stone.

The popular notion that the nectarine is a cross between a peach and a plum has no foundation in reality. In all probability, the nectarine is a natural mutation of the peach, although the famous botanist, Luther Burbank, believed that the peach developed from the nectarine, rather than the other way around. In any case, a very curious phenomenon sometimes takes place with nectarine trees producing one or several peaches, or vice versa.

The nectarine originated in China, where it continues to be a popular favorite. It is an extremely ancient fruit which was mentioned in Chinese written records of two thousand years ago. Following the usual route via Persia and the Near East, the nectarine came to Europe from China at an early date. Although cultivated to some small extent in ancient Greece and Rome, it was not well known at that time. Eventually, it spread to the Iberian Peninsula (Spain and Portugal), probably via the Romans. The Spanish introduced it to the New World, and some of the nectarines growing in California today are said to be the descendants of those brought by the Spanish.

Nectarines continue to be widely cultivated in China, the land of their origin. An exceptionally flavorful variety with a whitish pulp and rose-tinted skin is particularly esteemed by the Chinese. It looks and tastes very much like a rare type of peach known as the "babcock" in North America.

During the last twenty-five or thirty years, nectarines have become increasingly available in North American markets. Unfortunately, as is the case with so many fruits in the United States, they are often picked while still green and consequently never properly ripen.

New Zealand Spinach

Tetragonia expansa

This vegetable with its many spreading branches grows to a height of sixty centimeters (2 ft.). Its small green leaves are somewhat triangular in shape and it bears greenish yellow flowers that eventually produce seed pods. New zealand "spinach" is *not* a true spinach and is not even remotely related to it. It does, however, taste remarkably like spinach.

As its name suggests, new zealand spinach is a native of New Zealand where for centuries it has been a popular vegetable among the Maoris. From New Zealand, it spread to various South Pacific islands and to Australia long before European expansion into the Pacific area. It is still an important item of diet throughout that entire region.

Sir Joseph Banks is said to have been the first European to show any interest in this vegetable and he may have been the first to bring it to England, although Fitz-Gibbon, in *The Food of the Western World*, gives the honor to Captain Cook. In any case, during the late 1700s, new zealand spinach became a fashionable hothouse vegetable among the British. In some areas of southwestern England, along the Cornwall coast for instance, new zealand spinach can be grown outdoors.

New zealand spinach is not difficult to grow in a relatively warm temperate climate, and if only the ends of the branches are harvested, new leaves will develop again and again. People who have raised it observe that neither snails nor other insects show any interest in it whatever.

Twenty years ago, new zealand spinach was popular in both Canada and the United States. Although it could be grown in much of the United States, most of it was imported from New Zealand, the major producer of this excellent vegetable even today. While it remains widely available in Canada, unfortunately one encounters it less and less in the United States. Some is still cultivated in the British Isles where it is commercially available in many fine-quality produce markets. It remains, for the most part, unknown in continental Europe and the Near East.

New zealand spinach is prepared and used in the same ways as regular spinach.

Nutmeg
Myristica fragrans

Nutmegs are the seeds or kernels of a yellowish fruit that grows on a tree native to the Molucca Islands and elsewhere in Indonesia. It is also grown extensively in the Philippines, on the island of Mauritius, and in the West Indies.

A popular seasoning throughout much of southeast Asia, nutmeg first came to continental Europe and the British Isles in the twelfth century via the Near East. It was not, however, much used in European cooking until the sixteenth century. In Chaucer's England and well beyond, it was widely used as an addition to ale, but only gradually was it adopted for use in puddings and cakes.

By the seventeenth century, nutmeg had become *the* favorite spice of the Dutch who, from the viewpoint of most other peoples, developed an "inordinate fondness" for it during their monopoly of the spice trade and long occupation of the "Dutch East Indies" (today's Indonesia). In addition to using nutmeg in dessert dishes, the Dutch also use it lavishly on potatoes, vegetables, noodles, and nearly every dish imaginable. To a lesser degree, Norwegians also utilize nutmeg as an important seasoning.

Ground or powdered nutmeg is a pleasantly aromatic and flavorful addition to custards and other milk-based puddings, cakes, and cookies. Combined with cinnamon and honey, it makes an interesting addition to yogurt or sour cream.

Mace is the spice derived from the thin, reddish brown lacelike outer covering of the nutmeg seed. To many people, mace is simply a much stronger and less pleasant form of nutmeg. It is often used as a pickling spice.

Oat

Avena, many varieties

Oats are the "berries" or grains of a grass that is extremely hardy and thrives even in the dreariest of northern climates and worst of soils. *Avena fatua,* the common oat, is said to grow wild throughout much of central and western Europe as well as in the western United States; *A. brevis,* the European short oat, is grown in Germany and France; *A. sativa,* the common white oat, grows throughout northern Europe and, today, is cultivated worldwide; *A. orientalis,* sometimes called the siberian oat, was brought to continental Europe in the seventeenth century and to the British Isles in the eighteenth century. There are also many Mediterranean types including *A. strigosa, A. byzantina,* and *A. ludoiciana.* According to Anderson, in *Plants, Man, and Life,* oats began as a weed in fields of emmer wheat during the Neolithic period.

The Mediterranean peoples have never cared for oats and they are not used by the Greeks, Italians, or Spanish. In his *Natural History,* Pliny mentions that the barbaric German tribes of the North ate a gruel containing oats. Oatmeal porridge has been eaten for centuries in the British Isles, particularly in Scotland and Ireland. Oats are also widely grown and eaten in Norway and Sweden.

A hot, thick oatmeal porridge served with butter, sugar, and cream can be surprisingly good, especially with the addition of raisins and other dried fruits. Oatmeal can also be used as a base for vegetable loaves. Kale, spinach, or celery root all work out very well in such a dish. The Scots dip certain types of seaweed in oatmeal and fry it.

Oats are rich in protein as well as in vitamins B and E.

Okra

Hibiscus esculentus

Okra plants thrive in tropical regions where the temperature never goes below 15°C (60°F). The plant, which can reach a height of three meters (10 ft.), bears white and purple or pale yellow flowers with scarlet red centers. These flowers unfold just after sunrise during the warmest months of summer. They live only one day and by sunset have wilted, the new okra pods emerging from their centers. These seed-filled green pods can grow quite large, but are best when they are about seven centimeters (3 in.) long. They grow very rapidly and generally are ready to be harvested less than a week after they emerge from the flower.

Okra is indigenous to North Africa and spread at an early date over a large portion of the African continent where it now grows wild in many areas. From Africa, it also spread to the Arabian peninsula. Okra was a popular food among the ancient Egyptians, who cultivated it in the Nile Valley as early as 1000 B.C. From there, okra spread to the area known today as the Sudan and further southward into the very center of the African continent.

Its extensive use in both the Balkan and Turkish cuisines probably derives from the lingering influence of the thousand-year-old empire of the Byzantine Greeks which, for part of its existence, covered an area stretching from Syria to the Balkans and southern Italy. Okra reached Spain via the influx of Moors from North Africa and from there it spread into France. In the seventeenth century, it was introduced to Brazil where it thrived.

Okra, or "guba" as it was known among certain Africans, became particularly popular in the southern United States where it was first introduced by black slaves from West Africa in the seventeenth and eighteenth centuries. It is believed to have been first grown in the New World in Jamaica. Its use soon spread from the slaves to their captors. In Louisiana, where the French promoted its large scale cultivation, okra became particularly important in the local cuisine. In England and northern Europe, okra remains all but unknown as the climate is not conducive to its cultivation.

Okra pods may be eaten in their entirety but must be cooked. The somewhat mucilaginous texture of cooked okra is a natural feature of this mild, unique vegetable. It is delectable in vegetable stews with green peppers, tomato paste, onions, garlic, and potatoes. Okra is also excellent fried in cornmeal or garbanzo flour batter with garlic fragments placed inside the pods. Always be careful not to overcook okra. It is best before it becomes completely soft. In warm dry areas, okra can be dried for later use.

High-quality frozen okra is available in most parts of North America and is certainly preferable to the stale cold-storage specimens that all too often appear in North American markets. People who live in areas where it is available in a fresh-picked state are most fortunate.

Okra seeds have almost as much protein as soybeans, and the entire pod is rich in vitamins A and C as well as in calcium. An exceptionally nutritious vegetable, okra is also a very mild laxative.

Another vegetable, sometimes known as "chinese okra," externally resembles okra in the shape and contours of the pod, but is very much larger. Actually, it is not even remotely related to okra. Rather, it is a type of Old World gourd classified as *Luffa acutengula*.

Olive

Olea europa

Olive trees, which bear fruit only after eight years and can live for over one thousand years, have elongated pale green leaves with a somewhat grayish silvery hue. The olives themselves change from green to a deep purplish black as they ripen. Both green and ripe olives, as well as the oil derived from them, have been eaten from time immemorial.

Olea europa derived from the wild olive, *Olea chrysophylla*. There are approximately thirty-five different species of olive throughout the Mediterranean world. Although cultivated at a very early date in Greece, the olive is generally believed to have originated in the eastern Mediterranean area, which included both Phoenicia (Lebanon) and the ancient kingdom of Israel.

Olives are mentioned in both the Jewish scriptures and in the writings of ancient Greece. They were also known in Egypt some four thousand years ago. Homer, in the *Odyssey*, speaks of the olives growing in the gardens of Alcinous in Phoenicia. Indeed, olives may have been brought to Greece by the Phoenicians as they are generally credited with distributing the olive throughout the entire Mediterranean area.

Olive trees were viewed as symbols of peace, victory, and hope throughout the ancient Mediterranean world. In ancient Greece, olive branches—together with bay or laurel sprigs—were used to crown victorious athletes and to acclaim poets and kings. Royal scepters in Greece and throughout the Mediterranean world were generally carved out of olive wood to symbolize a long and benevolent reign. The ancient Greeks associated the olive with the goddess Athena.

The olive has been cultivated on the Italian peninsula ever since it was introduced there in the sixth century B.C. In his *Natural History,* Pliny mentions twelve varieties of olive known in the first century A.D. Although some types of olive were introduced to Iberia (Spain) and Gaul (France) by the Romans, there were apparently already certain wild varieties growing there which were probably descendants of Phoenician stock.

Throughout the Middle Ages and medieval period, olives were used by all classes of society in the Near East, throughout the entirety of Mediterranean Europe, and in North Africa. The olive was introduced to the New World by the Spanish, first to Mexico during the sixteenth century and later to Peru and Chile. Sometime after the middle of the eighteenth century, the Spanish began to cultivate olives in California. On the east coast of North America, extensive olive groves were planted in 1760 by the Greeks who founded the community of New Smyrna, Florida.

Italy, Spain, Greece, and Israel are all major olive growers. Greek kalamata and peleponisis olives are regarded as the finest available. There are time-honored and traditional methods used in the Old World to preserve olives in oil, salt crystals, lye, wine vinegar, or a strong brine. Americans simply can them in water! These American olives can be greatly improved by draining off the liquid, drying the olives out a bit, and placing them in oil and wine vinegar with some salt. Fine-quality Greek and Italian olives are always available in delicatessens and specialty shops. Italian olives are most often preserved in oil.

Whole or chopped olives go especially well with garlic, onions, and herbs such as fresh basil or oregano. Mixed with chopped parsley and garlic, they make an excellent garnish on noodles or pasta. They also go well with grated cheese, and can be added to cheese sauces, sandwiches, and salads. Throughout the Mediterranean world, a typical vegetarian repast consists of olives (with or without herbs and garlic) eaten with fresh bread, goat or sheep cheese, and a few figs or dates.

The oldest form of oil known to man is made from the olive. The finest type, excellent on salads, is a clear golden yellow. The greener the olive oil, the poorer the quality and the stronger the smell. Olive oil is also used in cooking, but some people do not care for the odor it creates when used for frying.

Onion

Allium cepa, many varieties

A member of the lily family, *Allium cepa* covers a number of different varieties of onion which have been cultivated since prehistoric times. Onions can be perfectly spherical, spherical with a flattened top, or oblong. They can be as small as a cherry tomato or as large as a grapefruit. They can be reddish purple, white, or yellow with a tannish skin.

The onion's place of origin is lost in obscurity. Regarded as a sacred symbol of life in ancient Egypt, the onion was known throughout the entire ancient world and is unquestionably the most universal seasoning used by man.

There can be little doubt that the most pleasing variety is the sweet, richly flavored "red onion," originally classified as *Allium cepa rubra.* These onions are purplish red to magenta in color, and can be either elongated or spherical with flattened tops. Always the most popular onion in Spain, Italy, and Portugal, the red onion was introduced into the New World by the Spanish not long after their conquest of Mexico.

White onions, originally classified as *Allium cepa alba,* tend to be somewhat stronger-flavored than the red ones, and are a favorite in the British Isles. The English introduced white onions to their North American colonies in the early seventeenth century.

Although onions of both red and white varieties are available in North America, the extremely strong, tan-skinned yellow onion is, for some inexplicable reason, the most commonly grown and eaten onion in the United States and Canada.

All varieties of onion are best when they are young and no larger than small lemons. In the United States there is an unfortunate tendency for onion-growers to wait until the onions have grown to an enormous size before harvesting. In addition to possessing an overpoweringly strong flavor and an unpleasantly slimy texture, these large onions are extremely inconvenient to use. Another practice on the part of onion growers that warrants strong public protest is their use of fish-based fertilizers which frequently imparts a strongly unpleasant fish taste to the onions.

The onion is so universally utilized as a seasoning that there is no need to enumerate its specific uses.

Onions contain vitamins A and C. They also contain allyl aldehyde, a chemical that destroys many types of bacteria. Hence, onions have generally been viewed throughout history as major deterrents to a variety of diseases, infections, and plagues.

See also **Chive; Chinese Onion; Egyptian Onion; Green Onion; Shallot.**

Orange
Citrus aurantius, C. sinensis, C. reticulata

There are approximately eighty different types of oranges included within three basic botanical classifications. The varieties have not been given secondary botanical names. *Citrus aurantius* applies to tart or sour oranges. The seville orange is the main variety. *Citrus sinensis* is the basic classification for all sweet oranges. These include the valencia, which is the most common orange in North America today; the navel orange, which was developed in Brazil and is distinguished by a navel-like protuberance on the bottom of the fruit; and the jaffa orange or "shamouti," which is grown in Israel and throughout the entire Mediterranean area. It is "seedless," has a greenish-hued skin, and is exceptionally flavorful. Unfortunately, this delectable orange is not available in North America. *Citrus reticulata* is the classification used for the "mandarin" oranges of the Far East, including the small tangerine which was developed in North Africa from a basic mandarin variety. All oranges within this classification have thin loose skins that are easily removed. The very sweet to sweet-tart flavor is quite distinctive.

In *Edible Plants of the World,* Sturtevant aptly stated a century ago that "The determination of the species of this genus seems to be in confusion." The situation in this respect has changed little, if at all. The Swedish botanist, Linnaeus, established the *Citrus aurantius* classification for both sour and sweet oranges. Later, botanical authorities introduced the *C. sinensis* category to cover all varieties of sweet oranges except the loose-skinned oriental type. Thus, *C. sinensis* includes not only the valencia and the jaffa orange, but also the very different and rather rare blood orange! (*See* **Blood Orange.**)

The somewhat sour seville orange was the first to be cultivated in the West. It is said to be indigenous to India where it was cultivated at a very early date. Around the ninth century A.D., Arab traders brought it to the Near East and North Africa. From North Africa, it spread to Spain, where, in the twelfth century, the Moors began to cultivate it in orchards around Seville. By the end of the thirteenth century, seville oranges were being grown in Sicily and in many parts of the Italian peninsula. The seville orange may have come to this area via crusaders returning from Syria and the Holy Land, but it is more likely that it first came via the Byzantine Greeks. In any case, by the fourteenth century, both oranges and lemons had become fairly common among the Italians.

According to Sturtevant, as early as 1290 the Spanish brought oranges of an unspecified type to Portsmouth in England and sold them to the queen of King Edward I. Within several centuries, the English were importing a vast quantity of seville oranges from Spain for the making of marmalade. The flowers of the seville orange are used to make "orange flower water," popular as a luxury item from medieval times right up through the last century.

The sweet orange, *Citrus sinensis*, originated in China, and there are references to it in Chinese writings dating from 2200 B.C. From the Far East, its cultivation spread westward. The Arab peoples introduced the sweet orange to North Africa and the Iberian Peninsula. From these lands, sweet oranges, particularly the valencia variety, were exported throughout Europe during the fifteenth and sixteenth centuries. Orange groves became widely established in many parts of the Italian peninsula, appearing even in many great paintings of the period, such as Boticelli's *Primavera* in which Mercury and the Muses are posed before a thick grove of almost mysterious orange trees, the fruits of which Mercury gathers in a net.

England began to import quantities of sweet oranges (probably the valencia variety) during the sixteenth century when they became a popular novelty food among the affluent. By the seventeenth century, English aristocrats were cultivating their own orange trees in "orangeries." The trees were left in the open air during the spring and summer, but glass-enclosed during the fall and winter. The famous Carew Orangerie of Surrey survived for 178 years, only succumbing to the cold during the bitter winter of 1740. At Wimbledon, Queen Henrietta Maria, wife of King Charles I and daughter of Marie de Medici and Henri IV of France, maintained some sixty tubs of orange trees. These were destroyed with savage abandon by the troops of Oliver Cromwell.

With the restoration of the monarchy under King Charles II, orangeries were revived in England and oranges became increasingly popular, being imported in great quantity from Portugal.

Regarded as a choice edible during that period, they were sold in theaters by "orange girls" who were often understudy actresses. One of these girls, Nell Gwyn, went on to become a leading actress of her day as well as the mistress of King Charles II.

Orangeries were even found in northern areas such as St. Petersberg and Stockholm. A famous orangerie was maintained for the French Court at Versailles, and in Dresden, the Elector of Saxony set up an orangerie of enormous size.

While sweet oranges were popular as a raw fruit, the British also imported ever-increasing quantities of seville oranges for use in marmalade—that favorite jam of English, Irish, and Scots alike.

Columbus brought orange seeds to the New World in 1493 on his second expedition to the West Indies. During the next century, the Spanish planted oranges in Mexico, Central America, and Florida. In South America, they were first introduced by Pizarro in Peru. Due to the ideal soil and climate conditions in the Caribbean islands and Florida, many wild orange groves developed simply through fallen or discarded seeds, eventually giving the impression that the orange was indigenous to these areas. During the late 1700s, the Spanish also brought oranges, probably valencias, to southern California, cultivating them in the mission orchards. Although the Portuguese brought oranges to Brazil, Sturtevant notes that Brazilian natives have long claimed that a small bitter variety of orange already existed there prior to the coming of the Europeans!

Mandarin oranges are indigenous to China, and are also cultivated in Japan. The only type of mandarin orange that is well known and widely available in North America and Europe, particularly during the Christmas season, is the tangerine, which was developed from a basic Chinese strain in the area of Tangiers in North Africa. Today, Japan is the world's main producer of this variety. Tangerines were unknown in Europe and North America until 1805. Today, they are grown on a minor scale in Florida.

Fresh oranges were considered a luxury item in North America and much of northern Europe until around 1915 when they became a common item of everyday diet. Oranges were first raised commercially in California in 1841. Today, California and Florida are major orange-producing areas. California oranges are almost exclusively of the valencia and navel varieties. Other important orange-producing areas include Spain, Israel, North Africa, Brazil, Italy, and Japan.

Fresh oranges blend beautifully with most other fruits in innumerable combinations. By themselves, they are best peeled, separated into segments, dipped in sugar, and eaten with a fork from a glass or goblet. Cream cheese goes remarkably well with oranges and added to this simple dish can turn it into a gourmet's delight.

Oranges are exceptionally rich in vitamin C content and are said to possess considerable antiseptic properties.

See also **Blood Orange; Tangelo.**

Oregano

Origanum vulgare, O. smyrnacium, O. onites, and others

Oregano is a small, green-leaved perennial that bears purple or white flowers. It is a member of the mint family, but has a totally different flavor.

There are many different varieties of oregano—each with its own unique flavor—found throughout the Mediterranean area from Asia Minor (Turkey) to Corsica. The majority, however, are Greek or Italian. A few of the main varieties are: *Origanum vulgare,* the basic wild oregano of southern Italy; *O. smyrnacium* from Asia Minor, a favorite seasoning of the Byzantine Greeks; *O. onites,* thought to be native to Sicily; and *O. heraclesticum,* which grows wild in Greece.

Greek oregano is particularly valued by connoisseurs, but there are also certain Italian types that are quite equal to the finest Greek varieties. In North America, imported Greek, Italian, and Mexican oregano are all available.

Oregano, with its pungent and very distinctive flavor, can be a marvelous seasoning in a variety of dishes. It is used either fresh or dried in the Italian, Greek, Spanish, and North African cuisines. It is especially good as an ingredient of tomato pastes and sauces, and combines well with garlic and lemon. It also enhances the flavor of green salads and zucchini. Combined with a generous portion of paprika and chopped garlic, and mixed with a bit of oil and wine vinegar, oregano is excellent as a garnish on a quality sourdough bread.

Whole-leaf oregano is far superior to the finely ground or powdered type. Oregano should be pinched between the fingers to release the aromatic flavor of the herb.

See also **Marjoram.**

Papaya

Carica papava

The papaya is an oblong yellowish fruit. The inside is pale orange with a "core" of tiny black seeds. It is indigenous to the West Indies in the Caribbean, as well as to Mexico and Central America. This fruit was brought to India, the Malay Archipelago, and Africa in the sixteenth century by the Spanish and Portuguese. Later, many people, ignorant of the papaya's origin, assumed it was native to those regions.

Today, the papaya is cultivated throughout most of the warmer areas of the world. In the United States, it grows only in Florida and Hawaii. Papayas can exceed nine kilograms (20 lb.), but the ones sold in North America usually weigh less than five hundred grams (1 lb.).

Fresh papayas are one of the most popular tropical fruits in all countries except the United States. Even Canadians consume more per capita than Americans.

Perhaps the best way to eat this mild and flavorful fruit is simply plain with a bit of fresh lemon juice and sugar, or served in a compote with other fruits. Dried papaya strips can be eaten as a candy or added to many dessert dishes. Many people find papaya juice to be an exceptionally refreshing drink.

The papaya is rich in vitamins A and C and contains more protein than any other fruit. As an aid to digestion, the papaya, which contains a considerable quantity of the enzyme, "papain," is an excellent food for people suffering from ulcers.

Paprika

Capsicum tetragonum, C. annum

Paprika, the "cayenne of Europe," is the aromatic powder derived from the ripe dried pods of several types of *Capsicum* peppers. Unlike cayenne pepper, paprika is used basically for flavor, rather than "hotness." The mild "sweet" type of paprika is the kind most frequently employed. A slightly hot type also exists. In this, a few seeds (removed for processing "sweet" paprika) of the dried pepper have been ground with the pulp.

All *Capsicum* peppers are indigenous to the New World, namely, South and Central America, Mexico, and the West Indies. In the sixteenth century, the Spanish introduced paprika to Europe, where it has become associated with various types of Old World cuisine. The Turks, Spanish, and Hungarians all use paprika in their cuisines. Indeed, it has become so identified with Hungarian cuisine that many people believe it is native to Hungary. The peppers from which paprika is made have, in fact, been cultivated in Hungary for several centuries, notably in the areas of Szeged and Kalocsa. An excellent paprika bearing the brand name "Szeged" is widely available in North America today.

Paprika adds considerable zest to lentils or dried beans, particularly when used in generous quantities. Combined with onions and garlic, it can be used as a substitute for tomato paste in pasta, noodle, vegetable, or legume dishes. The bright orange-red color of paprika lends a festive, decorative appearance to practically any grain or vegetable dish. It is particularly good with brussels sprouts or with fried barley and onion. Paprika should be used in reasonably large quantities in order to fully enjoy its unique flavor.

The long red peppers used for paprika are also delicious whole—either fresh or dried, raw or cooked—in innumerable grain, vegetable, and cheese dishes. They are particularly popular in the Balkans. A delicious sauce or "paste" is made by crushing fresh raw red peppers and mixing them with chopped garlic, parsley, and, if desired, some basil or oregano. This delectable thick sauce is used like butter on heavy dark bread.

Powdered paprika is widely available throughout North America, continental Europe, and the British Isles. It is not, however, a popular seasoning in the United States or Canada, except among those ethnic groups in whose cuisines it figures prominently. The long red peppers themselves are occasionally encountered in both dried or fresh forms even in North America and the British Isles. In using these, remember to remove most of the seeds unless your taste runs to the hot and piquant.

The vitamin C content of paprika is extremely high.

Parsley

Petroselinum sativim, P. hortense, P. crispum,
P. radicatum

Petroselinum sativim (in older botanical works, *Carum petroselinum*) is the basic wild parsley; *P. hortense* is the smooth-leaved "italian" type; *P. crispum* is the curly-leaved variety grown in North America; and *P. radicatum* is the hamberg or dutch parsley raised chiefly for its root.

Smooth or flat-leaved parsley was extensively used in the cuisine of the ancient Greco-Roman world. Curly-leaved parsley was primarily used for ornamental purposes, such as in the garlands used to crown athletes and poets. Parsley is native to a large area of the Mediterranean world, including Israel, Greece, the Italian peninsula, and the island of Sardinia. Indeed, Sardinia may well be "the island of parsley" mentioned by Homer (350 B.C.) in the *Odyssey*. The great botanist, Linnaeus, believed that parsley spread from Sardinia to the rest of the Mediterranean world. Among the Greeks and Romans, parsley was highly regarded as a seasoning as well as used in rites and repasts honoring the dead. In the Jewish Passover rites, parsley is eaten as a symbol of spring and rebirth.

Albertus Magnus mentions parsley as a kitchen-garden plant in the thirteenth century. By the fourteenth century, it was known throughout much of northern Europe. Although parsley is said to have been introduced to the British Isles by the Romans, it only became popular in 1548 when it was reintroduced directly from the island of Sardinia. According to certain persistent traditions, parsley was first planted in Cornwall by the Phoenicians. This may explain its more widespread use in Wales than elsewhere in Britain. The Spanish brought parsley to the New World in the sixteenth century as did the English in the seventeenth.

There is almost no dish, other than desserts, that chopped parsley does not enhance and it can be stated, virtually ex cathedra, that fresh chopped parsley transforms almost any salad or vegetable dish as well as any pasta or grain entrée into gourmet fare! A particularly delicious dish consists of sliced carrots simmered in oil with garlic and served with a generous amount of chopped parsley.

The smooth-leaved "italian" parsley is the type used throughout Europe and the Near East today, just as it has been for centuries. Twenty years ago, it was also widely available commercially in North America, but today it is less often encountered. This is most unfortunate as, without question, the flat-leaved variety is far more flavorful and has a more pleasing texture than the curly-leaved type. People with gardens are urged to raise this delectable herb.

More often than not, the frilled or curly-leaved variety available in North American markets consists of older, fully-matured sprigs that are even on the verge of turning yellow! This indifference to the quality of parsley in North America stems from the fact that most Americans do not eat this exceptionally nutritious herb at all, but use it only as a decorative garnish! In North America, many parsley lovers find it worthwhile to seek out Italian and Greek markets for high-quality parsley. Not infrequently, such shops may even have a private source for the delectable smooth-leaved type.

Hamberg or dutch parsley, which is believed to have originated in Holland during the sixteenth century, is grown primarily for its carrot-shaped white root that tastes something like a mixture of parsley and celery root. It is prepared in the same ways as the latter. Its delicious, although not very plentiful, smooth leaves can be used like regular parsley. Hamberg parsley root is commercially available in much of northern Europe, but is never seen in North America. It became quite popular in England during the eighteenth century. Today, it is occasionally still available there, although it can hardly be termed a popular vegetable.

Parsley contains large quantities of vitamins A (more than carrots) and C (three times the amount contained in oranges!), and is rich in minerals, particularly iron.

Parsnip

Pastinaca sativa

The parsnip is a long, cream-colored root vegetable that thrives in the cooler climates of the north, can withstand freezing, and even becomes more sweet and flavorful after being exposed to frost.

This ancient root vegetable has been eaten since prehistoric times and grew wild over a large area of the Old World. Its place of origin may have been the Caucasus or Asia Minor. At a very early date the wild parsnip found its way to northern Europe where it became a major cultivated vegetable during the medieval period. It became a popular basic vegetable food among the poor in much of northern Europe, and was a particular favorite among the Germans. Due to its high starch and sugar content, it not only filled the stomach, but provided needed energy and had a pleasant flavor besides.

Most ancient Greeks and Romans viewed the parsnip more as

a medicine than as a food, although Tiberius Caesar acquired a taste for it cooked in honey.

By the end of the sixteenth century in Elizabethan England, the parsnip had become popular among all classes of the population. It was, in fact, one of the few vegetables widely eaten there, the others being cabbage, kale, turnips, salsify, onions, and the ever-present dried green pea. English aristocrats even developed a taste for a dessert in which parsnips were combined with honey and spices in a custard.

Parsnips are still an English favorite and remain an important vegetable in much of northern Europe, although today they are seldom eaten by most Mediterranean peoples. Nor are they much favored by most North Americans. Although parsnips were introduced into North America by the British in the early seventeenth century, they never became more than a very minor vegetable crop there. Nevertheless, they are available in North America in small quantities throughout the winter months.

Parsnips are best steamed and eaten plain with butter and chopped parsley. They are also quite good broiled or in a cream sauce.

Pea

Pisum sativum and others

Pisum sativum, of the family *Legumnosae*, is the main variety of pea (also known as green pea and english pea). Other varieties include *P. arvense*, which grows wild in Georgia (Gruzhia), and *P. fulvum*, which is found in the eastern Mediterranean area.

Peas have been cultivated and eaten from ancient times over a wide area of the Old World. From northern India, they spread to the Near East and throughout the Mediterranean world, eventually reaching the British Isles and the northern part of continental Europe. They have been found in the famous excavations of Switzerland's Bronze Age lake dwellings, dating to 3000 B.C.; in Stone Age caverns in eastern Europe (Hungary); and in an excavation site at ancient Troy.

The Roman upper classes viewed peas as a food of ordinary country people and common soldiers. Dried peas were, in fact, among the main rations of ancient Greek and Roman soldiers, as they were easy to transport on long journeys and were an excellent source of protein.

Although the Romans may have brought peas to the British Isles, there is no indication that they were cultivated and eaten there prior to the Norman Conquest in 1066. Much used by the Norman French, peas gradually became an important crop among the English. Right up to modern times, "pease porridge" continued to form a regular part of the British diet, generally being cooked with onions and leeks.

Peas were apparently cultivated and eaten in Scandinavia considerably prior to their advent in the British Isles. In Norway and Sweden, peas were regarded as sacred to the god Thor, and were eaten in his honor on Thursdays. "Swedish soup," made from whole dried peas and seasoned with dill weed has remained a perennial Scandinavian favorite.

In most of northern and central Europe, whole dried peas, cooked in a soup or porridge, were used by the common people as a major source of protein during the entire medieval period and well into the nineteenth century, when they were largely replaced by the potato.

In the sixteenth century, the French introduced peas to Quebec, where their cultivation and consumption soon spread to the native Indian population of the entire region. In the early seventeenth century, the English introduced peas to their New England colonies.

Whole dried peas for use in pea soup and "pease porridge" are still popular and widely available in France, Scandinavia, the British Isles, and Canada, but in the United States whole dried peas are almost impossible to find except in the occasional organic food store. Americans generally use split peas, which have less nutritional value and less flavor. Not only have the skins been removed, but, being split, they cannot be sprouted and eaten raw after soaking.

Raw sprouted whole dried peas are particularly delectable and possess an even higher nutritional value than they do cooked. It is not necessary to actually let them sprout. Simply soak them for ten hours or more, drain, add a little sugar, and eat them as they are. They taste very much like fresh-picked peas, although the texture is somewhat harder.

Until the beginning of this century, pea flour was mixed with rye and barley flour to produce an exceptionally nutritious, heavy, dark bread common among the peasantry of northern, eastern, and central Europe. Unfortunately, pea flour is rarely processed in the

West today, although it may occasionally be found in organic food stores. In India, however, where it has been used for centuries in making a thin, dry "pancake" called a "papadum," pea flour continues to be produced in quantity.

In the ancient world, whole dried peas were softened by soaking, very briefly fried in oil, and sold by vendors in theaters, circuses, and other entertainment centers, much as popcorn is today. This custom apparently continued in the British Isles through Elizabethan times.

It was only in the late sixteenth and early seventeenth centuries that *fresh* peas began to be eaten in Europe, apparently first in France, where "petites pois" (very small fresh peas) became a fashionable dish among the aristocracy. In England, too, fresh peas became popular with the upper classes, but it was only during the eighteenth and nineteenth centuries that they began to be eaten by the general population.

Today, in North America, fresh peas are sometimes available commercially during the summer, but are not particularly popular. Both canned and frozen peas are, however, widely used. Both lack the exceptional nutritional value of whole dried peas.

According to Fitz-Gibbon, in *The Food of the Western World*, there were at least four varieties of peas growing in the British Isles in 1597. Today, many different types are cultivated throughout Europe. In the late eighteenth century, an Englishman, Thomas Andrew Knight, crossed a number of different strains to produce peas with optimum flavor, size, and productivity. Most peas grown today in the British Isles and North America derive from varieties developed by him.

A less familiar type of pea available dried in Canada and the British Isles, but unknown in the United States, is the "marrowfat," an extremely large, oddly wrinkled pea with a somewhat nutlike flavor. Marrowfats make exceptionally fine pea soup. Another type, the "common field pea" of ancient Egypt, is still much used in the Near East. These grayish-colored peas are much smaller than the green pea with which we are familiar. Its flowers are purplish rather than the white common to other varieties. Another extremely small variety is the one used exclusively for the processing of "split peas" in the United States.

Whole dried peas seasoned with dill weed and onion can be made into a delicious pea soup or "porridge." Peas, both dried and fresh, can be served simply with boiled potatoes and butter, or prepared in a milk or cream sauce with potatoes or noodles and served with dill weed or chopped parsley. Fried peas with a bit of mustard go nicely with rice, millet, or other grains or grain products, such as cous cous. Peas are one of those vegetables that offer considerable scope to the creative cook. It is worthwhile remembering that the addition of at least a small amount of sugar always enhances the flavor.

See also **Snow Pea.**

Peach

Prunus persica

A drupe or stone fruit, the peach originally grew wild in China. There are references to it in written Chinese literature even prior to 2000 B.C. At a very early date it was introduced to Persia and quickly became extensively cultivated by the inhabitants. From there, it spread westward to the area around Baghdad and then to Syria. It also spread north to Armenia, Georgia (Gruzhia), and the Caucasus, from there becoming known in Asia Minor and throughout the entire Mediterranean world.

Pliny, who lived from A.D. 23–79, says in his *Natural History* that the peach had only existed among the Romans from about one hundred years prior to his own day, although it had been known to the Greeks for many centuries. Theophrastes mentions the peach as early as 322 B.C., noting it as a Persian fruit. In any case, by Virgil's time (70–19 B.C.), it had been introduced to the Italian peninsula from Greece and had become a favorite luxury food among Roman aristocrats. In time, it was also introduced to the Iberian Peninsula (Spain and Portugal), Gaul (France), and even to some areas further north. Europeans generally assumed the peach was of Persian origin. Hence, the name *Persica* in the Latin nomenclature. In most areas, the peach remained a luxury item, except for those fortunate enough to possess their own trees.

The peach was brought to England by the Spanish and French during the 1500s. The English quite early introduced it to their North American colonies, but it was the second half of the 1800s before the peach became widely available to the general public. The Spanish introduced the peach in their New World colonies as well. The peach orchards that they planted in New Mexico and southern California proved to be especially productive.

Most varieties of peach can be either freestone or clingstone. The peach is closely related to the almond and there have been cases of flower pollen from peach trees producing peaches on almond trees! The "white" peaches of China and the Near East generally have reddish streaks in the skin, and a green-tinted, whitish inner pulp. With their tart sweet-sour quality, they are prized over all other peaches in both China and elsewhere. One variety of white peach, the "strawberry" peach, was very popular in parts of the United States thirty years ago. Today, for some inexplicable reason, it has all but vanished as far as commercial availability is concerned. A miniature type of this variety, the "babcock," does turn up occasionally and is highly recommended.

The most flavorful variety of "yellow" (actually yellow-orange would be a more appropriate description) peach is unquestionably the "elberta." Its delectable flavor is reminiscent of honeysuckle, pineapple, and the white "babcock" all combined. In *The Food Book*, Trager notes that, according to some sources, the elberta peach is Chinese in origin and was brought to the United States from Shanghai in 1850. Others believe that it was developed in the southern United States. The elberta is unquestionably one of the finest peaches for jams and preserves, for canning, and for eating fresh. Unfortunately, it is rarely, if ever, available in most parts of the United States or Canada today. It seems to be unknown in western Europe, although certain strains of the elberta are found in eastern Europe. In fact, Hungary produces what can only be termed the finest peach preserves in the world today!

The United States produces half the world's supply of peaches. Unfortunately, they all too often have been picked while hard and green, and placed in refrigerated storage for weeks before being made available to the public. By the time they are sold, these peaches have lost their flavor. Thus, one must look elsewhere for high-quality peach products—notably to Hungary, France, and China.

Dried peaches are excellent in a mixed dried fruit compote served with thick sweet or sour cream and either cinnamon or allspice. Fresh peaches, too, are traditionally served with cream and sugar. A very tiny dish of fine-quality peach preserves is pleasant eaten while drinking tea or served with a glass of water at the end of a meal.

Peaches contain exceptionally large quantities of vitamin A.

Peanut

Arachis hypogea

Originally termed the "groundnut," the peanut is actually a legume, which is to say that it is related to peas and lentils. Peanuts require a loose sandy soil and a warm climate to be productive. The peanut plant is a small, green-leaved bush bearing small yellow flowers and growing to a height of about sixty centimeters (2 ft.). Both the upright and trailing types produce their nut-containing pods beneath the earth. They are not part of the plant's root system as many people imagine. Rather, these pods extend from threadlike runners that are attached to the lower branches of the plant and burrow into the earth. From these runners grow clusters of 20–30 pods, each pod containing either two or four peanuts, depending on the particular variety. The *Arachis hypogea* is, in short, a highly unusual plant. The main varieties are the virginia and the "spanish" or valencia.

The peanut is native to Central America as well as to the Caribbean islands and large areas of South America—particularly Paraguay, Uruguay, and Brazil. At a very early date, the peanut spread to the Andean region where it became an important crop among the Incas (the Incan word for peanut is "mani," which simply means "groundnut"). They even made a type of peanut butter by grinding the peanuts with a pestle. The Incas also placed peanuts in tombs as offerings for the souls of the dead. The Aztecs and the Mayas likewise cultivated the peanut, although it was less important in their diets than it was among the Incas.

The Portuguese brought the peanut to Africa in the sixteenth century, and the Spanish—who first encountered it on the island of Haiti in the early 1500s—introduced it to the Philippines and the area that today comprises Malaysia. From the latter, the peanut was brought to China where it became popular from the seventeenth century onwards. In *Cultivated Plants and Their Wild Relatives*, Zukovskij observes that from China the peanut was even introduced into Russia, where, beginning in 1792, it was grown as a curiosity in the Odessa Botanical Gardens.

Apparently, the peanut was not known in North America until black slaves introduced it from Africa to an area ranging from Georgia to Virginia. However, it was not until George Washington Carver began his crop rotation reforms and soil enrichment programs in the late 1890s that peanuts became accepted as a food in the United States.

Eventually peanuts became one of the major U.S. crops as well as a pre-eminent food staple for millions—chiefly in the form of peanut butter. Peanut oil, too, became popular. Peanuts and peanut products also remain important foods in much of Africa. Peanut shells, it may be noted, are an excellent natural fertilizer for the soil.

The finest-quality peanut butter is derived from the valencia or spanish peanut, which is considerably smaller than the predominant virginia variety. One should only purchase peanut butter that has been processed without the addition of cornstarch or other "fillers." Peanut butter is one of the most nutritious of all popular foods, ranking higher in protein (26 percent) than many other vegetarian foods, including dried whole peas (24 percent protein), sesame seeds used for tahini or sesame butter (18 percent), millet (10 percent), and soybeans and soybean products such as tofu or bean curd (10 percent).

Today, peanut butter is primarily a North American and African food. It is seldom eaten by Europeans or even by Near Easterners, who, with the Greeks, prefer tahini or sesame butter. Peanut butter goes especially well with dates, prunes, and raisins—in sandwiches as well as in various confections. Bananas and shredded coconut are also to be highly recommended in peanut butter sandwiches. In many parts of Africa, peanut butter is mixed with oil and used as a sauce with various vegetables.

Pear

Pyrus communis, P. pyrifolia, P. sinensis

Pyrus communis is the common pear of Europe and the Near East; *P. pyrifolia* or *P. sinensis*, the chinese pear. There are many varieties of each. From very ancient times, pears have been grown from the Atlantic coasts of Europe to the Pacific coast of China. They are generally held to have originated in the region of the Caucasus and to have spread to both China and Europe from there. The Tien Shan Mountains and the Pamirs are viewed as secondary centers. The remains of a dwarf pear species have been found at the site once occupied by ancient lake dwellers in what is today Switzerland. Likewise, extensive pear orchards are known to have been maintained in both Phoenicia and ancient

Israel on the eastern shores of the Mediterranean. They were also grown and esteemed by the ancient Greeks. In the *Odyssey*, Homer praises pears as "a gift of the gods" and refers specifically to those growing on the island of Corfu.

Over the centuries, the Italians have taken the lead in developing the many different varieties of pear. In the first century A.D., Pliny, in his *Natural History*, mentions thirty-eight kinds that were known to the Romans. By the sixteenth century, there were no less than 232 varieties known to the Italians, and at the beginning of this century, over 800 different types were said to exist throughout the world!

The Romans are said to have brought the pear to England, although it is possible that the Phoenicians had already introduced the cultivation of pears to Cornwall. In any case, pears have proved to be a popular cultivated fruit in the British Isles right up to the present. In medieval times and well into the Renaissance period, a variety called the "warden" was generally viewed as the finest type grown there. There is even a reference to "warden pies" in Shakespeare's *Winter's Tale*. Until the Reformation, this pear was grown chiefly by monks in the extensive orchards of Warden Abbey in Bedfordshire. Over the centuries, pears grown on the isle of Jersey have also been regarded as particularly desirable, even today being viewed as the crème de la crème of the pear world. They are produced in exceptionally small numbers on extremely old trees and are sold to London gourmets at immensely high prices.

Both the British and the French brought pears to their respective colonies in the New World. Somewhat later, the Spanish introduced them to California. The chief variety of pear raised in North America today is the "bartlett," which was originally known as the "williams" in the British Isles. This bright yellow, shiny-skinned pear sometimes develops a slightly rosy, or even bright red, flush in the skin. Other commercially available pears in North America include the greenish-skinned, firm-textured, delicately flavored "anjou"; the rough-skinned, russet-colored "bosc" from Asian stock; a bright red type which has become popular only during the last decade; and the Oregon-grown "comice." A major crop in the Pacific Northwest, pears are also produced in considerable quantity throughout much of Europe—particularly in France, Belgium, Holland, Italy, Yugoslavia, and Germany.

Chinese pears, which are quite different from the Western varieties, are usually spherical in shape, hard and "crunchy" in texture, and have a pale yellow, rough-textured skin. At first glance, they almost give the impression that they are an exotic type of apple. The flavor is very delicate. Marco Polo mentions these chinese pears in his *Travels,* claiming to have seen one that weighed ten pounds (4.5 kg)! This is probably an exaggeration, although these pears are sometimes as large as grapefruits. In recent years, chinese pears have become increasingly available in Canada. In the United States, they are occasionally available in areas with large Chinese populations.

Pears are excellent fresh, baked, or canned. In fact, they are one of the few food items that survive the canning process quite well. In all their forms, pears are especially delectable with thick sweet or sour cream, cottage cheese, or cream cheese. Dried pears are particularly good in a fruit compote. Pears can be made into a very pleasing fruit "butter," which is very popular in much of Europe. Unfortunately, it is not produced in North America and is only very rarely available as an import from Europe.

Pecan
Carya olivaeformis

The pecan is indigenous to a wide area of the southern United States. Pecan trees, a species of hickory, grow to an enormous height of nearly sixty meters (200 ft.). The nuts are oblong in shape with highly "polished" shells. The inner nut is divided into segments. The pecan was a favorite of the American Indian peoples.

Pecans are often eaten plain, or used in candies, cakes, and other confections. The flavor is quite unique and is pleasing to nearly everyone.

Pecans are exceptionally high in a type of vitamin B known as pyridoxine.

Pepper. *See* **Black Pepper; Cayenne; Chili Peppers.**

Peppers
Capsicum, many varieties

This general pepper category includes the extremely hot, round cherry peppers, which resemble cherry tomatoes in appearance; the very long, green (turning orange-red as it ripens) anaheim pepper, which is medium-hot although sometimes classified as "mild"; the medium-long yellow wax pepper; and the quite long, pointed, very mild red pepper known as the "rumanian," "hungarian," or even "italian" pepper. This type is essentially the same as the paprika pepper and is widely used in Balkan cuisine.

In North America today various types of pepper are commercially available in a bewildering variety of shapes, colors, and sizes. Usually the smallest peppers are the hottest, while the long, pointed, orange-red hungarian type, which often reaches a length of twenty centimeters (8 in.), is usually very mild. It should be remembered, however, that the seeds of even quite mild peppers can be somewhat hot. Therefore, they should be tasted and removed if "hotness" is not desired.

See also **Bell Pepper; Cayenne Pepper; Chili Peppers; Paprika.**

Persian Melon

a variety of *Cucumis melo*

The persian melon is included within the basic melon category of *Cucumis melo*. As its name indicates, it is indigenous to Persia (Iran). It is globular in shape and resembles an exceptionally large cantaloupe or muskmelon with a greenish-hued outer rind. The inner pulp is a deep orange color. This large and outstandingly aromatic melon has for centuries been called the "king of the melons" by melon cognoscenti.

Persian melons were apparently introduced to the Italian peninsula via Byzantium sometime prior to the twelfth century. The Moors are said to have brought them to Spain. In North America, it is the Armenian farmers of southern California to whom we owe thanks for popularizing this superb fruit. Rather curiously, persian melons appear to be less popular in North America today than they were twenty-five years ago. They remain, however, major favorites in much of Europe and in Israel.

Persimmon

Diospyros virginiana, D. kaki

Diospyros virginiana is the North American variety of persimmon and *D. kaki*, the oriental variety. Both types are quite similar and it remains a mystery that this fruit, albeit in slightly different forms, is found growing wild in two areas so immensely distant from one another, namely, Japan and China on one hand, and the Atlantic seaboard of the central United States on the other.

The New World variety, which is much larger than the oriental version, is all but tasteless aside from its bland sweetness. Nevertheless, it was apparently enjoyed by the seventeenth-century English colonists in Virginia, probably simply because of its novelty.

The more flavorful oriental type is cultivated in Spain and Italy for jam. Today, it is also found in North America, where it was introduced from Japan by the returning Perry expedition in the nineteenth century.

Both varieties contain large quantities of tannin and are extremely astringent and unpleasant unless fully ripe. Ripe persimmons are cloyingly sweet and have a very "mushy" texture. Nevertheless, they contain a large quantity of pepsin, which is held to be beneficial to digestion. Persimmons can be used in puddings, pies, and other desserts.

Regardless of what one thinks of persimmons as a food, both varieties are very beautiful, especially in fruit bowl arrangements. People who have visited Japanese Buddhist temples in Japan or in North America will probably recall seeing bowls of beautifully arranged persimmons as offerings on temple altars.

Pineapple

Ananas comosus

The pineapple vaguely resembles a large pine cone with thick fibrous leaves emerging from its top. It is a deep golden yellow and the exterior is suffused with a brownish hue and covered with small prickly barbs.

The pineapple is indigenous to Brazil and Paraguay. Many centuries ago, it spread from these countries to a much wider area, including Mexico and the West Indies. The Incas, too, had it under cultivation. Pineapple was particularly associated with the Guarani tribe of Paraguay, from whose language the word "ananas" is derived. The French and most Europeans still refer to pineapple as "ananas."

Europeans have been enjoying pineapple ever since 1493 when Columbus brought this fruit back to Spain from the island of

Guadeloupe in the Caribbean. During the next two centuries, cultivation of the pineapple spread to many places outside the New World. In the sixteenth century, it was brought to China, southeast Asia, and the Philippines. Soon after the middle of the seventeenth century, both the English and the Dutch were successfully growing pineapples in glass hothouses. Indeed, the cultivation of pineapples became something of a fashionable pastime among British aristocrats after the Restoration. A well-known painting by Thomas Dankerts depicts a royal gardener presenting the first pineapple raised in England to King Charles II. Under James II in 1688, this fruit began to be grown in the Barbados. Somewhat later, pineapples were introduced in many areas of Africa, and in 1777 Captain Cook extended their cultivation to numerous islands of the Pacific.

In time, the Azores islands became the largest commercial producer of pineapples. From there, they were exported all over Europe. Even today, the Azores continue to produce fine-quality pineapples for the European market. In the early nineteenth century, the British began setting up large pineapple plantations in the West Indies, and in 1847 the first large shipment of 5000 pineapples reached England from the Caribbean. As pineapples became increasingly available and prices went down, they began to be eaten by the middle classes, but it was not until the twentieth century that pineapple became available to the general population of Europe and North America, namely as a canned fruit. Pineapple is among those few foods that turn out remarkably well in canned form, losing only a little of its delectable flavor.

Pineapples were first planted in Hawaii in 1790, and became a major Hawaiian crop by the 1880s. Today, Hawaii provides most of the world's fresh, frozen, and canned supply. The Philippines also produce a notably large quantity. English gourmets prefer pineapples grown in Bermuda and the Bahamas, claiming that the flavor is far superior to those grown in Hawaii or the Philippines.

Pineapple is usually eaten by itself, either fresh or canned. It can also be used in fruit salads, in mixed fruit compotes, or in combination with cheeses ranging from cream cheese and cottage cheese to rennetless Stilton.

Pineapple is rich in vitamins A, B, and C, and contains an enzyme that is valued as an aid to digestion.

Pine Nut

Pinus pinea

The "stone pine," *Pinus pinea*, which grows all the way from Portugal to the Black Sea, is the chief source of the protein-rich pine nut. There are also many other varieties of pine which produce "pine nuts," the latter being the seeds within the cones. Pines are native to both the Old and New Worlds.

Pine nuts have been a favorite food throughout the entire Mediterranean world since prehistoric times. They have also been eaten for centuries by the Chinese, the Japanese, and the Maoris of New Zealand, as well as the native peoples of the New World.

Ancient Romans employed the pine nut in various dishes, and, today, Italians still use pine nuts in "pesto," which is a fairly thick sauce consisting of pine nuts, fresh basil, garlic, black pepper, and grated cheese pressed into a paste for use on spaghetti or noodles. Pine nuts can also be pressed into a kind of thick white "milk," which is said to be exceptionally delicious. In the Spanish and Near Eastern cuisines, pine nuts are used in vegetable, rice, and grain dishes. In Greece, they are more frequently used in confections.

Pine nuts must be extracted from their very small, rather hard shells by hand. This makes them a very expensive luxury food and, today, in North America, prevents them from being popular.

Pistachio Nut

Pistachia vera

The pistachio tree grows to a height of about nine meters (30 ft.), and has grayish green leaves. The tree produces clusters of inedible wrinkled reddish fruits. Within the clusters are the edible bright green nuts, covered with hard white-tan shells. Following an ancient custom, pistachio shells are usually dyed a pinkish red color. This is how they frequently appear when sold commercially.

Indigenous to a wide area of the eastern Mediterranean, the pistachio nut has been cultivated for millenia, and was a favorite of the ancient Jews, Phoenicians, and Syrians. At an early date, pistachio trees spread to Persia (Iran), Afghanistan, and northern India. In Asia Minor (present-day Turkey), they were cultivated by the Byzantine Greeks. It is from the descendants of these Byzantine pistachio groves that the Turks derive the large quantities of pistachio nuts that they export to the world-at-large today. Iran is also a major supplier of the nut. Although some are grown in California, they remain a minor crop there.

The shelled nut, of exquisitely delicate fragrance and flavor, is used extensively in the finest Near Eastern, Greek, and Balkan confections. The best and, inevitably, the most expensive type of halva (a confection made of sesame seed "butter" and honey) contains pale green pistachio nuts. Pistachio nuts are also used to make a delicious ice cream and are excellent in "dry" cottage cheese pastries.

Plantain

Musa paradisica

The plantain is a variety of banana. It is a rather unpleasant reddish brown color and is generally baked or fried as it cannot be eaten raw.

The plantain is native to southeast Asia. The Portuguese and Spanish introduced plantains to their African and New World colonies during the sixteenth and seventeenth centuries. Today, they are grown chiefly in Mexico, Central America, and Africa. Some botanical authorities hold that plantain was already growing in the West Indies at the time of their discovery.

Many Europeans and North Americans do not find plantains particularly palatable. As Fitz-Gibbon points out in *The Food of the Western World*, the plantain, however well-prepared, is something of an acquired taste!

Plum

Prunus, many varieties

There are a vast number of different types of plum, including many hybrids, within the *Prunus* classification. The plum is a "drupe" or "stone fruit" that comes in a wide spectrum of colors and sizes. The majority of plums are varying shades of red. Others are bright or pale yellow, greenish-hued, blackish purple, and even grayish blue. Regardless of skin color, the pulp is usually a deep golden yellow, occasionally infused with reddish pink, especially around the stones.

The plum is indigenous to both the Old and New Worlds. Many

varieties continue to grow wild throughout the world. Many others have been cultivated for millenia in China, Japan, the Near East, and central Asia. Those growing in Europe are said to have originated with the Mongol hordes and the invading Turks who brought prunes (dried plums) with them when they overran eastern Europe. Time and again, plum trees grew up wherever the prune seeds were scattered by the invading armies. Consequently, plums became an important fruit throughout much of eastern Europe.

Crusaders returning to western Europe from Syria and the Holy Land are said to have brought damascus plum seeds, *Prunus institia*, with them. This delicately aromatic, round, dark, sweet plum is regarded as the most ancient and delectable of domesticated plums, having been cultivated for well over three thousand years in the eastern Mediterranean area. It was introduced in France by the Duke of Anjou upon his return from the Fifth Crusade. The present-day European "damson" plum is derived from this variety.

From the beginning of the 1600s, many European plum varieties—including the damson—were introduced into North America where many diverse types of plum were already growing wild from the shores of the Atlantic all the way across the continent to the Pacific. A number of hybrids were produced by mixing Old and New World varieties. The wild plums indigenous to North America were, of course, harvested and eaten in both fresh and dried form by the native Indian peoples. These plums were, in general, much smaller than their Old World counterparts, but not inferior in flavor. There are many varieties of wild plums. *Prunus americana* is a small red plum found in the eastern United States. *P. nigra*, the canadian plum, is an extremely hardy type that grows throughout southern Canada and in nearby areas of the United States. The native peoples dried these plums for winter use. *P. maritima* is very similar to the European damson, but has a more tart and spicy flavor. It grows only near the sea and in fairly sandy soil. *P. subcordata* is a red or purple Pacific coast variety found in California and Oregon.

California produces approximately 70 percent of the world's plum supply, much of which is dried for use as prunes. Unfortunately, none is used to make plum "butter." This product is occasionally available in North America as an import from eastern Europe, where it has long been a favorite fruit product.

In Europe, both Hungary and Yugoslavia are major producers

of the plum variety, *P. cerasifera.* The plums are used in a variety of ways, ranging from fine-quality jam and plum butter to plum brandy or "slivovitz." In Russia, *P. spinosa* is said to have been under cultivation from very remote times.

The greengage plum, extremely popular in the British Isles, was brought to England from France. Far Eastern plums are noted for their sweet-sour quality. The Chinese employ them to make a delectable sweet-sour plum sauce for use as a condiment. This sauce is available in the West wherever there is a sizable Chinese population.

Hundreds of varieties of plums have been developed during the last century. Luther Burbank, the famed horticulturist, developed about sixty different types. In the last half of the nineteenth century, *P. salicina* was introduced to North America from Japan, where it had been cultivated for the last five hundred years, although it was originally from China. Burbank developed several popular hybrid varieties by crossing it with native American plums. Many people consider oriental plums and varieties deriving from them to be superior to other plums due to their sweet-sour aromatic quality.

Many different varieties of plums are available in North American, British, and European markets. While nearly any type can be used for making jam and preserves, not all plums make satisfactory prunes. Nor are all plums to be recommended for eating fresh as some types are quite flavorless until they are dried.

Prunes are used in boiled puddings, such as the well-known British "plum pudding," which, in reality, is more like a cake than a pudding. Canned plum pudding is available commercially, but vegetarians should check the ingredients as some types are made with suet. Both prune juice and stewed prunes are delicious as a food and excellent as a natural remedy for constipation.

Pomegranate

Punica granatum

Pomegranate trees grow only in warm climates. This beautiful tree with reddish pink flowers bears the delectable—if arduous to eat—carmen-colored pomegranate fruit, which is spherical in shape, and has a small circular protuberance extending from one end. The thin external shell covers a segmented whitish labyrinth containing a vast quantity of seeds, each of which is surrounded by a delectable and very juicy translucent reddish pulp. This is the edible part of the fruit. The differences between pomegranate varieties are so slight as to be scarcely recognizable to any but botanical experts.

The pomegranate's actual place of origin remains something of a mystery. We do know that in prehistoric times the pomegranate was growing in the Near East and the Mediterranean world, from Persia and Armenia to ancient Israel and Phoenicia, as well as on the island of Cyprus and in the warmer parts of Greece. It was also known in Egypt and grew in particular abundance around Carthage in North Africa. Pomegranate trees still grow wild in parts of present-day Libya. In the ancient world, the exceptionally flavorful fruit from the extensive pomegranate groves of Carthage were exported in considerable quantity to the Italian peninsula for the Roman upper classes. Pomegranates also have been grown in China for centuries.

Many different sources attest to the importance of the pomegranate in the ancient world, including various biblical references to it. Solomon, for instance, had the pomegranate carved as a decorative motif on the pillars of the Temple in Jerusalem and Moses included pomegranates, together with figs and grapes, as fruits of the Promised Land. In the *Odyssey*, Homer refers to the pomegranates growing in the famous gardens of Alcinous in Phoenicia.

From Hellenic Sicily, pomegranates were brought to the Italian peninsula. In his *Natural History*, Pliny mentions nine varieties of pomegranate known in his day. The pomegranate became a major fruit in Spain after the influx of Arabs from North Africa. In Granada, it was even adopted in the city's coat of arms. "Granada" is, in fact, the Spanish name for the pomegranate.

The Chinese have a particularly high regard for the pomegranate, both medicinally and as a food. For Chinese Buddhists, it is also a symbol of Kwan-Yin, the Boddhisatva of Mercy, and often appears as a motif in Mahayana art works and temples. It is much used as a fruit offering at Chinese Buddhist shrines.

Pomegranate wine was the drink of kings and princes of the ancient Near East. Later, the unfermented juice became a favorite of those who could afford it. In its earliest form, sherbet or "sorbet"—a dessert that is thought to have originated in Persia—is said to have consisted of snow mixed with honey and pomegranate juice.

The Spanish brought the pomegranate to the New World, including both New Mexico and California. Although available when in season in North America, the pomegranate is not popular there and millions of North Americans have never tasted it. It remains a favorite fruit throughout the Near East, the entire Mediterranean area, and in China.

A dwarf flowering variety of pomegranate, which produces fruits so small as to be quite useless, has been grown as a decorative garden shrub in the warmer parts of the United States ever since the Victorian era.

Pomelo

Citrus grandis

The pomelo (also known as pommelo or shaddock) is the largest citrus fruit found on Earth. The majority of pomelos are about the size and shape of large grapefruits, but, in southeast Asia, they sometimes reach a gigantic 4.5 kilograms (10 lb.) or more. The pomelo differs from the grapefruit in many ways. Its skin, for instance, is considerably thicker, its inner fruit segments much firmer textured, and its flavor more delicate and aromatic. As the "membranes" enclosing the fruit segments are quite tough, it is best to remove them before serving.

The pomelo is native to Malaysia and Indonesia where it has been cultivated for several thousand years. Today, it is also grown elsewhere in southeast Asia as well as in China, various parts of the Near East, and in the West Indies.

Known to the Chinese for millenia, the pomelo is mentioned in the ancient Chinese *Book of Food Plants* (I-Yin) as being under cultivation in the Wan River region of China. Although grown in the Holy Land, Syria, and even in Byzantium since the early Middle Ages, it only became known in western Europe in the twelfth century when it was introduced by returning crusaders. It is cultivated occasionally in Spain, Italy, and southern France, but is viewed more as a rare garden curiosity than as the delicious fruit which it is. The pomelo is perhaps more highly regarded in Spain than elsewhere in Europe.

In the late seventeenth century, the British sea captain, Shaddock, acquired a large number of pomelo seeds in the East Indies and on his return trip to England in 1696, left the seeds to be planted on the island of Barbados in the Caribbean. These seeds formed the nucleus of the first pomelo plantation in the New World.

The Spanish, too, brought pomelos to the New World during the sixteenth and seventeenth centuries, or even later in the case of California, but only as single garden specimens. Occasional pomelo trees of very great age, probably dating from the days of Spanish rule, can be found in certain areas of California even today. There, and in other warm parts of the United States, a few pomelo trees also survive in the remnants of Victorian gardens from the last century, providing their fortunate owners with small crops of this delectable fruit every year.

Today, the pomelo is rarely to be found in much of the Western world, where it never became a popular fruit. In other areas, particularly in the Near East and in China, it is highly regarded and is regularly available commercially. The Chinese not only cherish the pomelo as a delectable fruit, but ascribe many medicinal properties to it. Today, according to the *China Daily* (December 26, 1991, p. 3), this king of citrus fruits is a major crop in the Zhejiang Province where some 2000 hectares are planted with pomelo trees, and over 9000 tons of the fruit were harvested in 1991.

In North America, pomelos can usually be found in cities with large Chinese populations, such as San Francisco, New York, or Vancouver, British Columbia. Elsewhere, it turns up occasionally in shops specializing in exotic produce. They are best eaten segmented and dipped in sugar, and go well with most other fruits.

In conclusion, it may be noted that the pomelo is said to be "the ancestor" of the grapefruit, the latter originating as a mutation of the pomelo. Yet, just how such a mutation occurred, no one has been able to explain. The curious fact remains that suddenly in the middle of the 1700s, trees bearing a hitherto unknown fruit—now termed the "grapefruit"—suddenly appeared in Barbados and elsewhere in the Caribbean area where no type of citrus was indigenous. For further information on this subject, *see* **Grapefruit**.

Poppy Seed

Papaver somniferum

The poppy seeds used for culinary purposes are produced by large poppies that are native to Asia Minor, and have long been grown in China and the Balkans as well. Their flowers are usually white, lavender, or sometimes a combination of both. The seeds of the white poppy common in eastern Europe are a gray-black color. Those produced by the lavender-colored poppy of the Orient are a creamy white. Both have a slightly sweet flavor.

Although opium is extracted from poppies, the tiny seeds are quite free from this narcotic substance. For centuries, poppy seeds have been used as a food and seasoning. Pressed together and mixed with honey, they are used as a filling in various pastries and confections common in Turkey, Greece, the Balkans, and even in lands as far north as Poland.

Poppy seeds are also used on the crusts of certain breads and rolls throughout eastern Europe, particularly among Jewish people, who use them on bagels as well. In India and the Far East, the seeds are used chiefly for producing oil. Poppy seeds are seldom used in western Europe and North America, except among those of the ethnic backgrounds mentioned above.

Potato

Solanum tubros

The potato is a New World tuber indigenous to the Andean regions of South America, notably to those areas encompassing Chile and Peru. Unlike corn and New World beans, potatoes were unknown in North America, Mexico, and the West Indies until introduced by the Europeans.

Potatoes were cooked fresh, sun-dried for later use, and even ground into flour by the Andean peoples for over seven thousand years. In Cuzco, the capital of the Inca empire, the Spanish found a vast variety of potatoes offered for sale along with different types of corn, beans, and tomatoes. The potatoes ranged from the red, white, and tan types common today to more exotic blue, purple, and yellow varieties. All are said to have been rather small by today's standards, with perhaps the majority being not much larger than plums or apricots. The shapes differed greatly.

A few of the more exotically-colored varieties are available today in specific areas. A type that is deep purple throughout the tuber, for instance, became popular in the Congo region of Africa and became known as the "congo potato." In Finland, the yellow potato became the favored type. Today, it is known as the "finnish potato." Both the congo and finnish varieties occasionally turn up in organic food stores and exotic produce shops in North America and elsewhere.

Soon after the conquest of Peru in the sixteenth century, the first potato was brought to Spain, apparently by one of Pizarro's priests. During the next 150 years, its cultivation spread slowly northward—to France, Germany, Scandinavia, and Russia. During the early seventeenth century, potatoes were imported from Holland and Belgium for cultivation in the British Isles. It was long believed that the potato was first introduced to the British Isles from Virginia by Sir Walter Raleigh. However, potatoes were unknown in North America at that time and the tubers brought by Raleigh to England could only have been jerusalem artichokes!

Initially, there was considerable European antipathy towards the potato, which was even condemned as causing leprosy and scrofula. In Scotland, many Calvinists objected to it because there was no mention of it in the Bible. Everywhere, there were rumors concerning its imagined toxicity. The toxins of the potato plant are, in fact, limited to its leaves and flowers.

It was not until well after the middle of the eighteenth century that the potato had established itself as a major food throughout most of Europe, particularly in areas where it thrived but many other crops barely survived. To be sure, the potato's Andean hardiness is one of its greatest assets. As early as 1681, the Royal Society in Restoration England urged the cultivation of potatoes as a means of preventing famine. It was only after a major grain famine in Europe in 1770, however, that the potato became established in many areas as a primary food of the poor. Unfortunately, in many parts of continental Europe and the British Isles, the potato began to replace the extremely nutritious dried pea as the basic food staple, much to the detriment of the general population's health. Nevertheless, one cannot overlook the fact that the potato did much to alleviate the terrible famines in France and elsewhere during the latter part of the eighteenth century. So important was the potato in Ireland that when a blight destroyed the potato crops there in the 1840s, the ensuing famine resulted in a massive emigration of the populace to North America.

Although eaten by both the Spanish and the Italians, the potato did not replace rice, pasta, or such nutritious legumes as lentils and garbanzo beans. Nor did the potato replace the all-important "bulgar wheat" in Turkey, the Balkans, and the Near East.

In North America, the potato was introduced by the Spanish in Florida a short time before the British started growing it in their colonies along the Atlantic coast. Irish immigrants began cultivating potatoes on a major scale in New England around 1719.

Potatoes can be prepared in many different ways. Scandinavians favor small whole boiled potatoes served simply with butter, pepper, salt, and, if desired, chopped dill weed or chives. Deep fried potatoes, either as English "chips" (not the dried, salted "potato chips" of the United States, but fairly large irregularly shaped chunks of deep-fried potato) or "french fries" (cut in fairly thin strips lengthwise) are popular in many parts of the world. So too, are diced, sliced, or grated pan-fried potatoes. These are all enhanced by the addition of chopped parsley, salt, black pepper or paprika, and a touch of vinegar or lemon juice.

Plain baked potatoes served with butter and sour cream are North American favorites. The French are fond of potatoes cubed or sliced and then sautéed or baked in a milk or cream sauce with cheese. Among Slavic peoples, plain boiled potatoes and salt are often served as a breakfast dish. Mashed potatoes, after being well mixed with cream or sour cream are delicious, particularly when served with dill weed and North Atlantic dulse. Potatoes go well with almost every vegetable in existence, and especially well with the *Brassicas*, including cabbage, brussels sprouts, mustard greens, and kale. Mashed potatoes with kale, known as colecannon in Scotland and Ireland, are especially delectable.

The potato contains vitamins C and B^1, as well as considerable amounts of potassium and phosphorous, which are both common to most vegetable foods.

Prune. *See* **Plum.**

Pumpkin
a variety of *Cucurbita pepo*

Like the other squash varieties within the *Cucurbita pepo* classification, the pumpkin lacks a more specific botanical designation. At one time, however, it was termed *Cucurbita indica*, sometimes with the addition of various suffixes.

There are a number of different varieties of pumpkin, all of them growing on vines extending over the ground. Most are more or less spherical in shape and have a slightly "ribbed" outer shell or rind. The color ranges from a pale yellowish orange to a very bright tangerine-orange. While pumpkins can exceed eleven kilograms

(25 lb.), they are usually sold at a more manageable weight of 2–4.5 kilograms (5–10 lb.).

The pumpkin is native to eastern North America. The French explorer, Cartier, observed it growing in great profusion in and around the native Indian settlement at Hochelaga (today's Montreal) in 1535. In the 1580s, the Englishman, Heriot, mentioned pumpkins thriving in Virginia, and in 1614, John Smith noted their cultivation by various native Indian tribes in New England. They were at that time generally referred to as "pompions" and it was observed that they were an important food in the diet of the native peoples.

From the New World, the pumpkin was introduced to continental Europe as well as the British Isles, although in most areas it was seldom eaten, but was grown only as a decorative garden curiosity. In Yugoslavia, however, the pumpkin (termed "bundeva" in Serbo-Croatian) became so popular as a food that one might think it native to that country! There, it is served fried with onions, as well as used in pies, strudel-type pastries, and puddings. The Japanese, too, adopted the pumpkin as a food and have even developed several curious varieties of their own. One of these appears to be black in color, but is actually a deep green. Another is a dwarf orange-colored type.

Considering both the delicious flavor and highly nutritious quality of the pumpkin, it is surprising that it is not a popular food worldwide, especially since it is very easy to grow. Even in North America, where this delectable food is at least extensively used in pies, it nevertheless is utilized chiefly to feed farm animals. Also, each year, millions of pumpkins are hollowed out for use as "jack o' lanterns" at Halloween, and then destroyed! This is an appalling waste of a nutritious and marvelous food.

Pumpkin can offer the creative cook a wide range of interesting possibilities. Cooked pumpkin, with the addition of sugar and spices—ranging from nutmeg and cinnamon to allspice or cardamom—can form a highly desirable base for pies, cakes, pastries, puddings, and even ice cream. Fried pumpkin is delicious served with sour cream, or chopped parsley, paprika, and sliced green or red peppers. A rich milk soup made with pumpkin and onion can also be very pleasing.

Pumpkin is extremely rich in vitamin A.

Purple Bean. *See* **Green Bean.**

Quince

Pyrus cydonia, Cydonia oblonga

There are about five different varieties of the fruit known as quince, all of which grow on fairly low, gnarled trees that bear fragrant white or pink flowers. The ripe fruit is a deep golden yellow. The shape can range from round to oblong, depending on the specific variety. In at least one particularly aromatic type, the surface of the fruit is "ribbed" or segmented. The smooth shiny skin of all varieties is covered with a layer of easily removed fuzz.

According to tradition the quince originated on the island of Crete or Cydonia, but it is more likely that this ancient fruit was indigenous to a fairly wide area stretching from the Greek mainland through Asia Minor (where it still grows wild) all the way up into the Caucasus and down into Persia.

The ancient Greeks were the first to cultivate it, both on the island of Crete and in the region of Corinth on the mainland. Perhaps because of the fruit's marvelous aromatic fragrance, the quince became for the Greeks a symbol of love, happiness, contentment, and even of the fabled "Golden Age" of the remote past. Later, the fruit spread throughout much of Europe, where it came to be viewed as a particularly appropriate food for kings and heroes. During the medieval period, quince was also much used as an ingredient of various dishes served at wedding banquets. What is more, it was traditionally held that the very presence or fragrance of a quince tree or one of its ripe fruits put evil doers, whether demonic or human in nature, to flight.

Cultivation of the quince apparently spread to Iberia (Spain and Portugal) at a very early date, long before its cultivation on the Italian peninsula, where it became so popular with Roman aristocrats that the fruits produced in their own land were insufficient for their need. Consequently, they imported quinces in large quantities from both Greece and Iberia. In time, the quince spread even to Gaul (France), where, in the year A.D. 812, Charlemagne had a quince orchard planted in his royal gardens. By the fourteenth century, the quince was known even in the British Isles. Mentioned by Chaucer, it was highly regarded and very popular throughout the Tudor and Elizabethan periods. It is said to have grown especially well in the temperately pleasant climate of Cornwall, from where it was taken to other parts of England and sold at very high prices.

Viewed as the finest and most desirable of fruits, the quince was brought to the New World by both the English and the Spanish. In much of North America, it remained popular until the end of the Victorian era. In fact, a few old, gnarled quince trees still survive in the remnants of Victorian or, even older, Spanish gardens in California and New Mexico. Today, however, the quince is not at all popular in either the United States or Canada. This lack of popularity may be because raw quince is exceptionally bitter and mouth-puckering! To be made edible, the quince must be cooked for some time with sugar or honey. In North America and even in the British Isles, fresh quince is only occasionally available in public markets, and most North Americans have never tasted this superb fruit.

Fortunate indeed is any person who has encountered a quince tree laden with ripe fruit that infuse the air with an aromatic fragrance evocative of some other world! No wonder that now and then one encounters someone who insists that the quince owes its existence to the "lost continent of Atlantis." Even a single quince can permeate an entire room with its pungent fragrance—a fact which alone should make the quince a desirable commodity.

Cooked quince tastes like a mixture of pear, pineapple, and apple. It is especially fine combined in a mixed fruit compote. Cherries, coconut, raisins, dried apricots, and prunes all go well with it. A considerable amount of sugar or honey is necessary in its preparation. Cinnamon, cardamom, or cloves (all used very sparingly) blend well with quince as does fresh lemon. It is best to use only one or two of these spices according to individual taste. Quince compote or preserves is excellent eaten plain or with sweet or sour cream. When sufficiently thick, it is also delectable on toast or served as a garnish with wheat, rice, or millet and eaten with cream. In England, quince is traditionally used in Christmas fruitcake. It is also sometimes used in Italian panetone. Delectable sandwiches can be made with quince preserves and cream cheese.

Quince preserves are still a popular item in Greece and the Balkans, but are seldom, if ever, available commercially in the United States. I can, however, remember the fine quince preserves my grandmother made from the fruit of an ancient tree in Santa Cruz, California, which may have survived from Spanish times. In Canada, fine-quality quince preserves imported from Greece, Bulgaria, and elsewhere in eastern Europe are often found in gourmet shops.

Quince produces a kind of gelatin when cooked. This has been used over the centuries to make quince candy, especially in Portugal and Spain where the quince remains a notably popular fruit and is widely available. "Marmalade," from the Portuguese word for quince, "marmello," originally designated not orange, but quince jam.

Quinoa
Chenopodium quinoa

Quinoa is an ancient New World grain that thrives in very high altitudes. It is native to South America, particularly to the region today comprising Peru, Bolivia, and Chile. The extremely small seeds of the quinoa plant have for centuries been eaten as a grain by the Incas and other native peoples of this area.

Quinoa is made into a flour or cooked and eaten like rice or amaranth. The leaves of the plant can be used as a fresh vegetable.

Despite its relative rarity, for the past decade quinoa, as a grain, has been available commercially in many North American organic food stores.

Radish
Raphanus sativum

Related to both turnips and mustard plants, radishes assume many different shapes and colors, ranging from the cherry-sized red or red and white radish popular throughout Europe and North America today to the large black Spanish radish and the enormous white Strasbourg. The Japanese daikon radish is listed separately under **Daikon**.

The radish is generally believed to be of oriental origin, but is nevertheless found growing wild in such diverse areas of Europe as the coast of Italy and the British Isles. The wild radish, which is quite hot and "peppery," is designated *Raphanus raphanistrum*.

The radish was widely eaten in ancient Egypt, Israel, and Greece. Spreading throughout most of Europe at an early date, the radish was a popular food during the Middle Ages and the entire medieval period, the leaves being valued as much as the root. The Spanish are credited with bringing it to the New World.

Today, the radish remains a favorite salad vegetable. The

French and other Europeans are fond of eating radishes plain with bread and butter.

Radish leaves are excellent in vegetable soups and stews, with dried beans and lentils, or eaten with rice, millet, pasta, or potatoes. They cook very quickly and should be added to soups or other simmering dishes not more than five minutes before such dishes are ready to serve.

The nutrient value of the root—the most commonly eaten part of the radish plant—is almost nonexistent. The leaves, however, are extremely nutritious, ranking with mustard and turnip greens in the high level of vitamins A and C which they contain.

Raspberry

Rubus idaeus, R. i. strigosus, R. i. occidentales

Rubus idaeus is the European raspberry; *R.i. strigosus*, the North American red raspberry; and *R.i. occidentales*, the black raspberry of eastern North America.

The raspberry is related to the blackberry but is quite different in both appearance and flavor. Most raspberries are bright red and grow on very soft-leaved bushes of 1.5–2 meters (5–6 ft.) in height. They can adapt to a very cold climate, thriving even in arctic regions, as long as they are assured of a brief warm summer.

The raspberry is native to both the Old and New Worlds. It is found throughout Europe and North America as well as in central and northern Asia. It is also frequently encountered in Mediterranean Europe. Pliny, the first-century Roman naturalist, believed that the raspberry originated on Mount Ida in Greece. Hence, the botanical name.

There are a large number of slightly differing varieties, many of which were developed in northern Europe and North America during the last century. Many of the varieties cultivated today are hybrids of mixed European and North American stock. The raspberry was popular in Elizabethan England, and continues to be highly regarded in the British Isles and throughout much of northern Europe. Today, Russia leads the world in raspberry production, and in North America, British Columbia is a major area of raspberry cultivation.

Raspberries are usually eaten fresh or made into jam or preserves. These are, in turn, used in tarts, cakes, and pastries, particularly in combination with whipped cream or dry cottage cheese. Raspberry jam is delicious on toast and combines well with cream cheese in sandwiches. Raspberry puddings, made with clear raspberry juice and fruit pectin are a favorite dessert in much of northern Europe.

All raspberries are rich in vitamins A and C.

Red Currant
Ribes sativim, R. rubrum

The red currant prevalent today is said to be a hybrid of eastern European and Siberian varieties. It grows throughout northern and central Europe. In general, the Mediterranean regions are too warm for it, although there are certain mountainous areas where a cooler climate permits it to prosper.

Rather curiously, currants were not mentioned in any written sources until the fifteenth century. By then, they were well-established favorites of the Hungarians, Germans, Danes, and the various Slavic peoples of eastern Europe. It was not until the sixteenth century that they were introduced to the British Isles.

Red currants have a delightfully tart, sweet-sour flavor, and can be eaten either fresh or as preserves. High-quality currant preserves from Hungary are sometimes available in North America. Red currant jam is excellent on toast and makes a superior sandwich, especially when combined with cream cheese. It is also superb eaten in small quantities while drinking strong, good-quality tea. In eastern Europe, red currants are often combined with dry cottage cheese in various pastry-type confections.

Red currants are "prohibited by law" in many areas of the United States as the bushes occasionally transmit a certain fungus that destroys pine trees. Thousands of acres of red currants have, in fact, been destroyed in order to prevent the spread of this fungus. They are, however, raised on a small scale in the Province of Ontario in Canada. The fairly rare white currant is simply an albino form of the red currant.

Rhubarb
Rheum rhaponticum

Generally regarded as having originated in China, rhubarb spread at a very early date to Mongolia, the Himalayas, far into the Siberian regions of northern Asia, and along the Volga in what is today the European area of Russia. A quite distinct variety is found in Asia Minor and other eastern regions of the Mediterranean. Today, rhubarb is grown throughout much of the nontropical world.

Rhubarb was originally cultivated in western Europe as a decorative garden plant, and in China, rhubarb was used primarily for medicinal purposes. It was in Russia that it was first widely utilized as a food. Although rhubarb first reached the British Isles directly from Russia in the early sixteenth century, it was only from the middle of the eighteenth century that rhubarb pies and tarts became a passion among the English. Introduced to North America by the British during that same century, rhubarb has been popular there ever since, particularly in pies and as a fruit sauce.

The pinkish red stalks are the edible part of the rhubarb plant; the leaves are highly toxic. As rhubarb is extremely acidic, a considerable amount of sugar must be used in its preparation. Not only is the sweet-sour flavor of cooked rhubarb very pleasing, but as a food, rhubarb contains vitamins A and C. It is also said to purify the blood.

Rice

Oryza sativa, many varieties

Rice is the seed or grain of a plant that is native to India and spread to southern China, Persia (Iran), and Babylon (Iraq). It also came to thrive throughout southeast Asia and in much of Africa.

Although it was first mentioned in Chinese written records dating from 2800 B.C. when the emperor of China established certain ceremonial rites which were to take place in conjunction with the planting of rice, it was known only to the ancient Greeks by the descriptions given by the troops of Alexander the Great, who had encountered it in India. By the time the Arabs expanded into Spain, however, rice had become common throughout the Arab world. It was the Arabs who introduced it to western Europe, namely to Spain, and from there it eventually spread to the Italian peninsula, where rice cultivation began in the area of Pisa in 1468. Much later, the Spanish introduced rice to South America, and, in 1685, the British planted it in North America. In time, the area of North Carolina became the center of rice production in British North America.

There are at least eighteen varieties of rice; *Oryza sativa* is the predominant species. Basmati is considered to be the finest type of East Indian rice; patna is a long-grain rice derived from basmati and today raised extensively in Texas; pearl rice is a very short, "round"-grained rice that was developed in the Piedmont area of Italy; ubisu is the Japanese equivalent of the Italian pearl rice, but is of a finer quality inasmuch as the grains do not tend to adhere to each other during cooking. The delectable Japanese ubisu is widely available in Canada, but is sometimes hard to find in the United States, except in areas with large Japanese populations.

Some kinds of rice (called "upland" rice) grow on unsubmerged land. The majority, however, grow on land submerged in water, especially in swampy regions, deltas, flooded river basins, and estuaries. Today, over 90 percent of the world's rice crop is grown in China, Indonesia, and the Philippines. Egypt, Italy, Brazil, Japan, and the United States also produce sizable quantities. Rice is a food staple in the Far East, southeast Asia, India, and most of the Caribbean islands. Nearly all rice is thoroughly milled or polished, causing it to be white or cream-colored. This milling process removes the nutritious hull and bran from the rice, which nevertheless remains an adequate food provided that it is eaten with fresh green vegetables, lentils, dried peas or beans, and products such as tofu or bean curd to provide needed vitamins, minerals, and protein.

"Brown" rice has become very popular in North America during the last twenty-five years, but not in such traditionally rice-eating lands as Japan. Brown rice is, quite simply, white rice in its nutritionally superior, natural, unpolished state. It has a richer nutlike flavor, which is, nevertheless, much disliked by Orientals and many westerners as well. It also takes considerably longer to cook.

Rice is particularly good with dried beans that have been cooked with garlic and onion in tomato sauce; with whole dried peas cooked with dill weed or bay leaves; and with various types of stewed vegetables and sautées, especially when okra is a main ingredient. It is also delicious with butter, grated cheese, and chopped parsley. The Spanish and Italians cook rice with tomato paste, onion, and garlic. This combination can also be briefly baked with cheese and diverse vegetables. In the Near East and in Armenian cuisine, rice is often mixed with bulgar wheat and used to fill grape or cabbage leaves. In preparing such dishes, the creative cook has many alternatives regarding sauces, seasonings, and additions. Oriental meals often consist of rice served with small portions of stir-fried, deep-fried, or steamed vegetables. Mizo and soy sauce are usually added, along with pickled lotus root, tofu, or tempeh. Many Scandinavians prefer rice in a dessert dish with raisins, cinnamon, sugar, and thick sweet cream. Other northern Europeans use rice extensively in custard-type puddings. In India, rice is used both as a base for various curried vegetables and in sweet dishes as well.

Romano Bean

a variety of *Phaseolus vulgaris*

Although the flat-podded romano bean or "italian" bean does not resemble the round-podded regular green or "french" bean, it is nevertheless classified within the same broad botanical designation, *Phaseolus vulgaris*.

Native to Central America and northern South America, the romano bean is a "pole bean," which was introduced to Europe by the Spanish in the sixteenth century and soon became popular throughout the Mediterranean area, particularly in Italy where it has remained a favorite for nearly five hundred years. Many people regard the romano as the finest of all fresh green beans, and consider it far superior to the french or ordinary string bean, both in flavor and texture. It is, in fact, very similar to the equally delicious scarlet runner bean. A bush variety of the romano, called the "roma," has also been developed.

Although popular as a home garden vegetable in the United States, the romano bean is infrequently available in U.S. markets. It is a far more popular vegetable in Canada, where it can sometimes be obtained fresh, and is always available frozen. The romano bean is one of those vegetables that retains its original flavor and texture when frozen.

Romano beans cook very quickly and one must be careful not to let them become too soft. They are delicious simply steamed and eaten with oil and garlic, either by themselves or with pasta. Also excellent eaten cold in salads with oil and wine vinegar, romano beans are particularly good when served together with boiled new potatoes.

Rose

Rosa damascena, R. centifolia, and many others

Roses are indigenous to much of the eastern Mediterranean area, ranging from Syria and Israel well into Asia Minor and even the Balkans. Today, they are cultivated as a garden flower throughout much of the world.

In the Balkans, Turkey, and the Near East, both the petals and the fruits or "hips" of roses are used in a variety of candies and confections. They are also employed in jams and preserves, as well as in rose water and rose oil, which, in turn, are used in dessert dishes ranging from cakes to sherbets and milk puddings.

Dried rose petals are occasionally added to regular tea, and pure rose hip "tea" has long been a European favorite in such diverse places as England and Bulgaria. More like a fruit juice than a tea, it is extremely rich in vitamin C and possesses a delicate flavor slightly reminiscent of apples.

Rose petal "loukoumi" consists of small squares of solidified pectin and rose petals which have been dipped in powdered sugar. This candy is said to date back to Byzantium and is a favorite of the Greeks. Today, it is sometimes available in Greek import stores in North America and Great Britain.

Aside from dried rose hips for use in "tea," other rose products, including both rose water and rose jam or preserves, can be rather difficult to find in North America, although they are exported from certain Balkan and other European countries. Today, Bulgaria is the largest producer of roses for commercial purposes, both culinary and otherwise. Rose oil or "attar of roses" remains a major Bulgarian export. It is used in many fine-quality perfumes.

Rosemary

Rosmarinus officinalis

Rosemary is a very aromatic evergreen shrub bearing thick clusters of bluish lavender flowers which bees find extremely attractive. The linear needlelike leaves, which are used as an herbal seasoning, are bright green with a pale grayish green underside. Native to the Mediterranean coasts, rosemary grows especially well near the sea. Rosemary still grows wild in Greece, Italy, Spain, North Africa, and along the Adriatic coast of Croatia. Today, it is also found along the coasts of Cornwall in

Great Britain and in fog-enshrouded northern California. Wherever it grows, it infuses the fresh sea air with its pungent fragrance.

Rosemary may have been brought to the British Isles by the Romans, who used it in the treatment of certain eye ailments. In any case, it has, for centuries, remained a very popular plant in England, although it is not used as much for culinary purposes there as it is in southern Europe. It is extensively used in Italian cooking and to a lesser degree by all Mediterranean peoples.

In many areas, rosemary is still used in funeral ceremonies, probably due to its powerful aromatic fragrance and to the fact that it has long been viewed as a symbol of "remembrance." Shakespeare mentions it in *Hamlet* where Ophelia exclaims, "There's rosemary. That's for remembrance." In certain parts of England, it is traditional to carry branches of rosemary in wedding processions as well as at funerals.

Fresh rosemary enhances green salads and goes well with chopped garlic. Only use the fresh, young tips of the rosemary sprigs—the older leaves (needles) are very tough and can be unpleasantly strong in flavor. Fresh or dried rosemary can also be used, very sparingly, in various cooked foods and sauces.

Today, rosemary is probably more widely grown as an odoriferous ornamental garden shrub or hedge plant than as a culinary or medicinal herb. Old plants can exceed two meters (6 ft.) in height with main stems resembling small twisted tree trunks! Rosemary, both fresh and dried, is widely available in European and North American markets.

Rutabaga

Brassica napobrassica

Rutabagas, also known as "swedish" or "lapland" turnips in much of Europe, are a pale tannish or orangish yellow vegetable, sometimes with a streak of purple around the top. Internally, their color varies from pale yellow to deep orange. A white type also exists, but it is rarely encountered today. Generally, the flavor of the rutabaga combines a decidely sweet quality with the sharp pungency of the turnip. Rutabagas bear yellow or orange flowers and have smooth cabbagelike leaves, which are quite edible but are rarely seen on market specimens.

Rutabagas grow with a minimum of care, even in the worst and coldest of climates. This fact alone made them popular in northern

Europe. They grow to an enormous size, eventually becoming as large as cantaloupes. Allowing them to grow to their full size does not seem to have any negative effect on their flavor or texture.

The rutabaga's precise place of origin is uncertain. Apparently, this mysterious vegetable, which is generally held to be the result of a hybridization between the turnip and some variety of cabbage, suddenly appeared during the seventeenth century in both north and central Europe from Bohemia (in present-day Czechoslovakia) to Swedish Lapland. There are no records of its existence anywhere prior to that time. In any case, it first became popular in Sweden. It spread from there throughout Scandinavia and was introduced among the Finns, Estonians, Poles, and Russians as well. Latin peoples evinced no liking for the rutabaga. Although it was known in France by 1700, the French apparently used it mainly as a food for farm animals. Nor did it fare much better in the British Isles where the turnip was preferred. It was introduced to North America in the early nineteenth century, but did not prove to be popular there either, except among the ethnic groups for whom it was an important vegetable staple in northern Europe.

Rutabagas are excellent in vegetable soups, but should be used sparingly as they possess a dominating flavor. Most frequently, they are simply sliced, steamed, mashed, and served with butter, black pepper, and chopped fresh dill weed.

Rutabagas have a high vitamin A content and are nutritionally superior to turnips.

Rye

Secale cereale

There are numerous varieties of the common rye. Rye is more disease-resistant than other grains. It can endure cold northern temperatures as far north as the Arctic Circle, and will grow in extremely poor rocky soil where other plants fail. The rye plant is usually about 1.5 meters (5 ft.) tall with spikelets resembling those of wheat, and roots that penetrate deeply into the soil.

Rye grain is said to have originated as a field weed in Asia Minor and to have spread to the Balkans and then northward throughout central and northern Europe. Originally considered an "intruder" in fields of wheat, rye eventually became a highly regarded, cultivated grain staple in much of the European world. It was not, however, eaten before the Iron Age and is not mentioned in the writings of the ancient world. It was only during the Middle Ages and the medieval period that rye became a popular grain flour for the making of bread.

Today, Russia produces 40 percent of the world's rye supply as compared with the 2.5 percent produced in North America. It is an important crop in many European countries ranging from Denmark to Hungary. Finland, Norway, and Germany are the major importers of this grain.

Most rye grain is processed into flour for use in making the different types of sweet or sourdough rye bread so popular throughout Scandinavia, Germany, and the Slavic countries. Rye breads are also especially popular among Jewish people of eastern European background. Some rye breads are made with fine-ground flour and others with fairly coarse-ground; some are lightweight and others are thick and heavy. Many are flavored with either dill or caraway seeds. In Sweden, a favorite type of rye bread is made with molasses, raisins, and spices. Up until twenty years ago, good-quality European-type rye bread was only obtainable in North America in Jewish, Slavic, or Scandinavian specialty shops. Today, it is widely available throughout the continent.

Rye flour can also be used to make excellent dumplings, traditional Scandinavian flatbread or "hardtack," pancakes, and pastries. Whole rye grains, soaked overnight and then cooked, make a delicious cereal dish that can be eaten with cream, raisins, cinnamon, and sugar. They are also good with mushrooms and various green vegetables.

Rye has the same protein content as wheat and less fat. Its vitamin B content is somewhat less.

Saffron

Crocus sativus

The yellow-orange powder known as saffron is derived from the dried flower stigmas of a crocus variety native to Asia Minor and elsewhere in the eastern Mediterranean area. Some people prefer to use the unground "threads," rather than the powder, to season foods.

Saffron was widely used in the ancient Near East, particularly by the Phoenicians. Solomon mentions it under the old Hebraic name, "carcoom." It was also known to the ancient Greeks,

Romans, and Persians. In his *Natural History,* Pliny notes that saffron grown in Sicily is of especially fine quality. The Byzantine Greeks used it extensively. For close to a millenium, the area around Corycus Cilicia, once a part of Byzantium and today, "Khorgoz" Turkey, was the chief saffron cultivation center. From there, it was shipped westward into Europe to be used in the foods prepared for kings and aristocrats.

According to Fitz-Gibbon, in *The Food of the Western World,* the Phoenicians introduced saffron to Cornwall, Wales, in pre-Roman times. Even today, "saffron cake," traditionally eaten at Easter and undoubtedly going back to some ancient spring festival, still remains a specialty in parts of Cornwall. Saffron did not spread to the rest of England, however, until crusaders brought some back from the Holy Land during the reign of Edward III. Soon after, Saffron Walden in Essex became the center of its cultivation in England.

In the contemporary world, saffron is cultivated throughout the Mediterranean world, in Kashmir, and in Iran. That which is grown around Valencia, Spain, is regarded as the finest available. Saffron is sold in very small quantities, and tends to be very expensive as it is entirely processed by hand.

In Europe and the Near East, saffron is used in cakes and other sweet dessert dishes. The Spanish and Portuguese employ it to flavor rice, as is the custom in parts of India. Saffron is also utilized as an ingredient in various Greek and Turkish dishes. Its unique, vaguely sweet flavor is very delicate and stronger spices should never be used with it.

Sage

Salvia officinalis

Sage is an herb of the mint family. It grows to a height of about thirty-eight centimeters (15 in.) and bears small attractive flowers that are purple, blue, or sometimes pink. The oblong gray-green leaves can be used either fresh or dried.

Native to the Mediterranean area, sage has been grown for centuries in much of northern Europe as well, more for medicinal purposes than as a seasoning. Today, it is also found throughout North America.

Sage has a strong, somewhat overpowering flavor that is not to everyone's taste. Some people, however, enjoy fresh sage in salads or cooked with zucchini, fava beans, and other vegetables.

Salsify

Tragopogon porrifolius

Salsify or "oyster plants" bear beautiful purple flowers on long stems emerging from the center of the plant, surrounded by long grasslike leaves. Eventually, the flowers evolve into globe-shaped, fluffy seed heads similar to those of dandelions and thistles.

Indigenous to much of the Mediterranean world, salsify was known in ancient Greece and, for centuries, its long white carrotlike root was regarded as a choice vegetable by the Italians and French as well as by the Germans and English.

Brought by the British to their North American colonies, salsify was grown as a vegetable there and continued to be eaten in both England and the United States right up to the beginning of the twentieth century when it suddenly and without explanation ceased to be a popular root vegetable. Today, more English people cultivate salsify as an ornamental garden plant than as a vegetable. It is still eaten in France and Italy, however, and is currently undergoing a revival as a "home garden" vegetable in the British Isles and, to a lesser degree, in the United States. It is even occasionally available in organic food shops, although rarely obtainable elsewhere.

A few flowering specimens of salsify can be seen in the overgrown remnants of Victorian gardens in out-of-the-way places such as Eureka, California.

Sassafras

Sassafras albidum

The sassafras is a large tree of the laurel family. It is indigenous to North America and thrives over a wide area extending from the Province of Ontario in Canada to Louisiana and Texas in the United States. The tree's yellow flowers and bluish berries are not used, apparently being all but flavorless. The individual, irregularly shaped leaves, which range from mitten-shaped to triune, however, are highly aromatic and are used as a seasoning.

Ground or powdered sassafras leaves were an important seasoning spice for many native Indian peoples in the eastern half of the North American continent. It also became the main ingredient of "filé powder," which is used in the Creole cuisine of Louisiana. Filé powder goes especially well with okra, green peppers, tomatoes, and garlic. It can also be used with other types of sautéed vegetables and legumes, such as black-eyed beans or lentils. Some people even enjoy filé powder combined with a little oil and lemon juice and eaten as a condiment on bread.

This delicious and unusual New World seasoning is not often found in continental Europe or the British Isles, but may be purchased in gourmet specialty shops throughout Canada and the United States.

Savory

Satureia montana, S. hortensis

Satureia montana is the winter variety of savory and S. hortensis, the summer. Indigenous to the Mediterranean world, the savory plant grows to a height of about thirty centimeters (1 ft.) and has purplish or lavender-pink flowers.

The ancient Romans used it in making various sauces as well as to flavor vinegar. Today, savory is extensively used by the French and Swiss, but is not particularly popular elsewhere. Although grown for centuries as a "pot herb" in England, its place in the cuisine of that land is minor. In North America, it is little used except among French Canadians.

The leaves are at their best before the plant flowers. Crushed savory has a distinctive peppery quality and is somewhat sweet. It goes well with fresh green beans and various sautéed legumes.

Savory plants possess an insect-repellent quality that makes them useful for planting near vegetables that are prone to insect attack.

Scalloped Squash

a variety of *Cucurbita pepo*

Scalloped squash is included within the very general squash classification of *Cucurbita pepo*, although at one time it was classified as *Cucurbita pepo laciniata*. In the British Isles, it is called the custard marrow, and in more archaic usage was often referred to as "cymling" or "symel." In North America, it is popularly known as "summer squash." This can be somewhat confusing since the term "summer squash" can also include zucchini and yellow crook-necked squash.

The pale green-white scalloped squash with its round scallop-edged shape develops very rapidly on a nontrailing vine. Like all summer squash, it should be eaten within four to six days of being picked. Without question, the delicately flavored scalloped squash is the most delectable of all summer squashes.

At the time of English and French colonization, the scalloped squash was a main vegetable in the diet of the various native peoples throughout much of eastern North America, particularly in New England and what are, today, the Maritime Provinces of Canada. It was first botanically described and accurately drawn by Mathias Lobel, a French botanist of the late sixteenth century. The seeds of this squash were brought to England early in the seventeenth century. The English became extremely fond of it and "cymling" or "custard marrow" was soon under extensive cultivation there.

Scalloped squash is best simply steamed and served with oil or butter, a little sea salt, and black pepper. Some people claim that a tiny amount of chopped garlic and parsley can be added without jeopardizing the squash's subtle and unique flavor.

Scalloped squash is fairly popular in North America and is widely available when in season. It also remains a favorite vegetable in the British Isles. The English are fond of it in a cream sauce topped with cheese, either by itself or served on toast or noodles.

In recent years, a yellow variety of scalloped squash—inferior to the traditional pale green type both in flavor and texture—has been developed through hybridization with the yellow crook-necked squash.

Scarlet Runner Bean
Phaseolus multiflorus

The scarlet runner bean is an exceptionally beautiful and decorative plant and was originally prized mainly for its scarlet-orange flowers. It is fast-growing, a prodigious climber, and very productive. What is more, the beans produced by this plant are perhaps the most delicious of all green beans, excepting only the romano, which it somewhat resembles.

Native to Mexico and Guatemala, the scarlet runner bean was introduced into Europe during the sixteenth century by the Spanish, but only became fairly well known there in the seventeenth century.

This bean, which is excellent dried or eaten fresh "whole pod," is a favorite with the Spanish and the Italians, and is also said to be the most popular green bean in the British Isles, where it is widely available commercially when in season. Unfortunately, these exceptionally flavorful beans are not normally available in North American markets. Hopefully, in the future, this extraordinary bean, that adapts well to a wide diversity of climates, will be cultivated commercially in North America on a large scale.

Scorzonera

Scorzonera hispanica

Also known as "black salsify," scorzonera is a root vegetable that is similar to salsify, but entirely unrelated to it. Scorzonera resembles a somewhat wizened, very thin, long, black-skinned carrot with numerous hairlike roots extending from the skin.

Scorzonera is native to the Mediterranean world, where it has been eaten since prehistoric times. Throughout the Middle Ages and medieval period, it remained an important European vegetable. It was especially popular in Italy, Spain, and France, and was a particular favorite of King Louis XIV, who apparently consumed it in prodigious quantities.

Although little known in contemporary France, scorzonera remains a highly regarded, if not actually popular, vegetable among both the Spanish and Italians. Recently, it has even begun to appear in public markets in North America, although the average North American has never heard of it, much less eaten it. It is also finding its way into the home gardens of those who are fond of the unusual.

Scorzonera should be scrubbed very thoroughly before cooking, but not peeled. It is perhaps best steamed or sautéed and served with oil and chopped parsley.

Sesame

Sesamum indicum

There are at least nineteen recognized varieties of sesame. The plant grows to two meters (6 ft.) in height and has white or pink flowers that produce pods containing the tiny blackish brown seeds. These seeds are a tan or whitish color after being hulled.

Sesame may have been native to India, spreading westward at a very early date to the Near East and much of Africa. Some botanical authorities, however, claim an African origin for sesame, designating India as a secondary center. In any case, sesame has been used as a food since prehistoric times. It was grown in large quantities by the ancient Egyptians and was an important food staple in ancient Greece. It was also known in China by the first century A.D., and probably arrived there at a considerably earlier date.

Today India and China produce most of the world's sesame supply, with a significant portion being processed into a high-quality salad and cooking oil.

In the Balkans and the Near East, the seeds are used in various breads and confections. Most important, however, is their use in tahini (or "tahina"), a semi-liquid "paste" that consists of the ground seeds. This sesame "butter" is, in a sense, the "peanut butter" of the East and, although it can be eaten with bread, with or without the addition of sugar or honey, its culinary uses are far more diverse than those of peanut butter.

Used as a major ingredient in various sauces basic to many Greek and Near Eastern foods, tahini goes particularly well in sweet dessert-type dishes consisting of a wheat or millet base and various dried or fresh fruits. Tahini can also be mixed with chopped garlic or green onion, and various herbs such as parsley or basil to provide a flavorful sauce for many vegetable and grain dishes. Capers can also be added to such a sauce. Mixed with water, lemon juice, and honey, tahini provides a delicious and refreshing drink. It is, in short, an extremely versatile product that can provide the creative cook with ample new ideas.

Tahini is also the chief ingredient of the well-known confection "halva" or "halwa," a candy enjoyed by all Near Easterners, from the Israelis to the Turks. It is also a favorite among the Greeks. Both tahini and halva were popular foods throughout the Byzantine Empire and major staples within the city of Constantinople itself.

Extremely rich in protein, tahini remains a food staple in Greece and the Near East. In the West, the importance of tahini in the diet of the vegetarian can scarcely be overemphasized. Tahini is widely available throughout North America, continental Europe, and the British Isles in ethnic specialty shops and "health food" stores.

Shallot
Allium cepa ageratum

The shallot was originally designated *Allium ascalonicum*, but was recently renamed *Allium cepa ageratum*. The shallot is a very small member of the onion family. Its skin is light brown and the onion within is white, but often infused with reddish purple hues. Shallots are milder and more easily digested than regular onions. Their clove-type structure resembles that of the garlic.

The shallot is native to the eastern Mediterranean, particularly to the regions that, today, comprise Israel, Lebanon, and Syria. It has been used by all the peoples of the eastern Mediterranean well back into prehistory. Its use spread to Europe in the thirteenth century when returning crusaders introduced it to France and the British Isles. The French developed a special fondness for it and have been cultivating it extensively ever since. The British aristocracy also found its mild flavor much to their liking and used it in a number of dishes. In the British Isles, it was generally called the "ascalonian onion."

In the seventeenth century, the French brought the shallot to Louisiana, where it is still cultivated and widely used in the local cuisine. In general, however, the shallot has not proved to be popular in North America except with people of French background. This is most unfortunate as the flavor of the cooked shallot is less obtrusive than that of regular onions. Shallots are also far more convenient to use, thanks to their small size.

Shallots are usually available in small quantities throughout North America and the British Isles. As they are very lightweight, they are not nearly as costly as their price may seem to indicate. They are recommended for use in all dishes that require onions.

Shanghai Bok Choi
a variety of *Brassica chinensis*

A dwarf variety of *Brassica chinensis*, shanghai bok choi was developed in the area around Shanghai and gradually spread throughout most of China and even to Korea,

Japan, and eventually North America. Shanghai bok choi differs from the more usual large bok choi in size, appearance, and flavor. Its somewhat gourdlike shape tapers up from a very wide base. It is usually about ten centimeters (4 in.) high and its leaves tend to be pale green.

Shanghai bok choi has a delicate, subtle flavor, so it should never be eaten with onions or garlic. It is perhaps best simply steamed, either whole or halved, very briefly, and served with a bit of lemon juice and a small amount of oil.

Shanghai bok choi became widely available in Canada sometime before it made its appearance in the United States. Today, it can be purchased throughout North America, although it is never stocked in very large quantities. In the United States, it is sometimes erroneously sold as "baby bok choi." Shanghai bok choi is a light vegetable by nature, and some sellers set it in trays of water to increase the weight. These specimens should be avoided, not only because this can double the cost, but because this practice results in almost total loss of their subtle and unique flavor.

Shitoke. *See* **Mushroom.**

Snow Pea

Pisum sativum macrocarpum

The snow pea is also known as the "chinese snow pea." It is widely used in Chinese cuisine, but is not actually of Chinese origin. While the snow pea is sometimes held to have been developed by the English in the eighteenth century, it was, in fact, first mentioned by the naturalist, Ruellius, in 1536. According to Sturtevant, in *Edible Plants of the World*, the original type came from Holland and was introduced first to France, and then to England around 1600.

Soon after the snow pea's appearance in Europe as a developed or mutant type, it was brought to China where, within a short period of time, it became thoroughly integrated into the Chinese cuisine. In fact, by the mid-1800s, many Chinese themselves were convinced that the snow pea was indigenous to China!

Snow peas are eaten "whole pod." These sweet, tender pods contain peas so tiny that the pod is almost flat. As the pods of the snow pea are skinless, they cook very quickly and, consequently, should be steamed or sautéed for no more than a few minutes. They go especially well with ramen (oriental noodles), millet, or rice, and are often served with sliced water chestnuts and tiny slivers of fresh ginger in a sweet-sour sauce.

Snow peas are widely available today in North America, even in areas without large Chinese populations. They are much less frequently encountered in Britain or continental Europe. The buyer should not be alarmed by the seemingly high price of snow peas as they are extremely lightweight.

Snow peas are high in vitamins A and C.

Soybean

Glycine max

The soybean is one of the few Old World beans. Indigenous to China, the different varieties of soybeans come in a wide spectrum of colors ranging from black to white and yellow. The tan-colored variety, however, is the major type grown today. One of the richest sources of vegetable protein known, the soybean was first brought to Europe in the eighteenth century and was introduced into the United States around 1800, but not extensively grown there until the twentieth century.

For thousands of years, the soybean has been of major importance in the Chinese diet, being utilized in the making of both bean curd and soy sauce as well as for bean sprouts. Likewise, the importance of soybean products for contemporary vegetarians can scarcely be overemphasized. Such products include tofu or bean curd, tempeh, soy "milk," soy flour, and the various soybean sauces and pastes that play such a prominent part in the oriental cuisine. Soybeans are also a major source of a high-quality vegetable oil used in many parts of the contemporary world, including North America, where it has become the most frequently encountered vegetable oil available. It is equally recommended for use in salads, on cooked vegetables, and for frying. Combined with rice, wheat, millet, or corn, soybeans and soybean products provide a complete protein.

Tofu or bean curd, perhaps the most important soybean product, is usually cut into cube-sized pieces and sautéed with vegetables in a soy sauce or miso preparation. Its delicate flavor is enhanced by chopped chives and minute fragments of fresh ginger. Like another soybean product, tempeh, tofu is also delectable fried in vegetable oil until a light golden brown and then eaten with chives and fresh grated daikon (oriental radish). A very simple cold dessert dish—and one to be highly recommended—is made by cutting tofu into fairly thick strips and adding sugar and cinnamon. This delicious dessert resembles a solid-textured custard pudding.

In many areas of Europe, soybean products are not always easy to find. In Canada and the United States, however, where these products are widely used by the large Chinese populations in major urban centers, and where health food stores promote their nutritional value, soybean products have become widely available and even, to a degree, popular.

Spinach

Spinachia oleracea

Spinach is said to be of Persian origin. Rather surprisingly, this delectable deep green leaf vegetable was apparently unknown among the ancient Greeks and Romans. Given the popularity of spinach in the respective cuisines of contemporary Greece and Italy, this fact is all the more amazing. Spinach may have become known to the Greeks during the existence of the Byzantine Empire, perhaps via the Arabs, who had adopted it from the Persians. In all probability, spinach first spread to Sicily and the Italian peninsula via Byzantium sometime prior to the twelfth century. The Arabs probably introduced it into Spain, and from there its cultivation became widespread throughout much of western Europe. By the thirteenth century, it had even reached Germany, and was mentioned in the writings of Albertus Magnus. Spinach became known in the British Isles when crusaders brought it back to England in the late fourteenth century. At that time, it came to enjoy a certain popularity at the court of King Richard II. Gradually, its use began to filter down to the common people. During the sixteenth and seventeenth centuries, both the Spanish and English introduced spinach to their colonies in the New World, where it became a fairly popular vegetable.

The Armenians make an excellent salad that combines raw spinach with oil, lemon juice, and a little chopped garlic. A favorite Greek dish, inherited from Byzantine times, consists of a pastry filled with chopped spinach, cheese, garlic, and oregano. In Italy, the city of Florence became especially noted for its spinach dishes involving cream and cheese sauces. Anyone can experiment with

making an Italian "deep dish" cheese and spinach pie without fear
of culinary catastrophe. One should, however, cook it very slowly
and at a very low temperature to avoid burning it. Fresh basil or
garlic can be added to this dish to enhance the flavor. A perennial
favorite is plain steamed spinach served with butter and lemon
juice.

Spinach is rich in iron, calcium, and vitamin A. It also contains
a very small quantity of oxalic acid, but not enough to be harmful.

Strawberry

Fragaria virginiana, F. chiloensis, F. vesca, and many
others

Fragaria virginiana is the North American strawberry; *F. chiloensis,* the Chilean; *F. vesca,* the Alpine
or Swiss; *F. rosaceae,* the English; and *F. moschata,* the central
European. Wild strawberries are indigenous to both the Old and
New Worlds. They are found from Alaska to Chile and from Italy
to Ireland. Although strawberries were apparently unknown to the
ancient Greeks, in his *Natural History,* Pliny, who lived from A.D.
23–79, mentions a wild strawberry growing on the Italian peninsula. Strawberries were being grown in private gardens by the
fifteenth century in some areas of Europe, but were not widely
cultivated until the eighteenth century.

The exceptionally flavorful wild strawberries of North America
and Europe are quite small. Seventeenth-century English colonists
noted their abundance in Maryland as well as in Virginia. In 1624,
the wild North American variety was brought to France, and from
there to various other European countries. It soon became far more
popular than the wild European varieties, as it was considerably
more productive.

In the eighteenth century, another, larger variety was discovered in Chile, where it had been cultivated for centuries by Chilean
Indians. The Chilean strawberry grew to the size of a large walnut,
but was not as flavorful as the tiny North American and European
types. Consequently, new strains combining the Chilean strawberry with other varieties were produced through cross-pollina-
tion. Throughout the nineteenth century, widespread cultivation
of these new strains occurred, both commercially and in private
gardens, particularly in North America. Thriving in soils ranging
from sandy to claylike, strawberries had by the turn of the century

become a major North American crop and one of the most popular fruits produced.

Strawberries are perhaps most frequently eaten fresh with cream. They are exceptionally delectable in combination with other fresh fruits, ranging from melons to peaches and apricots. They are delicious sprinkled with sugar and served with pomelo or grapefruit segments. In North America and the British Isles, strawberries are particularly popular served with thick sweet cream and shortcake. Sour cream, with sugar, works equally well in this dish. Strawberry jam and strawberry ice cream are popular everywhere.

A word of caution! Many commercial strawberry growers try to produce exceptionally large berries through the use of animal-based fertilizers which, in fact, negatively affect the flavor of the fruit. Such strawberries can be avoided by purchasing only the smaller "organic" strawberries guaranteed to be free from both toxic pesticides and animal-based fertilizers.

String Bean. *See* **Green Bean.**

Sugar Cane

Saccharum officinarium, S. barberi, S. sinensis, and others

Sugar cane, a member of the grass family, is native to the East Indian subcontinent and southeast Asia. It was being cultivated in India by 300 B.C., and at a very early date its cultivation had spread to southern China. Sugar cane is referred to in the Chinese classic, *"Tao Chung King"* and Marco Polo mentions its use in the China of his day.

The Arabs introduced sugar cane to Egypt and Spain during the seventh and eighth centuries. Columbus brought it to the Canary Islands in 1515 and Cortez had it planted in Mexico in 1531. By the seventeenth century, sugar cane was being cultivated throughout much of Central America and on many of the Caribbean islands as well. In fact, the Spanish, the English, and the French all planted sugar cane in those of their New World colonies that had a sufficiently warm climate. Sugar was commonly used in much of Europe during the seventeenth and eighteenth centuries. Thus, sugar cane plantations and the exportation and processing of that commodity played a major role in the economy and trade of that period.

The processed sugar that we use today is derived from berries and sugar beets as well as sugar cane.

Summer Squash. *See* **Scalloped Squash; Yellow Crook-necked Squash; Zucchini.**

Sunflower Seed

Helianthus annus

Who has not stood in absolute awe before a large sunflower plant in full bloom? Growing to a height of 2–4.5 meters (7–15 ft.), its enormous golden yellow flower heavy with its honeycomblike disk of seeds, the sunflower is a plant of extraordinary beauty. Beholding it, who has not been left musing that if any plant on Earth is from another planet, it must surely be the sunflower!

There are said to be 1081 different species within the genus *Helianthus*. The "common sunflower," *Helianthus annus*, is the most numerous. Sunflowers are indigenous to a wide area of North America and are particularly prevalent in the Great Plains region. They adapt well to northern climates, and have for millenia grown in profusion throughout much of Canada. In 1615, Champlain noted the extensive use of sunflower seeds among the Hurons. There are also several varieties of sunflower found in Peru, Chile, and Brazil. Sunflower seeds have even been found in Andean Indian remains dating back 3000 years.

In the first half of the sixteenth century, the Spanish introduced the sunflower to continental Europe, using seeds taken from the New Mexico area. From Spain they were dispersed throughout Europe and it was not long before they were being cultivated in areas as diverse as the Netherlands and Russia, to which land Peter the Great introduced them in the early eighteenth century. Ukrainians and Russians soon developed a particular fondness for the beautiful sunflower and its seeds, as well as for the nutritious oil extracted from them.

Sunflower seeds also proved to be extremely popular among the Balkan peoples and the Chinese. Brought to China soon after their discovery in the New World, sunflower seeds came to be used there extensively as a food. In addition, the sunflower soon made its appearance as a stylized motif in Chinese porcelain decoration as well as in fabric design. So much a part of Chinese culture did the sunflower become that many Chinese came to think of it as unique to China, not realizing how recently that it had been introduced there.

Sunflower seeds are delicious simply hulled and eaten by themselves, either plain or after they have been soaked and sprouted. The flavor resembles that of pine nuts, and if soaked in water for awhile, they develop a mildly smoky flavor that appeals to some. Sunflower seeds blend well with a variety of vegetable and grain dishes. For a particularly delectable and unique dish, sprouted sunflower seeds can be cooked with wild rice. This dish has its basis in the often neglected native American Indian cuisine. Another native method of preparation is to simmer sunflower seeds in a thick corn soup or "chowder."

Hulled sunflower seeds are widely available in health and natural food stores throughout North America. Although their availability in western Europe and the British Isles has increased in recent years, hulled sunflower seeds are not always easy to find there.

Today, sunflowers are cultivated in China, North America, Russia, and the Ukraine. In the future, sunflower seeds will likely become an increasingly important food staple throughout the world. A "butter" made from the pulverized seeds has become available in recent years and certainly ranks with peanut and sesame "butter" as an extremely nutritious and pleasing food.

Sunflower seeds contain large amounts of protein, as well as vitamins B, D, and E.

Sweet Potato

Ipomoea batatos

The sweet potato, which can make a rather pretty houseplant, has long trailing vines and eventually produces a flower that resembles that of the morning glory—a plant to which it is related. The sweet potato is not related to the regular potato, although both are New World tubers.

The sweet potato is native to the West Indies, Central America, and northern South America. The Incas, Mayas, and Aztecs all cultivated it as a food staple. The Incas also extracted a deep golden yellow dye from it to color fabrics.

Centuries before the Europeans came to the New World, the sweet potato had spread to various Pacific islands and even to today's New Zealand, where the Maoris were cultivating it at the time of Cook's discovery. According to Maori tradition, sweet potatoes, which were known by the Inca name, "kumar," were brought to New Zealand in canoes coming across the Pacific from the East. Sweet potatoes are said to have been cultivated in the Hawaiian Islands as early as 500 B.C. The Spanish introduced them to the Philippines in the sixteenth century, and from there they spread to much of the Far East.

During the sixteenth and seventeenth centuries, cultivation of the sweet potato spread to many warm-climate areas of the Old World. It was first introduced to Europe in Spain just after Columbus encountered it in the West Indies. As early as the 1500s, Spain was exporting small quantities of sweet potatoes from their New World colonies to the Iberian Peninsula and to other parts of Europe for the tables of the aristocracy. Henry VIII of England, for instance, enjoyed imported sweet potatoes baked in pies with honey, ginger, and cloves. During the reign of Elizabeth I, Sir Francis Drake is said to have brought sweet potatoes back with him from the West Indies, but attempts to cultivate them in England failed due to the British climate.

The sweet potato—unlike beans, corn, and various types of squash—apparently had not spread to North America prior to European colonization, despite the fact that it was a major food staple in the Caribbean area. It was first introduced by the English in Virginia during the seventeenth century. Later, its cultivation spread northward into New England where it did not thrive, and southward to the Carolinas where it did. It became a favorite food of the black slaves in the Carolinas who had, in fact, known it in Africa since the sixteenth century. The sweet potato was introduced to California by the Spanish and is still popular there. It has been grown in China since the sixteenth century, and spread from there to Japan where it is most commonly sliced, dipped in rice flour, and briefly deep-fried. It is only in Africa, however, that it became a major dietary staple.

There are a large number of sweet potato species in South America that are never seen elsewhere, including some that are purple, red, or even white in color. The best sweet potatoes grown in the United States are a very pale yellow inside, with a light tan skin.

Sweet potatoes can be baked or steamed, and eaten with butter and chopped parsley; or they can be pan-fried in butter until slightly crisp. Some people like them with cream, sugar, and cinnamon while others use them, with excellent results, as an ingredient in cookies, ice cream, or heavily spiced puddings. In many parts of Africa they are eaten with a peanut-butter sauce, particularly as holiday fare.

What North Americans commonly call a "yam" is actually an inferior variety of sweet potato which has an extremely soft, moist, cloyingly sweet, deep orange pulp. The skin is reddish purple. It is not related to the true yam, *Dioscorea*.

The regular yellow sweet potato is rich in vitamins A and C as well as in protein.

Swiss Chard. *See* **Chard.**

Tangelo

This extremely delectable fruit is a hybrid of *Citrus reticulata* and *C. grandis* or *C. paradisi*. Some types are descended from tangerine-pomelo hybrids, and some from tangerine-grapefruit hybrids. Others involve a crossing of these two basic types. The tangerine heritage usually predominates. Most are a deep orange color, while some are a lime green or have irregular areas of a greenish hue. Tangelos are usually the size of a small-to-medium orange, with a somewhat spherical shape that rises to a little caplike peak on top. In certain types, this characteristic is very pronounced.

The skin of the tangelo is thinner than that of the pomelo or the grapefruit, but is thicker than that of the tangerine. This skin, which sometimes retains a trace of the pomelo or grapefruit fragrance, usually adheres quite tightly to the pulp of the fruit. The pale orange inner fruit segments taste like an exceptionally good, but considerably more tart, tangerine, with just a hint of the pomelo or grapefruit, depending on the specific type.

According to Fitz-Gibbon, in *The Food of the Western World*, the tangelo was first developed as a hybrid in Florida by W. T. Swingle in 1897. This original tangelo was named the "Sampson." Other later varieties include the "Orlando" and the popular "Minneola."

A grapefruit-sized citrus fruit known as the "ugli" (pronounced "ougli"), which originated in Jamaica, is also sometimes classified as a tangelo, although it is very different from the above types. It is green or greenish yellow and develops brownish blotches as it ripens. The delectable inner segments are a very pale orange and the grapefruit heritage is much more apparent than in other tangelo hybrids. Although something of a luxury in North America, the ugli is appearing with increasing frequency in American markets during its winter season.

Like blood oranges, pomelos, and even grapefruits, tangelos are best served after being peeled, segmented, placed in an aesthetically-pleasing frosted glass goblet, and sprinkled with sugar. If desired, a bit of cream cheese or a few slivers of fresh ginger can be added.

Tangerine. *See* **Orange**, section dealing with *Citrus reticulata*.

Taro Root
Colocasia antiquorium

Taro is the "root" or tuber of a tropical plant apparently indigenous to Burma. From there, it spread throughout southeast Asia as well as to the numerous islands of the Pacific where it has, for centuries, been a basic food of the Polynesian peoples. Even today, it continues to be widely eaten in Hawaii as the basis of "poi." Taro root is also cultivated and eaten in Japan and the West Indies. Although it is sometimes found in U.S. markets, taro root remains unknown to the vast majority of the North American public.

This mild tasting, highly nutritious root can be prepared in the same ways as the potato.

Tarragon
Artimisia dracunculus, A. dracunculoides

Tarragon is a bushlike plant with long narrow leaves and tiny greenish gray flowers. It grows to a height of about one meter (3 ft.). *Artimisia dracunculus* is native to the Mediterranean world, including southern France; *A. dracunculoides* is found in the former Soviet Union and Iran.

Tarragon is not a popular herb among most Mediterranean peoples, but it is widely used in French cuisine, particularly in cheese, mushroom, and vegetable dishes served with cous cous. It is also a favorite vinegar herb.

Tarragon and tarragon vinegar are not to everyone's liking. As its unique, somewhat sweet flavor, although fairly mild, is quite penetrating, tarragon should be used very sparingly.

Thyme

Thymus vulgaris, T. serpyllum

Although thyme originated in the Mediterranean area, it has for centuries been more cultivated and used in northern Europe than in the lands of its origin. Thyme grows in almost any climate and is known to thrive in places as diverse as Iceland and Mauritius.

Often employed in various medicinal preparations, thyme is also put to occasional culinary use. Lemon thyme, *Thymus serpyllum*, is the type preferred as a seasoning. It greatly enhances tomato paste and some people like it in salads or chopped on fried potatoes. Icelanders use it to flavor sour milk. Mixed with powdered sassafras, it is an important ingredient of the "filé" seasoning used in Louisiana cuisine.

Tomatillo

Physalis ixcarpa, P. pruinosa

The tomatillo or husk tomato is native to Mexico and resembles a small green tomato with a dry husk around it. It thrives in extremely high temperatures and dry rocky ground.

Very solid in texture, the tomatillo is excellent sliced and served as a garnish with fried foods such as potatoes, eggplant, sweet potatoes, or vegetable cakes made with garbanzo bean flour and wheat germ. It can also be cut into segments and either eaten plain with a little sea salt, or added to salads.

The main use of the tomatillo, however, is in making sauces, particularly "salsa verde," the piquant green sauce used as a garnish or condiment with so many Mexican dishes. Salsa verde is made by combining tomatillos with garlic, onion, hot chili peppers, lime juice, and parsley or cilantro. The entire mixture is then thoroughly chopped and mashed into a semiliquid sauce. Although most Mexicans use cilantro (actually coriander leaves) in their salsa verde, smooth-leaved italian parsley is an excellent substitute. Salsa verde can be used as a relish for a wide variety of foods.

Tomatillos stay green for a considerable period of time. As they ripen, they turn purple and become somewhat sweet. At this stage, with the addition of lime or lemon juice as well as sugar, they are

sometimes made into preserves. In dried form, the versatile tomatillo can be used in cakes and puddings.

Excellent quality tomatillos, imported from Mexico, are often
available in North American markets. In Europe, they are a rarity
and are seldom encountered.

Tomato
Lycopersicum esculentum

The tomato is native to northern South America, but
was also cultivated in Central America and Mexico
many centuries before the Spanish arrived. In certain areas of the
Andes, wild tomatoes can still be found. Rather curiously, tomatoes
were not part of the North American Indian diet at the time of
European colonization.

The Spanish introduced the tomato to Spain as well as to North
Africa in the sixteenth century. From Spain, it was brought to Italy
and eventually to France. The tomato is a member of the deadly
nightshade family and most Europeans originally believed it to be
poisonous. Others believed it to be not only toxic, but to be an
aphrodisiac as well. Thus, it was dubbed the "love apple" and was
even condemned as a "corrupter of morals"! For a considerable
period of time it was grown in Europe only as an ornamental
garden plant. These early garden "exotics" were chiefly of the small
yellow cherry tomato variety.

The Italians were the first Europeans to begin eating the tomato. They were followed by the Spanish and the French, who
introduced it to Louisiana where it came to play a prominent part
in New Orleans cuisine. It was not until around 1850, however,
that the tomato became universally adopted as a food. The English
and the North Americans were the last to start eating it. In India,
tomatoes never became popular, for they had the ill fortune to fall
under the interdiction of the Brahmanic religious authorities and
hence were regarded as "impure."

Over the years, an immense number of tomato varieties have
been developed. Among these, there is considerable difference in
size, shape, texture, and color. Although most are a deep scarlet
red, others range from a pale rose to various shades of orange and
even a golden yellow. Regardless of variety, however, sun-ripened
tomatoes all possess the same superb flavor. What is more, they
are a major source of vitamin C.

The tiny cherry tomato, *Lycopersicum cerasifolium*, does possess a certain pleasing "sharpness" of flavor that differentiates it from its larger relatives. Another specific variety worthy of special mention is the oblong, quite small, and often vaguely pear-shaped roma or italian tomato, which was developed in Italy for use in tomato paste. These flavorful tomatoes are dried in the sun for later use, and sometimes are preserved in oil. The latter type are delectable eaten with vegetables or served with rice or cous cous. The creative cook will find other uses for them as well. They are available in many delicatessens in North America and can also be found in British cities where there are large Italian populations.

The diverse culinary uses of the tomato hardly need to be described here. Suffice it to say that raw tomatoes are used in an almost infinite variety of salads as well as in sandwiches. Cooked, either puréed or whole, tomatoes are a major ingredient in numerous dishes eaten throughout much of the world. Various herbs ranging from dill weed to parsley, oregano, and basil all go extremely well with them, as do both garlic and onion.

Unfortunately, in the United States, except for guaranteed vine-ripened tomatoes available in natural food stores and at roadside stands, tomatoes are generally picked prematurely and refrigerated for so long that they are all but tasteless by the time they reach the consumer.

Turk's Turban. *See* **Winter Squash.**

Turmeric

Curcuma longa

Turmeric is of the ginger family and, like ginger, the spice is derived from the rhizomes of the plant. This mild unique spice—which tastes nothing like ginger—blends well with other spices and seasonings, and is often used for its golden-yellow color as much as for its flavor. It is indigenous to an area encompassing southern China, Vietnam, and parts of India. For centuries, it has been used in curries and certain processed mustards. Today, turmeric is also grown and much used in the West Indies.

Although turmeric is not widely used in western cuisines, it can provide an interesting base for various flavorful and unusual sauces. For instance, an extremely pleasing sauce can be made by mixing turmeric with dill weed and chopped garlic. This sauce is excellent on a variety of vegetables including potatoes, beets, and celery.

In addition to turmeric, most East Indian curries also contain cumin, ground coriander, cayenne and other chili pepper powders, black pepper, fenugreek, cloves, ginger, cardamom, and garlic. Some curries, such as "madras" also contain "karipatta" or "curry leaves," which resemble a mild bay leaf. A tremendous variety of curries can be made simply by altering the quantities and combinations of the basic ingredients.

Turnip
Brassica rapa

The turnip is a sharp-flavored, somewhat sweet root vegetable that is one of the most ancient and universally-used vegetables known to man. The turnip is thought to have been indigenous to a wide area of the Mediterranean world, ranging from Asia Minor to Greece and the Italian peninsula. It is even possible that the turnip's native habitat extended well into Gaul (present-day France). In his *Natural History*, Pliny, in the first century A.D., describes several varieties common among the Romans of his day. Some botanical authorities, including Sturtevant, maintain that the turnip of northern Europe developed from a wild species that was common to the Northern Hemisphere from Siberia in the east to the Baltic in the west. In any case, at a very early date, the turnip spread to both northern Europe and the Far East.

During the Middle Ages and medieval period, the turnip was a major vegetable staple throughout northern Europe. Over the centuries, it has become no less popular in China and Japan. In all areas, the delectable "greens" or leaves of the turnip have traditionally been valued as a food as much as the bulbous root itself. No doubt people sensed, even in the Middle Ages, the nutritional value of the leaves, which contain exceptionally large quantities of vitamins A and C. Turnips were first introduced in the New World by Jacques Cartier in 1541, at which time they began to be widely cultivated in the French colony of Quebec, presently a province of Canada. Less than a century later, the English brought the turnip to Virginia and New England.

Turnip greens are best steamed and eaten with oil and lemon

juice, either by themselves or combined with mashed potatoes, cous cous, or pasta. They are also very good cold in salads.

As a root vegetable, turnips can be eaten either cooked or raw. Raw grated turnips can be added to salads, or combined with chopped parsley and eaten as a "garnish" with fried vegetable cakes, tofu, or rice. Baked or roasted turnips, a favorite in Tudor England, are excellent served with roasted or broiled potatoes, carrots, and onions. Turnips provide a flavorful addition to various vegetable soups and stews. They can also be steamed and eaten as an individual vegetable dish, with butter, pepper, and fresh dill weed.

The most delicious type of turnip frequently encountered today is chalk-white with a lavender-purple coloration around the top. Other types, which are entirely white, cream-colored, or even somewhat yellowish, are hybrids derived from cross-breeding the turnip with the rutabaga.

Vanilla Bean

Vanilla planifolia

The plant that produces the vanilla "bean" is a type of orchid that is native to Mexico and nearby areas. Today, it is extensively cultivated in many other parts of the world, including Tahiti, Java, the Malagasy Republic (Madagascar), the Seychelles, and the Comoro Islands. Vanilla beans are the fruit or pods of the plant. These are dried for use as a seasoning, either as they are or in the form of vanilla extract. The distinctive aromatic odor and flavor develop during the drying and curing process.

The Aztecs used the vanilla bean to enhance the taste of chocolate and other foods. In the early sixteenth century, the Spanish introduced vanilla to the Old World and within several centuries it had become a major flavoring used in dessert dishes throughout Europe.

Vanilla is widely utilized in puddings, cakes, cookies, and ice cream. It also brings out the flavor of chocolate. A particularly delectable fruit dish consists of dried apricots cooked with sugar, lemon juice, and vanilla. This dish is enhanced by the addition of thick sweet cream.

Many people do not realize that the superbly aromatic vanilla bean can be used with superior results in any dish calling for vanilla extract. After using the vanilla bean in some particular item such as cream, remove it, wash it off, and let it dry out for future use. A single vanilla bean can be used several times, depending on the heat of the item in which it has been immersed or steeped. For a highly aromatic sugar that can be used as a flavoring, place a vanilla bean in a container of sugar until the latter is thoroughly infused with the vanilla flavor.

Vanilla beans are universally available throughout Europe, but are not always so easy to find in North America, particularly in smaller communities. They are, however, always obtainable in larger cities with sizable European populations, as most Europeans simply refuse to use the vastly inferior vanilla extract so popular with the average North American.

Walnut

Juglans regia, J. nigra

Walnuts are indigenous to both the Old and New Worlds. *Juglans regia* is native to a wide area of the Near East, reaching from Israel to Iran. Walnuts were highly regarded by the ancient Greeks and Romans. According to Pliny, in his *Natural History*, the walnut was introduced to the Italian peninsula from Persia. Eventually, it spread to Gaul (France) and the British Isles where a particular strain, the "english walnut," was developed and became the dominant type.

The New World representative of this nut, *Juglans nigra*, is known as the "black walnut" and is indigenous to eastern North America. It was important in the diet of many native peoples of that area.

Walnuts are widely used in candies and confections, and are particularly good dipped in sugar and cinnamon or placed within dried figs or dates.

Walnut wood is regarded as one of the finest woods available for making high-quality furniture and other wood products.

Water Chestnut

Trapa bicornis, T. natans

The water chestnut, or "chinese water chestnut," comes from a floating plant that grows in ponds and inland waterways. It is native to China, where it is cultivated in wooden tubs.

A variety of water chestnut was also grown in ancient Greece and Rome. In his *Natural History*, Pliny mentions that the natives of Thrace in Greece used water chestnut flour in making bread. In Italy, water chestnuts were grown in and around Venice right up to the present century, when they apparently vanished altogether.

Boiled or roasted water chestnuts possess a pleasantly crisp texture and delicate flavor that can enhance a variety of vegetarian dishes, including soups and salads. Extensively used in the Chinese cuisine, both canned and fresh water chestnuts are available in Chinese markets and specialty shops everywhere.

Watercress
Nasturtium officinale

According to some botanical authorities, watercress is native to both the Old and New Worlds. Others believe that it is indigenous to the Old World and became "naturalized" in North America. In any case, today, watercress grows wild throughout the Mediterranean area, the Near East, France, Germany, the British Isles, and a considerable portion of North America. It was highly regarded by the ancient Greeks, Romans, and Persians.

Watercress grows near fresh water sources, including riverbeds with only a trickle of water. In flavor, it possesses a mustardlike sharpness. People who prefer to gather their own should be aware that if the water source is in any way polluted, serious illness may result from eating the watercress. Thus, it is wise to eat only commercially-raised specimens, which are frequently available in both Europe and North America.

The Irish and the Welsh traditionally use watercress only as a cooked vegetable. In most places, however, including England, watercress is eaten raw as a salad vegetable. Without question it greatly enhances any green salad. The English are also fond of watercress sandwiches made with toast. Chopped, it is a pleasant garnish on fried potatoes.

Watermelon
Citrullus vulgaris

The watermelon grows on a trailing vine and can weigh up to twenty-two kilograms (50 lb.). Externally, it is dark green, often with vaguely yellowish or pale green stripes. The sweet inner pulp, which is imbedded with hard black seeds, ranges from a pale pink to a deep scarlet.

The watermelon is native to Africa where, in some areas, it still grows wild. It was esteemed by the ancient Egyptians and, even in prehistoric times, had spread throughout the Near East. It was also introduced into much of southern Europe as well as China where its cultivation began during the Middle Ages. The Spanish brought watermelon seeds to the New World as also did innumerable black slaves from Africa.

Watermelon remains a major crop throughout a considerable portion of Africa where it has been used for centuries as an invaluable emergency water supply during periods of drought and in areas where water is scarce. The watermelon is also extremely popular in both Russia and the United States.

Apart from its importance as a source of water in hot, dry climates, the watermelon has very little nutritional value.

Welsh Onion. *See* **Chinese Onion.**

Wheat

Triticum, many varieties

Wheat is the grain of the genus *Triticum. Aegilops* and *Agropyron* are related types, and all of these genera mix. Some varieties of *Triticum* include *T. paleocolchicum,* a very ancient form; *T. duram,* which originated in the Mediterranean area and is considered to be the most important type of wheat cultivated today; *T. polonicum,* an exceptionally large-kerneled type of wheat that apparently originated in Poland; *T. vulgare,* widely grown in Canada, Russia, and the United States for use as bread flour; *T. einkorn,* a primitive wild variety; and *T. emmer,* a very ancient type found in warm climates. These last two types are believed to have crossed to produce most of the wheat cultivated today. There are also many other hybrid varieties. In fact, hybridization is believed to have begun as early as the Neolithic and Bronze ages.

The genus *Triticum* is generally held by botanists to be indigenous to a wide area that includes the present-day lands of Turkey, Armenia, Afghanistan, Iran, and Pakistan. Today, it is found from the Arctic Circle to Argentina.

In many areas of the world, wheat is *the* basic food staple. Its cultivation may be viewed as concomitant with civilization itself. Although wheat may have been cultivated as early as the Paleolithic age, it only became a major crop with the expansion of agriculture that occurred during the Neolithic period between 6000 and 7000 years ago. Ever since then, it has been of supreme importance in the human diet. Rich in protein (12 percent), wheat is a primary source of human energy, both mental and physical. As such, its role in the development of civilization can scarcely be overestimated.

A wheat dish known as "frumenty" or "fermenty" was for millenia one of the most basic and widespread foods known to man, eaten from India to northern Europe, from the remote Neolithic past right up to Elizabethan times. Frumenty consists simply of whole wheat kernels soaked in water for several days in a mildly warm temperature (as near a hearth) until the wheat begins to sour and becomes somewhat gelatinous. The grain should be soaked long enough to become pleasantly "sour" in odor but not so long that it becomes too "gummy" for use. A great deal depends upon the temperature. Traditionally, frumenty was then either eaten cold with milk and honey or was mixed with vegetables and fried as a main dish. Frumenty is well worth trying today, although somewhat odd to the modern palate. Fried or steamed frumenty is excellent with such vegetables as brussels sprouts or kale. Chopped garlic, dill weed, oil, and paprika all make flavorful additions to this dish.

After rice, wheat is the most widely eaten grain of our planet. It is used primarily to produce flour for diverse types of bread, pasta, pastries, and cakes. It is also eaten as a whole grain in certain areas. "Bulgar wheat," which is a split-grain, is popular throughout the Near and Middle East as well as in the Balkans. Dried parsley, lemon mint, and onion mixed with bulgar wheat constitute a product called "toubouleh." Soaked briefly in water, toubouleh makes an excellent addition to vegetable salads. It is greatly enhanced by the addition of chopped garlic, lemon juice, and oil. Added to cous cous, toubouleh creates a dish which many people find quite pleasing.

White Pepper. *See* **Black Pepper.**

Wild Rice

Zizania aquatica

The grain known as "wild rice" is not a wild variety of regular cultivated rice. It is a separate species that is native to a wide area of Canada and the United States.

Wild rice is the grain of a marsh or "water grass" that grows up to 2.5 meters (8 ft.) tall. There are several varieties, some of which even grow in brackish water. The black-brown or black-purple grain somewhat resembles a very thin *Oryza* type of long-grain rice.

Eaten by various native Indian peoples of North America for centuries, wild rice grows in swamps and marshes as well as along rivers and lake shores in an area ranging from the Atlantic coast and the St. Lawrence River all the way to the Mississippi River valley and the lakes of Minnesota. Native Indians still gather wild rice by approaching the plants in their canoes and shaking the grains from the plant by hand. This accounts for the fact that wild rice is generally rather expensive.

It is perhaps best to soak wild rice before cooking it. It should then be simmered over a low heat in a small amount of water until the water has evaporated and the rice is sufficiently soft. Onion, mushrooms, and various vegetables can be added while it is cooking. Corn or chopped chard go especially well with it as do hulled sunflower seeds.

According to Sturtevant, in *Edible Plants of the World*, this same grain plant is also found in certain regions of China, particularly in Manchuria. There, it is known as "kaw-sun." It would be interesting to know if it was growing there antecedent to its discovery by the Europeans in North America.

Winter Squash

Cucurbita maxima, many varieties

A number of different varieties of "winter squash" are included within the general botanical designation, *Cucurbita maxima*. No individual Latin suffixes are assigned to differentiate one type from another. Although varied in external appearance, the many types of winter squash are all very similar in flavor, possess the same texture, and are prepared in basically the same ways. They are also all trailing plants. The fruits are harvested in autumn and keep for up to six months.

The chief varieties of winter squash are the banana squash, the hubbard, the so-called "danish" or acorn squash, and the colorful, exotic-looking turk's turban. They are all extremely hard-shelled. The edible inner pulp ranges from a pale or golden yellow to a deep orange. In size and external color, the varieties differ considerably, ranging from the enormous, pale orange, oblong banana squash, which can reach a length of well over forty-five centimeters (1.5 ft.), to the relatively small, ridged, dark green acorn squash and the rather bizarre turk's turban with its swirling mound of green and bright orange.

The different varieties of winter squash are indigenous to South America, namely to an area ranging from the valleys of the Andes to the coastal regions of Chile and northern Argentina. Unlike the soft-skinned summer squashes, the winter squashes were not found in North and Central America at the time of European colonization. The reasons for this remain a mystery.

In the sixteenth century, the Spanish introduced the winter squashes to Europe as well as to Central America and Mexico, but they never became at all popular in Britain and northern Europe. They apparently first became known in North America during the early decades of the nineteenth century, being brought around the Horn from Chile by New England sea captains. It is unclear which specific types were included, but the hubbard squash did not appear until the 1850s. About the same time, the turk's turban reached France via Brazil and, for a while, aroused much interest as an exotic decorative garden plant rather than a food. In more recent times, certain types were taken to Japan and the Japanese have developed several unusual varieties of their own.

Although not a major North American crop, winter squash is available in markets throughout the United States and Canada, being more popular in the latter than the former.

Unlike summer squashes, the winter squashes can grow to their full sizes without the taste or texture suffering any detrimental effects. All types of winter squash are best either baked or broiled after being cut into convenient-sized pieces. Mild and somewhat sweet, cooked winter squash is best served with butter, black pepper, and chopped parsley. Hubbard and banana squash can also be grated, combined with chopped onion and garbanzo bean flour, molded into small cakes, and fried in oil.

The pale orange "winter crookneck," sometimes termed the "canadian crookneck," has its own separate designation of

Cucurbita moschata. It is native to Central, rather than South, America and is totally different from the thin-skinned, yellow, crook-necked summer squash.

Winter squash contains reasonably large amounts of vitamin A and even some protein.

Yam
Dioscorea

Less than ten of the approximately two hundred species of *Dioscorea* are commonly eaten. The plants have long trailing stems with leaves and clusters of greenish flowers. Only the tubers, which differ greatly in size and shape, are eaten. The edible varieties of yam are indigenous to both the Old and New Worlds. In West Africa, Fiji, and other Pacific islands, the yam is an important food staple. One Fijian variety can weigh over forty-five kilograms (100 lb.). Another species is widely eaten in China and southeast Asia. Still others exist in the tropical regions of Central and South America. There is even a variety that grows wild in the Pyrenees!

Yams have a sweet, rather bland flavor, and an extremely high starch content. They can be roasted, fried, or steamed. Lemon juice helps to make yams more palatable, as does the addition of a garnish such as grated daikon or oriental radish.

In North America, the term "yam" commonly refers to a decidedly inferior form of sweet potato rather than to the true yam, *Dioscorea*. During the last few years, the true yam has become increasingly available in Europe, as well as in North America, where it is mainly eaten by immigrants from Fiji, Samoa, and other Pacific islands.

Yard-long Bean. *See* **Chinese Green Bean.**

Yellow Crook-necked Squash
a variety of *Cucurbita pepo*

The yellow crook-necked is a summer squash that falls within the general *Cucurbita pepo* category but does not seem to have any further botanical designation. In North America, it is also popularly known as "summer crookneck" or "bush crookneck." It can be either smooth-skinned or somewhat "warted." Like the scalloped squash, it is a New World vegetable that was widely cultivated by the various native peoples of the northeastern regions of North America for centuries before European colonization. It was described by Champlain in 1605, and, among the French, it was valued more as an ornamental plant than as a food. There is also a pale green crook-necked variety and a straight-necked yellow squash. Aside from color or shape, these are essentially the same as the yellow crook-necked squash.

Yellow crook-necked squash is similar in flavor and texture to zucchini and scalloped squash, but, today, is not as popular as either of them, although throughout the nineteenth century, it was a favorite vegetable in much of North America. It has never been very popular in the British Isles and continental Europe. For suggestions as to preparation, *see* entries for **Scalloped Squash** and **Zucchini**.

The yellow crook-necked squash should not be confused with the pale orange, hard-shelled, crook-necked winter squash described in the entry for winter squash.

Zucchini

a variety of *Cucurbita pepo*

Included in the rather broad classification of *Cucurbita pepo*, the zucchini grows on a trailing vine that has large green leaves and lovely golden yellow flowers. The squash, which develops out of the flowers, is oblong in shape and dark or light green in color, sometimes with pale greenish yellow speckles and sometimes with yellowish green stripes running through it. This stripe pattern becomes more noticeable as the squash matures. The pulp is a whitish cream color infused with green near the thin outer skin. The skin, by the way, is quite edible and is never removed before cooking. Zucchini should be harvested when only 10–12 centimeters (4–5 in.) long. Very large specimens are mushy, tasteless, and full of hard seeds.

Although descended from squash native to the New World, zucchini was actually developed in Italy, perhaps from a green straight-necked type. No doubt, it was through Italian immigrants and their descendants that zucchini became a popular vegetable throughout the United States and Canada. The zucchini is also eaten in France, where it is known as the "courgette," and in England, where it is termed the "italian marrow."

Although zucchini lacks the delicacy of scalloped squash, it is an excellent and pleasing vegetable when prepared correctly. It should never be boiled or prepared without seasonings and herbal additions. Zucchini can be broiled, steamed, fried, or sautéed in oil. Chopped garlic, black pepper, oregano or basil, grated cheese, parsley, and wine vinegar all enhance the flavor of this squash. These may be used in whatever quantities and combinations desired. Zucchini can also be served in a tomato paste on pasta, or pan-fried in slices after having been dipped in moistened garbanzo flour. In short, the creative cook will find numerous and often unexpected ways of utilizing zucchini in a variety of tantalizing dishes.

Appendix

Vegetables

The category "vegetables" is extremely broad and includes many diverse families of food plants. Some of our vegetables are "leaf vegetables" such as cabbage, spinach, or lettuce, and each belongs to a totally separate and unrelated family. Others are "root vegetables" such as the carrot, turnip, onion, or beet, and once again, each is of a different family. Still other vegetables such as the lentil, pea, and various types of bean ranging from the Old World fava (*Vicia faba*) to the New World *Phaseolus* are "seed vegetables," which all belong to one family, the *Leguminosae*.

A few of the items listed here, such as dulse, are "sea vegetables" harvested from the ocean. While some tubers, such as water chestnuts, are grown in fresh water ponds or tubs, others, such as potatoes or jerusalem artichokes, are grown beneath the surface of the earth. Some unrelated vegetables—for example the artichoke and cauliflower—take certain unique forms, growing into "heads" well above the ground.

Then, there are the New World squashes: the soft-skinned *Cucurbita pepo* varieties ranging from the scalloped squash to the zucchini, and the hard-shelled "winter squashes" classified as *Cucurbita maxima* and native to South America. All belong to the vast *Cucurbitaceae* family, which includes both squashes and melons!

Among the most popular of all vegetables are those belonging to the *Cruciferae* family. These include the diverse species of the genus *Brassica oleracea* consisting of the cabbage, brussels sprout, kohlrabi, broccoli, and kale. The mustard plant and watercress also are of this family.

Certain vegetables harbor many surprises for us. For instance, the different varieties of onion (*Allium cepa*), garlic (*Allium sativim*), and leek (*Allium porrum*) are all members of the *Liliaceae* or lily family, which includes flowers of such delicate fragrance as the lily of the valley! Many people do not realize that carrots, parsnips, and celery are all within the *Umbelliferae* or parsley family. Likewise, who would suspect that the eggplant, which grows above the surface of the earth, is of the same family (*Solanaceae*) as the tuberous potato? Nor would one expect the lettuce and the artichoke to be related. Yet, they both belong to the *Compositae* or thistle family, which also includes among its members that beautiful flower, the common garden thistle, so abhorred by some gardeners but so highly regarded by the Scots as a symbol.

Lastly, there are certain foods that, while taxonomically are classified as fruits, are nevertheless viewed and eaten as vegetables. These include the tomato, the cucumber (which shares the same genus [*Cucumis*] as melons), and the avocado, which actually belongs to the *Lauraceae* or laurel family.

Amaranth: *Amaranthus gangeticus viridis* (the type used as a leaf vegetable)

Artichoke: *Cynara scolymus*

Asparagus: *Asparagus officinalis*

Avocado: *Persea americana, P. drymifolia* (although a fruit, the avocado is widely used and regarded as a vegetable)

Azuki bean: *Phaseolus angularis*

Banana squash. *See* Winter squash

Beans. *See* specific type of bean

Beet or beetroot: *Beta rubra*

Belgian endive. *See* Endive

Bell pepper: *Capsicum annuium*

Black bean: included within the general *Phaseolus vulgaris* classification

Black-eyed bean or Black-eyed pea: *Vigna sinensis*

Bok choi: *Brassica chinensis*

Boletus mushroom: *Boletus edulis* (actually a fungus, but used as a vegetable)

Broad bean. *See* Fava bean

Broccoli: *Brassica oleracea botrytis, B. o. botrytis cymosa, B. o. italica*

Brussels sprout: *Brassica oleracea gemnifera*

Cabbage: *Brassica oleracea capitata* (regular), *B. o. bullata major* (savoy cabbage), *B. o. pekinensis* (chinese or napa cabbage)

Cardoon: *Cynara cardunculus*

Carrot: *Daucus carota*

Cassava plant (also termed manioc or yuca): *Manihot esculenta, M. aipi*

Cauliflower: *Brassica oleracea botrytis caulifloris*

Celery: *Apium graveolens dulce*

Celery root or celeriac: *Apium graveolens rapaceum*

Chard or swiss chard: *Beta vulgaris cicla*

Chayote or chayote squash: *Sechium edule*

Cherry tomato. *See* Tomato

Chicory: *Cichorium intybus*

Chinese green bean (also termed the long bean or yard-long bean): *Vigna sesquipedalis*

Chinese onion: *Allium fistulosum*

Chinese snow pea. *See* Snow pea

Corn: *Zea mays*

Cos lettuce. *See* Lettuce

Cucumber: *Cucumis sativas* and *C. vulgaris* (the "common" cucumber); *C. longus* (includes the english, armenian, and chinese types); *C. anguria* (the gherkin)

Custard marrow. *See* Scalloped squash

Daikon: *Raphanus sativas longipinnatus*

Dandelion: *Taraxacum officinale, T. erythrospermum,* and others

Danish or acorn squash. *See* Winter squash

Dulse: *Rhodymenia palmata* (an Atlantic sea vegetable)

Eggplant: *Solanum melongena*

Egyptian onion: *Allium cepa viviparum* or *A. canadense*

Endive: *Cichorium endiva*

Fava bean: *Vigna faba*

Garbanzo bean or chick pea: *Cicer arietinum, C. judaicum, C. pinnatifidum*

Garlic: *Allium sativim, A. scordoprasum* ("elephant garlic")

Green bean: within the general *Phaseolus vulgaris* classification

Green onion: within the general *Allium cepa* classification

Hubbard squash. *See* Winter squash

Husk tomato. *See* Tomatillo

Irish moss: *Chondrus crispus* (an Atlantic sea vegetable)

Italian bean. *See* Romano bean

Italian marrow. *See* Zucchini

Jerusalem artichoke: *Helianthus tuberosis*

Jicama: *Pachyrrhizus erosus, P. tuberosus*

Kale: *Brassica oleracea acephala*

Kidney bean: within the general *Phaseolus vulgaris* classification

Kohlrabi: *Brassica oleracea gongylodes* or *B. o. caulorapa*

Laver: *Porphyra laciniata* (an Atlantic sea vegetable)

Leek: *Allium porrum*

Lentil: *Lens escuelenta, L. nigricans, L. culinaris*

Lettuce: *Latuca sativa*

Lima bean: *Phaseolus limatus, P. limensis*

Lotus or water lily: *Nelumbium nelumbo* (a fresh water tuber)

Mung bean: *Phaseolus aureus* or *P. mungo*

Mushroom: *Agaricus bisporus* (the common edible mushroom raised commercially; actually a fungus but used as a vegetable)

Mustard (as a leaf vegetable): *Brassica juncea*

Navy bean: within the general *Phaseolus vulgaris* classification

New zealand spinach: *Tetragonia expansa*

Okra: *Hibiscus esculentus*

Olive: *Olea europa*

Onion (purple, white, and yellow varieties): *Allium cepa* is used to designate all three types

Parsnip: *Pastinaca sativa*

Pea: *Pisum sativum* (the chief variety in use today)

Peanut: *Arachis hypogea* (a vegetable related to peas and lentils)

Potato: *Solanum tubros,* many varieties

Pumpkin: within the general *Cucurbita pepo* classification

Purple bean. *See* Green bean

Radish: *Raphanus sativum*

Roman or italian bean: within the general *Phaseolus vulgaris* classification

Rutabaga: *Brassica napobrassica*

Salsify: *Tragopogon porrifolius*

Scalloped squash: within the general squash classification *Cucurbita pepo*

Scarlet runner bean: *Phaseolus multiflorus*

Scorzonera: *Scorzonera hispanica*

Shallot: *Allium ascalonicum* or *A. cepa ageratum*

Shanghai bok choi: a dwarf variety of *Brassica chinensis*

Shitoke: *Lentines exodes*

Snow pea: *Pisum sativum macrocarpum*

Soybean: *Glycine max*

Spinach: *Spinachia oleracea*

String bean: *See* Green bean

Summer squash. *See* Scalloped squash; Yellow crook-necked squash; Zucchini

Sweet potato: *Ipomoea batatos*

Swiss chard. *See* Chard

Taro root: *Colocasia antiquorium*

Tomatillo: *Physalis ixcarpa* or *P. pruinosa*

Tomato: *Lycopersicum esculentum, L. cerasifolium* (the cherry tomato)

Turk's turban. *See* Winter squash

Turnip: *Brassica rapa*

Water chestnut: *Trapa bicornis* or *T. natans* (a water tuber)

Watercress: *Nasturtium officinale*

Welsh onion. *See* Chinese onion

Winter squash: *Cucurbita maxima,* many varieties

Yam: *Dioscorea,* many species

Yard-long bean. *See* Chinese green bean

Yellow crook-necked squash: within the general *Cucurbita pepo* classification

Zucchini: within the general *Cucurbita pepo* classification

Fruits

The category "fruits" covers many diverse families and species. Nearly all fruits are to some degree sweet and are characterized by a soft edible interior pulp. They include the following varieties:

1. The drupes or "stone fruits" of the *Rosaceae* family; all of the genus *Prunus*, namely, the peach, nectarine, apricot, plum, and cherry
2. The apple, crab apple, and quince are also of the *Rosaceae* family, but of the genus *Pyrus* (sometimes given the variant designation *Malus*). The pear also is classified with the *Pyrus* genus
3. The citrus fruits of the *Rutaceae* family and the genus *Citrus*, namely the orange, lemon, lime, pomelo, grapefruit, and the hybrid tangelo and ugli
4. Melons of the *Cucurbitaceae* family. These include the cantaloupe, casaba, cranshaw, and persian (all designated *Cucumis melo*), as well as the watermelon, which is of African rather than Middle Eastern origin and is of the genus *Citrullus*
5. Fruits of varying types and families which are termed "berries." These include blueberries and cranberries of the *Ericaceae* family and the genus *Vaccinium*; raspberries and blackberries of the *Rosaceae* family and the genus *Rubus*; and gooseberries, which, together with red and black currants belong to the *Saxifragaceae* family and the genus *Ribes*. The kiwi fruit of the genus *Actinidia* is also a berry and is sometimes described as a "chinese gooseberry." It, however, belongs to the *Actinidiaceae* family

6. Bananas—regular, dwarf or finger, and the plantain type—are of the *Musaceae* family and the genus *Musa*
7. Lastly, there are a number of diverse, mostly one-of-a-kind fruits of unrelated genus and family. These include the fig of the *Moraceae* or mulberry family and the genus *Ficus*; the pomegranate of the *Punicaceae* family and the genus *Punica*; the pineapple of the *Bromeliad* family (familiar to many in the form of several species of decorative tropical houseplants) and the genus *Ananas*; the grape of the *Vitaceae* family and the genus *Vitis* in its thousand or more varieties; the rare cherimoya, which is of the *Annonaceae* family and the genus *Annona*; the many varieties of mango of the *Anacardiaceae* or cashew family and the genus *Mangifera*; the papaya of the *Caricaceae* family and the genus *Carica*; and various others, including those termed "medlars," of which the loquat is an example.

Apple: *Malus pumila, M. sylvestris, Pyrus pumila*

Apricot: *Prunus armenica*

Banana: *Musa sapientum* (the regular banana), *M. nana* (the dwarf or finger banana)

Blackberry: *Rubus*, many varieties. *Rubus canadensis* (trailing), *R. cunifolius* (upright)

Black currant: *Ribes nigram*

Blood orange: within the basic sweet orange classification *Citrus sinensis*

Blueberry: *Vaccinium*, many varieties, the most important being *V. angustifolium* and *V. coryboscum*

Cantaloupe: *Cucumis melo reticulatus* (the regular variety popular today), *C. m. cantaloupsis* (the much smaller "true cantaloupe" of the ancient world)

Casaba melon: within the general melon classification *Cucumis melo*

Cherimoya: *Annona cherimola*

Cherry: *Prunus avium* (the "sweet" cherry), *P. cerasus* (the "sour" or "sweet-sour" cherry); and many varieties

Crab apple: *Pyrus baccata, P. rivularis, P. coronaria*

Cranberry: *Vaccinium macrocarpon* (North American), *V. oxycoccus* (British)

Cranshaw melon: within the general melon classification *Cucumis melo*

Currant. *See* Black currant and Red currant

Date: *Phoenix dactylefera*

Fig: *Ficus carica*, many varieties

Gooseberry: *Ribes grossularia* (Old World), *R. hertellum* (New World)

Grape: *Vitis vinifera* (Old World), *V. rotundifolia* and *V. labrusca* (New World); over 1000 varieties

Grapefruit: *Citrus paradisi*

Guava: *Psidium guajava* (common), *P. lucidum* (yellow), *P. catteiamum* (reddish)

Honeydew melon: within the general *Cucumis melo* classification

Kiwi fruit: *Actinidia chinensis*

Lemon: *Citrus limonium*

Lime: *Citrus aurantifolia*

Loganberry: *Rubus loganobaccus*

Loquat: *Eriobotrya japonica*

Lychee: *Nephelium litchi*

Mango: *Mangifera indica*, many varieties

Muskmelon. *See* Cantaloupe

Nectarine: *Prunus persica nectarina*

Orange: *Citrus aurantius* (tart or sour oranges), *C. sinensis* (sweet oranges), *C. reticulata* ("mandarin" oranges)

Papaya: *Carica papava*

Peach: *Prunus persica*, many varieties

Pear: *Pyrus communis* (European), many varieties; *P. pyrifolia* or *P. sinensis* (the chinese pear)

Persian melon: within the general basic melon classification *Cucumis melo*

Persimmon: *Diospyros virginiana* (North America), *D. kaki* (China and Japan)

Pineapple: *Ananas comosus*

Plantain: *Musa paradisica*

Plum: *Prunus institia* (the damascus plum), *P. americana* (eastern United States), *P. nigra* (Canadian), *P. subcordata* (Oregon and California), *P. spinosa* (Russia), *P. salicina* (Japan), *P. cerasifera* (Balkans), and many others

Pomegranate: *Punica granatum*

Pomelo or pommelo (the shaddock): *Citrus grandis*

Prune. *See* Plum

Quince: *Pyrus cydonia* or *Cydonia oblonga*

Raspberry: *Rubus idaeus* (European), *R. strigosus* (North American red raspberry), *R. occidentales* (North American black raspberry)

Red currant: *Ribes sativim* and *R. rubrum*

Rhubarb: *Rheum rhaponticum* (used as a fruit, rhubarb is actually a vegetable)

Rose (hips and petals): *Rosa damascena, R. centifolia,* and many others

Strawberry: *Fragaria virginiana* (North American), *F. chiloensis* (Chilean), *F. vesca* (Swiss), *F. rosaceae* (English), *F. moschata* (Central European)

Tangelo: a hybridization of *Citrus reticulata* and *C. grandis* or, in some cases, of *C. reticulata* and *C. paradisi*

Tangerine. *See* Orange, *Citrus reticulata*

Ugli. *See* Tangelo

Watermelon: *Citrullus vulgaris*

Grains

Although there are only a few basic grains, they are very important in the human diet throughout the world. Dried grain of various species is either cooked whole or prepared in ground form as a dietary staple in both the East and the West, although in the latter it is less used today than in the past. Throughout most of the Far East, a meal without rice is all but inconceivable. The same is true of cracked wheat in much of the Middle and Near East. Among the Slavs and other Eastern Europeans, buckwheat or "kasha" has, over the centuries, formed a very central part of their diet. In pre-Hispanic Central and South America, amaranth grain and quinoa were widely used. Among the

North American native peoples, wild rice was in many areas a food of major importance.

Most grains can be processed into flour for use in a wide variety of bread products, noodles, and pastas. Wheat and rye have long been the favorite grain flours of European countries and, by extension, of North America. In South and Central America, corn flour is widely used in the making of tortillas—the "bread staple" of many Hispanic Americans. In the ancient world, barley, buckwheat, and millet were extensively used as flours. In some areas, such as North Africa, the use of millet flour remains widespread even today.

While buckwheat is of the *Polygonaceae* family and amaranth of the *Amaranthaceae* family, most grain types belong to the *Gramineae* family. Corn, too, is of the *Gramineae*, but belongs to the subfamily *Maydeae*. Some varieties of millet belong to the *Poaceae* family.

Amaranth: *Amaranth hypochondria*

Buckwheat: *Fagopyrum esculentum, F. sagittatum* (sometimes termed "groats" or "kasha")

Corn: *Zea mays, Z. mays indentata* (used dried and as a flour, corn may be viewed as a grain)

Millet: *Panicum mileaceum, P. molissimum, Setaria chaetochia, Penisetum glauchim,* and many others

Oat: *Avena fatua, A. brevis, A. sativa, A. orientalis,* and many others

Quinoa: *Chenopodium quinoa*

Rice: *Oryza sativa,* many varieties

Rye: *Secale cereale*

Wheat: *Triticum,* many varieties. *T. duram* (the major type cultivated today), *T. polonicum, T. vulgare,* and *T. emmer* are the most important

Wild rice: *Zizania aquatica*

Nuts

For the most part, "nuts" belong to totally different families and are even less homogeneous as a group than vegetables or fruits. The walnut and pecan, however, are members of the same family, namely the *Juglandaceae*. So, too, the cashew and pistachio both belong to the *Anacardiaceae* family of which the mango fruit is also a member.

The almond is actually of the family *Rosaceae* and the genus *Prunus*, to which so many "stone fruits" belong. It is, in fact, very closely related to the peach. Unlike the latter, however, the fruit never develops, and functions only as an external covering of the seed or nut within it.

The strange and fascinating brazil nut belongs to the *Lecythidaceae* family. The coconut, which is sometimes regarded as a fruit, belongs to the *Arecaceae* or palm family. It is certainly the largest nut or seed in existence. Among the peoples of the Pacific Islands, it functions as a dietary staple.

Unlike many vegetables, fruits, and grains, most nuts are not indispensable to our diets. They are, for the most part, simply pleasant additions or "luxuries," eaten either as between-meal snacks or used as garnishes or fillings in desserts ranging from cakes and cookies to puddings and confections.

The pine nut is an exception to the above. The Italians use it in making "pesto," a sauce combining crushed pine nuts with basil, black pepper, and other ingredients for use on pasta. In the New World, pine nuts were widely used by the native Indian peoples in areas ranging from Canada to Chile.

In the last several decades, certain nuts—notably almonds, cashews, and pecans—have become available, particularly in organic and health food outlets, processed into a high-protein paste or "butter" that can be used on bread.

Almond: *Prunus amygdalus*
Brazil nut: *Bertholleta excelsa*
Cashew nut: *Anacardium occidentale*
Chestnut: *Castenea sativa* and *C. dentata*
Coconut: *Cocos nucifera*
Hazelnut: *Corylus avellana*
Lychee nut: *Nephelium litchi* (used as a nut when dried, but viewed as a fruit when fresh)
Macadamia nut: *Macadamia integrifolia*
Peanut. *See entry under* Vegetables
Pecan: *Carya olivaeformis*
Pine nut: *Pinus pinea*
Pistachio nut: *Pistachia vera*
Walnut: *Juglans regia*

Culinary Herbs

Any attempt to differentiate between culinary herbs and spices and seasonings is, to some degree, arbitrary. They could, in fact, all be included in one category. For the purposes of this book, however, I will include in "culinary herbs" those plants with leaves that are used, either fresh or dried, as seasonings in non-dessert foods. Also included are certain seeds.

Culinary herbs, for the most part, differ from spices and other seasonings inasmuch as they do not have to be imported from distant and exotic lands. Nor are they accordingly costly. The culinary herbs listed here have never been luxury items. Rather, they can be grown in home gardens, window boxes, and pots. Some—such as parsley, basil, and, in some areas, dill—are available fresh in produce markets. In dried form, they are all obtainable at reasonable prices in food outlets everywhere.

Certain culinary herbs are associated with specific ethnic groups and their cuisines. Oregano and basil are connected with the Italian cuisine. Dill is chiefly a northern European seasoning characteristic of the Swedish, Danish, Baltic, Polish, and Russian cuisines. Marjoram, tarragon, and chives are all favorites of the French. Perhaps the most widely used culinary herb in the Western world is parsley. It is extensively utilized from the Mediterranean to the British Isles and the New World as a chopped garnish on a variety of dishes.

The majority of culinary herbs are of two plant families. For example, caraway, dill, fennel, and parsley are all within the *Umbelliferae* family, although some botanists classify dill and fennel as of the *Apiaceae* family. Basil, marjoram, oregano, sage, and thyme are all members of the mint or *Lamiaceae* family. Of the various items listed here as culinary herbs, only bay leaves, tarragon, and chives are of families different from the two above. Bay is of the laurel or *Lauraceae* family; tarragon is of the *Asteraceae* or *Compositae* family; and chives of the *Liliaceae* family.

Basil: *Ocimum basilicum, O. minimum*

Bay leaf: *Lauris noblis*

Caraway seed: *Carum carvi*

Chive: *Allium schoenoprasium*

Cilantro. *See* Coriander

Dill or dillweed: *Anethum graveolens*

Fennel: *Foeniculum vulgaris* (one type is also eaten as a vegetable)

Marjoram or sweet marjoram: *Origanum marjorana*

Mint and peppermint: *Mentha viridis, M. longifolia, M. rotundafolia, M. piperata, M. citrata*

Oregano: *Origanum vulgare, O. smyrnacium, O. onites, O. heraclesticum*

Parsley: *Petroselinum sativim* (wild), *P. hortense* (the smooth-leaved Italian type), *P. crispum* (the curly-leaved type), *P. radicatum* (the hamberg variety eaten as a root vegetable)

Rosemary: *Rosmarinus officinalis*
Sage: *Salvia officinalis*
Savory: *Satureia montana, S. hortensis*
Tarragon: *Artimisia dracunculus, A. dracunculoides*
Thyme: *Thymus vulgaris, T. serpyllum*

Spices and Seasonings

Spices and seasonings differ from the items in the "culinary herb" category in a number of ways. They are not—with one exception—derived from the leaves of the plants involved, but rather from the barks, "berries," seeds, roots, peels, pulps, or, in the case of saffron, petals. In most cases they are used in ground or powdered form. Many, like allspice, cardamom, cinnamon, cloves, and nutmeg, are used in dessert dishes. There are also those that are utilized in vegetable and grain dishes. These include black pepper, cayenne, paprika, and cumin.

Other items included here among spices and seasonings are further processed into a derivative product or flavoring. Chocolate, vanilla, mustard, horseradish, sugar cane, and sesame seeds are all examples. Still other items are candied in sugar (for example, ginger and citron) or marinated in brine or vinegar, as are capers. A few are utilized in both dessert and non-dessert dishes. These include saffron, ginger, sunflower seeds, and nutmeg. Sesame seeds are utilized by themselves on bread products or are processed into tahini or halva.

Many spices were, for much of human history, luxury items imported at considerable cost from the exotic lands of the East. These spices played an important part in the development of human commerce while the search for a shorter "spice route" inspired major voyages of discovery and the opening up of the New World. The spice trade was also a major factor in the development of cross-cultural relations between East and West and the resultant expansion of human knowledge.

Unlike culinary herbs, which were used by everyone, the spices and seasonings listed here were for many centuries, at least in the West, costly luxuries known only to the few. They also differ from culinary herbs in that they derive from a large number of totally different plant families. Vanilla, for instance, is of the orchid or *Orchidaceae* family; cassia, cinnamon, and sassafras are of the laurel or *Lauraceae* family; cardamom and ginger are of the *Zingiberaceae* family; anise and cumin of the *Umbelliferae*; cayenne of the nightshade or *Solanaceae* family; horseradish of the *Cruciferae*; citron and bergamot of the *Rutaceae*; capers are of the *Capparidaceae* family; allspice and cloves are of the myrtle or *Myrtaceae* family; sugar cane of the *Granineae* or grass family; sunflowers are of the *Compositae*; sesame of the *Pedaliaceae*; saffron of the iris or *Iradaceae* family; and carob, rather surprisingly, is of the pea or *Leguminosae* family.

Allspice: *Pimenta officinalis*
Anise: *Pimpinella anisum*
Bergamot: *Citrus bergamia*
Black pepper: *Piper nigrum*
Capers: *Caparis spinosa*
Cardamom: *Eletteria cardamomum*
Carob: *Ceratonia siliqua*
Cassia. *See* Cinnamon
Cayenne pepper: *Capsicum frutescens longum*
Chili peppers: including *Capsicum frutescens longum,*
    C. f. abbreviatum, and *C. f. conoides*
Chocolate: *Theobroma cacao*
Cinnamon: *Cinnamomum zeylanicum*
Citron: *Citrus medica*
Clove: *Eugenia caryophyllata, E. aromatica*
Cumin: *Cuminum cyminum*
Fenugreek: *Trigonella foenum graceum*
Ginger: *Zingiber officinale*
Horseradish: *Cochleania amoracia, Amoracia lapthifolia,*
    A. rusticana

Mace. *See* Nutmeg

Mustard: *Brassica nigra* or *Sinapis nigra, Brassica alba,*
   B. juncea

Nutmeg: *Myristica fragrans*

Paprika: *Capsicum tetragonum, C. annum*

Pepper. *See* Black pepper, Cayenne, etc.

Poppy seed: *Papaver somniferum*

Saffron: *Crocus sativus*

Sassafras: *Sassafras albidum*

Sesame seed: *Sesamum indicum*

Sugar cane: *Saccharum officinarium, S. barberi, S. sinensis*

Sunflower seed: *Helianthus annus*

Vanilla bean: *Vanilla planifolia*

White pepper. *See* Black pepper

SELECTED BIBLIOGRAPHY

Adams, Ruth. *Eating in Eden: The Nutritional Superiority of Primitive Foods*. Emmaus, Pa.: Rodale Press, 1976.

Anderson, Edgar. *Plants, Man, and Life*. Boston: Little, Brown and Co., 1952.

Aries, Philippe, and Georges Duby, editors. *A History of Private Life* (a series): *Vol. A. From Pagan Rome to Byzantium*. Cambridge, Mass. and London: Belknap Press, 1987.

———. *Vol. B. Passions of the Renaissance*. Cambridge, Mass. and London: Belknap Press, 1989.

Bailey, Liberty Hyde, and Ethel Zoe. *Hortus Third*. rev. ed. Bailey Hortorium, a College of Cornell University. New York: Macmillan Publishing Co., 1982.

Bianchini, F., and F. Corbetta. *The Complete Book of Fruits and Vegetables*. New York: Crown Publishers, 1976. (Entries are nonalphabetical)

Boxer, Arabella. *The Encyclopedia of Herbs, Spices, and Flavorings*. New York: Crown Publishers Inc., 1984.

Camp, Wendel, Victor Boswell, and John Magness. *The World in Your Garden*. Washington, D.C.: National Geographic Society, 1957.

Cato, Marcus Porcius. *On Agriculture*. Trans. by William David Hooper. Loeb Classical Library. W. Heinemann Ltd. London: 1936.

Colin, Jane. *Herbs and Spices*. London: Arlington Books, 1969.

Coyle, L. Patrick. *World Encyclopedia of Food*. New York: Facts Press, 1982.

Darby, William J., and Paul Ghalioungui. *Food: The Gift of Osiris. Vol. 2* (only). London: Academic Press, 1976.

Fitz-Gibbon, Theodora. *The Food of the Western World: An Encyclopedia of Food from North America and Europe.* New York: Quadrangle. New York Times Book Co., 1976.

Friedlander, Barbara. *The Secrets of the Seed: Vegetables, Fruits, and Nuts.* New York: Grosset and Dunlop, 1974.

Halprin, Anne Moyer, ed. *Unusual Vegetables: Something New for This Year's Garden.* Emmaus, Pa: Rodale Press, 1978.

Howe, Robin. *The Mediterranean Diet.* London: Weidenfeld and Nicolson, 1985.

Kraft, Ken, and Pat Kraft. *Exotic Vegetables.* New York: Walker and Co., 1977.

McPhee, John. *Oranges.* New York: Ferrar, Straus, and Giroux, 1967.

Magness, J. R., and Else Bostlemann. *"How Fruit Came to America."* National Geographic, September 1951, 325-77.

Marcus, George, and Nancy Marcus. *Forbidden Fruits and Forgotten Vegetables. A Guide to Cooking with Ethnic and Neglected Produce.* New York: St. Martin's Press, 1982.

Pliny the Elder. *Natural History.* Trans. by H. Rackman. 10 Volumes. Cambridge, Mass.: Harvard University Press, 1938-63.

Schwanitz, Franz. *The Origin of Cultivated Plants.* Cambridge, Mass.: Harvard University Press, 1966.

Soyer, Alexis. *Pantropheon.* Paris, 1853. Reprint. London/New York: Paddington Press, 1977.

Stobart, Tom. *The International Wine and Food Society's Guide to Herbs, Spices, and Flavorings.* New York: McGraw-Hill Book Co., 1973.

Sturtevant, Edward Lewis. *Edible Plants of the World.* Edited by U. P. Hedrick. New York: Dover Publications, 1972.

Szafer, Wladyslaw. *General Plant Geography.* Translated for the Smithsonian Institute in Washington D.C. by the Paristwowe Wydawnistwo Naukowe. Warsaw, 1975.

Tannahill, Reay. *Food in History.* New York: Stein and Day, 1973.

Trager, James. *The Food Book.* New York: Avon Books, 1970.

Vietmeyer, Noel D. *"The Captivating Kiwifruit."* National Geographic, May, 1987.

Zukovskij, P. M. *Cultivated Plants and Their Wild Relatives.*
USSR State Publishing House, 1950. Trans. and abridged
by P. S. Hudson. Bucks, England: Commonwealth Agricul-
tural Bureaux, 1962.

Index

ABOUT THE AUTHOR

Jon Gregerson is a graduate in Humanities of the University of California at Berkeley. Presently a resident of Eugene, Oregon, he has traveled extensively and lived abroad. He is a member of the Vegetarian Union of North America, an organization affiliated with the International Vegetarian Union which has members throughout the world. He also belongs to the 1745 Association, which is dedicated to the memory of Prince Charles Edward and Culloden. His interests include the history and culture of Stuart Britain, music of the English and French baroque, and vegetarian cuisine. He is presently working on a history of vegetarianism.